PRESSURE

HOW THE PEOPLE
WHO POWER FORMULA ONE
THRIVE AT THE LIMITS

SIMON LAZENBY

EBURY
SPOTLIGHT

EBURY SPOTLIGHT

UK | USA | Canada | Ireland | Australia
India | New Zealand | South Africa

Ebury Spotlight is part of the Penguin Random House group of companies
whose addresses can be found at global.penguinrandomhouse.com

Penguin Random House UK
One Embassy Gardens, 8 Viaduct Gardens, London SW11 7BW

penguin.co.uk
global.penguinrandomhouse.com

Penguin
Random House
UK

First published by Ebury Spotlight in 2025

1

Typeset by seagulls.net

Printed and bound in Great Britain by Clays Ltd, Elcograf S.p.A.

The authorised representative in the EEA is Penguin Random House Ireland,
Morrison Chambers, 32 Nassau Street, Dublin D02 YH68.

A CIP catalogue record for this book is available from the British Library

ISBN 9781529939293 HB
ISBN 9781529939323 TPB

MIX
Paper | Supporting
responsible forestry
FSC
www.fsc.org   FSC® C018179

Penguin Random House is committed to a sustainable future
for our business, our readers and our planet. This book is
made from Forest Stewardship Council® certified paper.

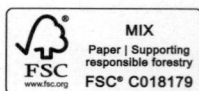

To my family.
Thank you x

CONTENTS

FOREWORD
BY DAMON HILL

have been a friend and colleague of Simon since 2012, when we both embarked on a great adventure with Sky Sports F1 covering Formula One like it had never been covered before. I knew next to nothing about TV, and he knew almost everything. I had a lot to learn, so having him alongside was a huge bonus. He taught me everything about being in front of a camera and millions of viewers. I was an expert on being a Formula One World Champion, so at least I had something to give in return!

His reaction to Formula One, for the first couple of seasons presenting it at least, was tinged with a slight scepticism which, at times, I too have felt and that we bonded over. He viewed Formula One cautiously in those early years, unsure whether it was a completely 'true' or 'pure' sport. Maybe it was a wise scepticism, born of a journalistic stance of never taking things at face value.

That said, he threw himself into it with a commitment of the highest Formula One standard. Always utterly professional and thorough, he managed to absorb the entire history of the sport, together with the names and faces of all the key protagonists and personnel in less than six months in preparation for his debut. His ability as a live sports TV broadcaster cannot be matched. He was battle-hardened to the excitement and adrenaline rush of live events from his work with rugby and across many sports and could steer a straight course through even the most chaotic of mayhems, of which there are plenty in Formula One – thankfully!

During all those occasions he has never, in my experience, ever 'lost his cool'. What he can do is listen to four different voices in his head at the same time and make sense of them all, remember his lines and deliver them on cue, to the split second, every time. He also has a unique insight and inspiration when it comes to the ad-lib.

The Formula One world is a travelling circus. After 14 years of going through airports, hotels, promotional events and being in the paddock from dawn to dusk, you develop close friendships and strong professional relationships. More importantly, you acquire a huge respect for the hardworking and talented individuals who make this sport happen, from travel co-ordinators and caterers to engineers and mechanics, designers, marketing and media teams. There really is a job for anyone in Formula One, if you are prepared to work hard and with passion. So, it is no surprise to me that Simon has felt the need to write a book that celebrates all those people, of which he is now one. His initial scepticism has evaporated, Formula One has got into his blood and he'll never be able to get it out. The 'pure sport' within the sport has been revealed to him! And over the years, we even found the time to have a few drinks, play a lot of golf and even make a film together.

This book is about the people of Formula One who, like Simon, are as much a part of Formula One, as Formula One is part of them.

INTRODUCTION

The past 14 years have been an absolute blur. In the time that I've been working in Formula One, I've managed to marry a very patient wife who single-parents our two kids while I travel the world, reached 50, celebrated my parents' golden wedding anniversary and bought a spaniel who unfortunately – when the low summer sun illuminates her orange fur and bleached blonde crown – bears a striking resemblance to Donald Trump. Life is flashing before my eyes as quickly as the cars that we follow around the world race around the track. While most of the other sports I have covered last 80 or 90 minutes, Formula One is always a four-day event that is totally immersive and becomes an addiction.

I, like many of my age, first got into it in the mid-1980s, when Nigel Mansell was oiling his tache and going wheel to wheel with the other titans of the sport. It didn't occur to me then that I might get the opportunity to follow it from country to country and across continents. You never know how long your career will last in television and when the axe might fall, but while it hasn't, the sole aim of everyone who I work with is to enjoy each minute and bring you as close to the sport as we possibly can. Therefore, when the chance came along to write a book on the subject, the first idea that came to mind was to introduce you to some of the remarkable people that I have met along the way.

This is my attempt to decipher a world in which, almost by accident, I found myself hurled into in 2012, when Sky won the rights to broadcast Formula One in the UK. At that point I was presenting Sky's rugby coverage and had been doing so since 2002. My boss in the rugby department was TV legend Martin Turner. He had given me, as he had so many others, my big break in TV by taking me on as a runner in the rugby department in 1998 and guiding me through my early career – something for which I am eternally grateful. Before then, my first job out of university was as a commercial management trainee for a large commodities firm called Cargill. It would be fair to say that I was an extremely average trader, haemorrhaging cash daily as I stared blankly at the numbers ticking up and down on the screen in front of me. Futures, spreads, options, arbitrage – the terminology was a different language and one in which I was nowhere near fluent. I would like to take this opportunity to apologise to the many Lincolnshire farmers who seemed constantly perplexed as to how I priced their grain, and especially to the stevedores of Antwerp and Ghent, who stood idle on the docksides as boats of different sizes arrived in the wrong order or not at all.

Inevitably, I walked before I was pushed (most likely into a vat of the soya bean oil that I was attempting to trade). Only 18 months out of higher education I stood at a career crossroads, KFC or McDonald's, but thankfully inspiration came from within my own family. My sister was working as a runner on *The Big Breakfast* and thoroughly enjoying herself. I'm not ashamed to say that I followed her lead and made the move into the creative rather than the fast food sector by applying to Sky Sports for some work experience. In those days, there were opportunities everywhere as Sky grew rapidly by mopping up major global sports rights, but I had studied natural sciences at university and dissecting dog fish was in no way preparation for a career in the media … or trading, now that it springs to mind.

I started off making the teas and coffees and then got a chance reporting on some really terrible third-division rugby. Slightly encouraged by what they saw, they gave me what is known in the trade as a screen test. I had mine at the same time as Kirsty Gallacher.

You've probably seen her on things like *Ant and Dec's Saturday Night Takeaway* and she now hosts her own show on a major UK radio station. Anyway, I can't have done too badly as the bosses persevered with me. Then, one day, while sitting in an edit suite, having received a grand total of about 30 minutes autocue training, I got a call from the deputy head of Sky Sports. His broad Scottish accent boomed through the receiver with a very simple message: 'Gae home, son, get your suit, you're on!'

Patting my Turkish editor friend Murat on the back, I drove at breakneck speed in my one-litre Volkswagen Polo Fox Coupe to my parents' house to fetch a suit that I didn't possess. I had to borrow one off my dad, which was a couple of sizes too big. As you might have noticed, if you watch Sky F1, style has never been one of my fortes but in the late nineties I'm pretty sure 'baggy' was in. I returned to the studios in Isleworth, was dabbed down with some make-up and then moved to the set of Sky Sports News. I was to partner a very experienced presenter that night who was extremely supportive despite the sweat that was running freely down my back.

And then the countdown came into my earpiece from the production assistant, '10 ... 9 ... 8 ... 7 ... 6 ... 5 ... 4 ... 3 ... 2 ... 1'. It's not rocket science or blast off, it's speaking out loud, but to a 24-year-old it was about as terrifying a thing as you can possibly imagine.

'And we're on air!'

I don't remember what the stories were, I don't really remember much at all about the whole experience, but I definitely spoke out loud and continued to speak out loud for the next four hours until it finished. It was sink or swim. Thankfully, I didn't sink but I may well have soiled my dad's suit!

From there, the powers that be moved me around a variety of sports to learn on the job. There was ice hockey from Nottingham, bowls from somewhere in Wales, golf weekly, Super 12 Rugby, England cricket Test matches with some great characters like Phil Tufnell, Bob Willis and Clive Lloyd. I even did an endurance race from Donington with Perry McCarthy when Keith Huewen turned up at the track instead of the studio! I've asked Perry since about this seminal televisual moment, but he doesn't remember it. From there, I moved into outside broadcasts covering cricket and golf, before eventually getting the main rugby job in 2002.

That was a great decade: covering two Lions' tours to New Zealand and South Africa, England internationals at Twickenham, plus loads of Heineken Cup and Premiership matches. And then, when the F1 rights came Sky's way in 2012, I thought, *Wow, that would be good fun.*

Turner was a massive petrol head and Arsenal fan (sadly). He wanted to bring me across from rugby with him and I jumped at the chance.

My years in Formula One have been some of the best of my life and I've experienced things that I will never forget. Whether it has been hurtling down an Olympic bobsleigh run, jumping out of planes and helicopters, jet skiing with drivers in Monaco or being driven around iconic circuits by some of the greats, it has all been in an attempt to make entertaining television. But it's not lost on me how lucky I am, and they are opportunities that I never take for granted. I often share these experiences with my travelling band of colleagues with whom I spend as much time as I do with my family. It's a good job we all get on so well and I hope that comes across on screen.

That's pretty much how I arrived at where I am today … and most definitely enough about me.

In the book, I return to the race that people still talk about to this day, Abu Dhabi 2021, several times because many of those I talked to were so close to the drama and have their own unique perspective. The title of the book is *Pressure* and that race encapsulated it for so many reasons. It wasn't just the drivers who were feeling it, everyone was.

What follows are the stories of the men and women who make up the Formula One paddock. The unsung heroes and heroines. Of all the sports that I have reported on or presented over my 27 years in television, Formula One is, without doubt, the ultimate team sport. To produce the fastest racing cars on the planet requires the dedication of, in some cases, teams of over 1,500 people. I can't, for obvious reasons, cover every role, but I do hope to give you an overview of what makes the teams tick, how individuals learn to thrive under pressure and what makes the whole ecosystem work. From one race to the next, the show moves on. It is an enormous logistical, as well as sporting, challenge. Every team member has a specific part to play and each is, arguably, as important as the next. This is about them. It's about a few of the people that I've had the privilege to get to know and who are extremely good at what they do.

I hope you enjoy it.

CHAPTER 1
THE MEDICAL CAR

S unday, 5 October 2014 is a day that no one who was there in the paddock will ever forget. It was one of those dark Suzuka afternoons where the rain tumbles out of the Pacific sky and the cold chills you to the bone. It can be such a bleak and desolate venue when the rain sets in and yet so much has happened there over the years that it remains an iconic track, where championships have been decided in a range of heroic and villainous ways.

With a typhoon approaching and daylight fading, on lap 43 of the Japanese Grand Prix Jules Bianchi lost control of his Marussia and collided with a recovery vehicle at the Dunlop curve. Immediately, everybody feared the worst. As a broadcaster, the death of a driver was not something I had given too much thought to when I entered the sport, as no one had lost their life due to injuries sustained at a track since Senna in 1994. When Bianchi crashed, few of us were prepared for how to deal with it. There is very little you can say and little information flows, as Formula One goes into crisis mode. You simply report the facts and don't attempt to speculate.

The memory of Anthoine Hubert's fatal crash as he climbed the Raidillon curve at Spa in 2019 is equally numbing. Lewis Hamilton was going through the motions of a pen interview after qualifying when the crash happened; his eyes were immediately drawn to the big screen in the paddock. As he caught sight of the shunt in the Formula Two feature race for the first time he lost his train of thought. 'Jeez, I hope that kid is OK,' he stuttered. But he wasn't.

Lewis knew how dangerous that part of the circuit could be and as Juan Manuel Correa ploughed into the side of Hubert's car at 218km/h, Hubert was subjected to an impact force of 65G. He didn't stand a chance: 90 minutes later, he was pronounced dead.

Then there was Romain Grosjean's crash on the opening lap of the Bahrain Grand Prix in 2020. I was sat in the TV compound watching with Karun Chandhok and Damon Hill when Grosjean veered right after contact with Daniil Kvyat's Alpha Tauri. As his car ploughed through the barrier at high speed it was torn in two and erupted into a fireball. We all looked at each other open-mouthed and Damon shook his head. He has witnessed as much loss in Formula One as anyone. Damon was Ayrton Senna's team-mate on that fateful day at Imola in 1994 and, as the son of Graham Hill, had endured the deaths of so many of his father's friends behind a steering wheel, as well as his dad, in a plane crash, when he was only 15. He had seen this all before. As the inferno raged, every second counted and we held our collective breath as we waited to see if Grosjean would emerge from the blaze.

As is the way in Formula One, when there is a bad accident, there are no replays and the director immediately cuts away from the incident. Everyone watching was in the dark and praying Grosjean was OK. Miraculously, within a few moments, news emerged that the French driver was out of the car and being treated. And then, eventually, the world saw the pictures that highlighted just how lucky he had been – but also of the remarkable work of a few men who were simply doing their job. Two men in particular had been there in Suzuka in 2014, Spa in 2019 and at every Grand Prix in between: the crew of the Fédération Internationale de l'Automobile (FIA) medical car.

Dr Ian Roberts was appointed the FIA's medical rescue co-ordinator in 2013 having served as chief medical officer at Silverstone since 2008. Originally a consultant in anaesthesia and intensive care, he had been part of the helicopter emergency medical service and originally wanted to be a Royal Marine. Vastly experienced in trackside emergency response before he made the step up to the top job, Roberts's interest in medicine came from his mother, a nurse, while his background in emergency medicine and in particular neuro-intensive care served as the perfect grounding for working in motorsport. First and foremost, though, Roberts is a fan of racing and used to attend club meetings regularly at Silverstone in the 1990s while he was still working as a registrar.

'I'm one of those people who can't stand back and watch for long, I have to get involved. So I went to meet the chief medical officer at Silverstone at the time, David Cranston, and he invited me to join the Grand Prix medical team.'

Roberts spent most of his weekends, when not on call, standing on the banking at a range of different meetings, learning to be a trackside doctor and providing cover for those with more experience.

'I believe in serving an apprenticeship and that is always my advice to any doctors who are trying to get into motorsport. I get suspicious of those who want to come straight in at the top. I started in the chase car behind a grid of 30 Minis. You learn so much at club meets, appreciating track craft and just being immersed in it, smelling the Castrol GTX!'

He progressed to working in the medical car at Silverstone, spent time in the medical centre, and eventually became Cranston's deputy until he took over from him in 2008. During that time, Roberts saw first-hand how dangerous the sport can be.

'I dealt with a significant number of deaths on track. Every one is a tragedy. I'm not trying to put a value on this but when you see those that come to the circuit as part of their hobby and they don't go home at the end of it, don't turn up for work on a Monday morning, it's incredibly sad. With professional drivers there is a different understanding. At these club meets often there are fatalities and horrific injuries but they don't get reported and they are even more heart wrenching as a result.'

Over the years Roberts has learnt to compartmentalise what he has witnessed.

'I was a paediatric anaesthetist at a children's hospital as part of my training and I have looked after some severely ill children, some who were damaged by their parents to such an extent that they required intensive care treatment and yeah, I found those much more difficult to deal with, particularly as some of them were the same age as my own kids. In motorsport I have found a way to concentrate on the needs of the patient. I tend to be very focused on what the problem is and trying to solve it, because by doing that, I'm doing my best for the person involved.'

Roberts was offered the job as medical rescue co-ordinator for the FIA by its president, Jean Todt, in 2012 and took over from Gary Hartstein, who had succeeded the late, great Professor Sid Watkins. Watkins was the original FIA medical delegate and stayed in the role that Roberts now occupies for 26 years. He is rightly lauded as a legend within motor racing. Nicknamed simply 'The Prof', he helped save the lives of many drivers, including Gerhard Berger, Martin Donnelly, Rubens Barrichello and Mika Häkkinen, as well as being on the scene and treating those who weren't so lucky, including Ayrton Senna.

'Sid was this mythical person, who had operated at the top level of motorsport for so long. All the things that he put in place in Formula One, the quality of the medical centres, the equipment, the procedures all filtered down and were adapted to the smaller race meetings, so his influence was huge.'

Watkins was a tough act to follow and so, when Roberts made the step up to Formula One, he knew the responsibility that he was taking on. The medical car was commissioned by Watkins after Swedish driver Ronnie Peterson lost his life following a huge first-lap incident in the 1978 Italian Grand Prix at Monza. It lines up at the back of the grid ahead of the start of every Formula One race, the thought process being that major incidents are more likely to happen at the start of the race when the field is bunched up and everyone is jockeying for position. These days it is either an AMG Mercedes or an Aston Martin DBX and they are primed to get to any first-lap incident as quickly as possible. At the time when Roberts first arrived in Formula One it was driven by South African racer Alan van der Merwe.

A former winner of the coveted Formula Ford Festival at Brands Hatch back in 2001, van der Merwe topped that by winning the British Formula Three championship two years later. It was clear that he had the talent to succeed and he began to believe he had a shot at becoming a Formula One driver. As is the way with so many hopefuls though, the stars just never quite aligned for him.

'I got called the day before I was supposed to go out and test with this particular Formula One team and I was under the impression that they were going to announce me as one of their drivers. It was six in the evening and it was a Milton Keynes number and I thought, oh great, they are going to give me my flight details. It was a really nice guy on the phone, I won't name names, but he said, I'm really sorry, we've given the drive to someone else. I had one thought: *Fucking hell!* That was my introduction into Formula One. it's a cut-throat environment. And yes, talent really matters, you need to be good to get there but once you past a certain point, it's not just about that. You need to have the right surnames, the right manager, the right sponsors, even the right nationality.'

Van der Merwe's is a familiar tale for aspiring drivers trying to reach the pinnacle of motorsport. After his hopes were dashed on a couple of other occasions he became disillusioned and was struggling to figure out what he was going to do next when, out of the blue, he got a call from Charlie Whiting, the FIA race director. It was midway through 2008 and Whiting asked to meet him at the first-class check-in at Heathrow. There he offered van der Merwe the opportunity to drive the medical car. It wasn't the drive he wanted but it was a chance to have a role within Formula One. He took the opportunity, and his first race was the Australian Grand Prix in 2009, alongside Dr Gary Hartstein.

'I knew nothing about anything, particularly on the medical side, at that stage. Driving the car is incredibly easy for a high-calibre driver because it's a road car and I was probably a bit overqualified for that part! But I remember at that first race sitting in the car and Nico Rosberg and Nelson Piquet Jr pulled alongside me at the pit exit to do their practice starts. I had a very intense, bitter feeling. That was my realisation that it was not a fair environment because I had kicked these guys' arses in Formula Three.'

After that he learnt to cast off – or at least bury – any jealousy, and instead threw himself into learning all about his latest drive, serious about creating a more stable career for himself.

'The medical car itself is the tip of the iceberg, it's what everyone sees on TV, but the stuff that goes into it before then is this long chain of events. It's all about the development of the safety equipment, the training of people around the tracks, the design of the cars and the circuits and it was the start of an incredible new chapter in my life.'

When the FIA didn't renew Hartstein's contract at the end of 2012, Roberts stepped in, and over the next decade the pair were to form a unique, unbreakable bond.

'Gary was a very impressive individual, he knew his job inside out, but he had a very fiery temperament and he probably didn't play the political game well enough. When Ian turned up and we started together, I thought, bloody hell, this is different. Ian wasn't there for the glory, he never walked round with his chest puffed out. There's a huge amount riding on you, he knew that and I knew instantly that he was the right person for the job.'

Roberts and van der Merwe had been working together and developing an understanding for a couple of years before they had to put everything into practice in Suzuka in 2014 after Bianchi's horror crash.

Roberts – 'I remember the conditions were worsening and we could hear chatter over team radio. I thought this is going to be red-flagged very soon. On my screen I saw a yellow sector pop up.'

VDM – 'We were watching how the cars were behaving as they came past us and we knew that something was going to happen.

We saw the Sauber of Adrian Sutil go off and I said to Ian, "It's fast, it's blind and there's a car off in that area, it needs to be red-flagged immediately." Just 20 seconds later we got an impact advisory. The deployment went really well. Bernd Mayländer, the safety car driver, let us past straight away and I drove the best five corners of my life. But when we arrived at the incident we knew instantly that it was bad. You develop a bit of a sixth sense for whether it's a serious accident for the human, just by looking at the car.'

Roberts – 'I could see there was a Formula One car, but in my head I thought, *What's wrong with this picture?* Something didn't feel right. And then I suddenly realised it. The top of the car had gone. As it hit the recovery vehicle it had sheared the top off Bianchi's car. And at that point your heart sinks.'

VDM – 'We just looked at each other, shook our heads and cursed. I know it sounds harsh but you just let your emotional response come out and we're on the intercom speaking only to each other. But it didn't change our approach. We knew that he had probably hit the JCB in fifth or sixth gear at close to 130km/h. The line of survivability has been compressed with all the safety systems in place and 99 times out of 100 a driver in an accident will be absolutely fine. They might have a concussion but you don't usually arrive at a crash and see broken bones anymore. It's kind of a binary event nowadays with the survival cell. You either get there and they are OK, in the grand scheme of things; or they don't survive. This, unfortunately, was the first one where we got there and thought, *This is not survivable.*'

Roberts – 'I could feel Jules's breath on my hand so I secured an airway whilst he was still in his seat. We gave him oxygen and he had a pulse, so at that point we reverse all the things that are reversible, i.e. good airway, breathing, oxygenation. Once he's out of the car there is nothing more we can do on site, so we properly extricated him, ensuring that his neck was well supported because if he's had a big hit he's almost certainly going to have some problems with the C spine, and then he's put into the ambulance and onto a ventilator.

But you could tell by looking at the eyes, the pupils, that he had had a catastrophic head injury.'

VDM – 'The JCB was there to pick up Sutil's Sauber so he saw the whole thing and he just kept asking, "Is he going to be OK? Is he going to be OK?"'

Roberts – 'I got a message on the radio to tell us that the race had been stopped but that there was going to be a podium ceremony and I remember saying, "I strongly recommend that you do not celebrate on the podium."'

Under normal circumstances, Roberts's duty of care would have been handed over to the medical team in the helicopter or ambulance, but on that occasion, because of the severity of Bianchi's injury, he decided to remain with him until he got to the hospital in Yokkaichi. Upon viewing the initial CT scans, Roberts's worst fears were confirmed. Bianchi was put into a medically induced coma to give him the best possible chance of survival. The drugs he was given calmed his brain activity down, reducing its oxygen requirements in the hope that the swelling would reduce and allow the blood to be reabsorbed. It was about preventing the secondary injury that the inflammation had caused. Bianchi was taken out of his artificial coma in November 2014 and began breathing unaided. It meant that he was able to be transported to hospital in Nice, but it was to no avail. There he remained unconscious and in a critical condition with his family by his side at their daily vigil, but on 17 July the following year Bianchi passed away as a result of the injuries he had sustained nine months earlier.

In the days and weeks that followed, the pair went through a lot of soul-searching and questioned every action that they had taken that day in forensic detail. Did they get there fast enough? Could they have got the driver out of the car any quicker? Were all of the medical interventions carried out at the right time? Were they supporting each other with the right equipment at the right time? It was a string of endless questions that they needed to go through to process what they had just encountered, with the ultimate aim of being able to say to themselves, yes, we did all that we could do to help the patient. In the case of Bianchi, after exhaustive self-analysis, they arrived at that conclusion and it provided them with an element of closure.

But they always prepare for the worst.

It starts with both of them knowing the location of the equipment that they have in the car like the back of their hands. Roberts carries gloves, a tourniquet, airways and scissors in his race suit, a few pieces of emergency equipment that he can call upon when he first arrives at a situation. Under his seat he places a small trauma bag with ventilation, cannulas, basic monitoring and burns dressings. In the back of the car he has further tools that enable him to undertake more invasive interventions, including a video laryngoscope, a defibrillator, oxygen and intraosseous needles to get fluid into drivers' bones if it is too difficult after an accident to locate the patient's veins. If the driver is losing blood this allows him to get an IV into the driver as soon as is possible. As well as all the medical devices, they carry two fire extinguishers that can deal with any kind of blaze, even electrical, and a cutter to cut bodywork such as the halo device in order to get the driver out of the car as fast as possible.

They are supported at the track by a number of local teams including a regional doctor who always makes up a third person in the medical car and carries their own trauma kit. There are two or three extrication teams who specialise in the safe removal of drivers from the survival cell, as well as intensive-care-standard ambulances with ventilation and monitoring onboard.

No stone is left unturned and that dreadful afternoon in Suzuka further focused their minds on what they could do better next time. It is impossible for them to prepare for every situation but they never stop trying. They know from experience that there are certain points at different tracks where accidents are more likely to occur. Eau Rouge at Spa, the exit of the tunnel at Monaco and, on the faster street circuits such as Baku, at the end of the long straight. They also know which drivers are accidents waiting to happen.

VDM – 'Ian and I spent a comical amount of time in the car being paranoid about being unprepared. We did so many dry runs in our minds. We were always working through scenarios that we had never witnessed before and, because incidents are less frequent these days, there are always long periods where nothing happens and everybody's patting themselves on the back, saying how well everything is going. Ian and I were always the pessimists. It's coming, something is coming and we're going to have to deal with it. And that's a brilliant motivator.'

Roberts and van der Merwe's responsibilities extended to all Formula Two and Formula Three sessions over Grand Prix weekends and one of those scenarios van der Merwe mentions occurred on the second lap of the Formula Two feature race in Spa on 31 August 2019, five years on from Bianchi's crash, at one of the most dangerous points on any circuit, anywhere in the world. Any driver who has raced around Belgium's iconic circuit will tell you just how fast the Eau Rouge combination is. The circuit dips down and the left, right, left series of turns is often taken flat-out. The blind uphill section out of Eau Rouge is technically called Raidillon, and it was here that Anthoine Hubert suffered a fatal collision where once again Roberts and van der Merwe were first at the scene.

The slightest miscalculation at this section can have terrifying consequences. It wasn't the first time that they had seen a crash of this magnitude. Kevin Magnussen had a horrible shunt at Raidillon in 2016 when his Renault ploughed into a tyre wall at 180mph. The Dane was lucky to hobble away with an ankle injury and was fit enough to race the next week in Monza. Other drivers down the years have not been so lucky, including German driver Stefan Bellof, who was killed in a World Sportscar Championship there in 1985 after colliding with Jacky Ickx.

Hubert's crash occurred as a chain reaction after Giuliano Alesi suffered a puncture and crashed. Several cars behind him braked but Hubert was unsighted, clipped one of the slowing cars, hit the barrier and then rebounded onto the track. As he came back on,

American/Ecuadorian driver Juan Manuel Correa T-boned the cockpit area of Hubert's Arden, sending it into the air and splitting it in half.

Roberts – 'When we arrived, the scene we were presented with was a huge debris field, lots of bits of cars but also lots of big chunks of cars, so the idea was for me to find all the stricken drivers as rapidly as possible. The first question I asked myself was how many cars do we actually have here? It looked like two cars were involved but the debris was sufficient for three. You just hope that you're going to pick up the driver that's in the worst condition first. Thankfully I went straight to Anthoine.'

VDM – 'I parked between the remains of the two cars that we could see and Ian went straight to Hubert because it looked like he had the most acute injury. I went over to Correa and I could see that he was fully conscious. It's actually a nice thing when you arrive and the driver is screaming and very angry or in a lot of pain because you know that it's salvageable.'

Roberts – 'As soon as I looked at Anthoine though, my heart sank. Once the local medical team arrived I ensured that the simultaneous resuscitation and removal of the driver was going on, so that I could go and check the rest of the field. My task as part of the rescue co-ordination is to be very careful not to drill down on one particular driver, I have to understand the whole scene. I have to prioritise. Anthoine was unconscious and unresponsive, but Correa was talking and in a lot of pain from his ankle but he was conscious and so I first had to ensure Anthoine was receiving CPR.'

VDM – 'The local doctor in the back of the medical car was Teddy, a huge bear of a man, always smiling, always laid back, and with Ian tending to Anthoine, he looked after Correa. It was hard to get him out of the car and made so much harder by the people that were arriving. The scene filled up quickly with people that were in shock. It looked like an aeroplane crash. We kept getting rescue trucks and things we didn't need. Ian and Teddy needed space to do their job and I remember that a lot of people with a lot of experience sort of fell apart that day. Seasoned rescue workers, who have worked at Eau Rouge for 20 years, their overalls faded but who had never seen a young kid who's not going to make it. It was one where Ian needed support. He's only got two eyes and two hands and he needed to deal with Hubert and Correa. That weekend was as dark as the Bianchi weekend. Hubert was a lovely kid, such a gentle individual, and to see him in that state wasn't nice and it affected me. It's a miracle that Correa got out of that as he did.'

Correa 'got out of it' with fractures to both his legs and a minor spinal injury and after being transferred to an intensive care unit in London was placed in an induced coma after falling into acute respiratory failure. He recovered but his rehabilitation took over a year. He has since returned to racing. Hubert wasn't so lucky and despite the administered CPR continuing until he reached the medical centre, Hubert was pronounced dead at 18.35, just an hour and a half after the crash.

The following day saw the motorsport community pulling together as only they can, with Hubert's family all present at the front of the Formula One grid ensuring that the show would go on. It's always confusing to some why, when tragedy strikes, racing always continues. You ask any driver though and they would say the same thing. They know the risks when they start on their racing journey. That risk in motorsport is as high as it comes and yet every single one of them would say it was all worth it, to feel as alive as they do, while doing the thing that they love. Some have died for it and others will in the future. That is motor racing. The quest for it to be risk free is Sisyphean but doctors like Roberts will keep on pushing boulders up hills until the end of time, because they love the sport as much as those who take the risk.

The pair didn't have to wait that long before they were next called into action for another extreme event. Their presence on the scene so quickly in Bahrain the following year, the night Grosjean's car exploded on live television in front of a global audience, emphasised just how innate and telepathic their actions had become when something serious happened. Years of preparation and discussion about improvement had become totally engrained.

Van der Merwe knew he was able to cut the first complex of corners via a service road in order to shave off a couple of seconds and stay close to the pack ahead of them. When they turned the corner they saw the fireball erupt in front of them. They were at the incident almost as it happened.

'My first thought upon arrival was, *Holy shit, where's the car?* It had split in two but there was only one half on the track.'

The front of the car had pierced the two sections of the Armco like a tin opener. That in itself would have likely decapitated Grosjean had it not been for the introduction of the Halo device in 2018. As it penetrated the barrier, the car was ripped in two and erupted in flames.

'I ran over and could see through the gaps in the Armco, it was like looking inside a furnace and I could see Romain and I thought, *He's done!*'

Trapped inside his survival cell, Grosjean knew the clock was ticking.

'It felt much longer than 28 seconds. I saw my visor turning all orange, I thought about a lot of things, including Niki Lauda and I thought that it wasn't possible to end up like that. Not now. I couldn't finish my story in Formula One here. And then for my children, I told myself that I had to get out. I put my hands in the fire, so I clearly felt them burning on the chassis, then I felt some-one pulling on my suit, so I knew I was out. My escape was like a second birth.'

The man pulling at his suit, of course, was Roberts. They had arrived at a raging inferno and his immediate reaction was to direct a marshal with a fire extinguisher to rebuff the flames. It was suffi-cient for him to get close enough to the barrier to give Grosjean a helping hand as he jumped clear and was in position to treat his burns immediately. As Roberts directed him away from the blaze, van der Merwe had already collected another extinguisher from the back of the car and deployed some of it on Grosjean's body to ensure there were no residual flames. It helped that the driver had had the clarity of thought to extricate himself from the car in under 30 seconds. Any longer and it would have been horrific. Roberts's approach to the fire was enough to singe his face.

'I put my hands up to protect me but I couldn't afford for him to fall back into the flames.'

Thankfully Grosjean didn't, but Roberts knew that he had to work quickly to assess the damage. One of the first things he had to figure out was whether Grosjean had suffered any internal burns through inhalation. Roberts had had experience of this a few years previously when on call in the emergency room at the hospital where he was training. A worker had been admitted after walking past a furnace in a factory just as the door had accidentally swung open. As well as suffering serious external burns he had also sustained a severe inhalation injury. When Roberts tended to him his first thought was to check his airway and upon doing this he realised that the swelling was closing the patient's throat up. He just managed to get a ventilator into him before it closed completely. It bought the other doctors treating him some time, although unfortunately it still wasn't enough to save his life. Burns are often fatal in the hours after the immediate trauma.

'When we got Romain at a safe distance from the flames, I just wanted to get his helmet off and get him talking to me, so that I could assess if there was any damage to his airway. Then we assessed him for a head injury and immediately got his gloves off and applied some cooling gel to limit the damage to the part of his body that had the thinnest fire-resistant clothing over it, the gloves. Then it was into the back of the car as we thought that it was the quickest way to get him to the medical centre.'

Grosjean suffered burns to his hands in the accident but returned to the wheel in IndyCar and is still racing at one of the top levels in the US. Life goes on for him, and for others that Roberts has tended to over the years; his commitment to the Hippocratic oath is to be admired. When he wasn't working at race tracks around the world he continued to work for the NHS in the off season up until the end of last year. People think that he must be a millionaire working as the main doctor in Formula One, but he's not. In fact he's been paid less over the years than if he'd been working full time for the NHS. He stopped private work 12 years ago so that he could see his kids grow up. His sacrifices for the love of the sport he grew up watching have been as great as anyone up and down the paddock.

'I gave up a lot of practice to come and work in Formula One, but I knew that right from the start. The decision was either to continue to work full time for the NHS and miss this opportunity, or have something to talk about to my grandkids when I'm 90. And that's what I decided to do. So, you know, I'm not complaining, I'm just explaining.'

Van der Merwe left the sport in 2021 when, like many, he refused to take the Covid vaccine. He was replaced by Portuguese driver Bruno Correia, but he and Roberts still stay in touch and remain good friends. For a decade they worked tirelessly together to continue the work of Sir Jackie Stewart, Sid Watkins and all those who had committed to making the sport as safe as is humanly possible. And with Roberts still in charge and continuing to push in his role as hard as any driver would on track, you know that those who choose to risk their lives are in the safest pair of hands. They help the show go on even in the most trying of circumstances. The job of putting on that show falls to the promoter.

CHAPTER 2

THE PROMOTER

The British Grand Prix. A magnificent gathering of like-minded folk in the heart of this green and pleasant land. Where the glitz and the glamour of the paddock are forced to get down and dirty for the weekend and embrace whatever our summer weather can throw at them. Where the smell of a thousand sausages wafts up your nostrils, music reverberates from every corner of the circuit and passionate fans wrapped in colourful flags consume warm beer by the gallon, while the badgers and foxes of these particular shires stay underground for the weekend wondering what on earth that infernal racket is taking place above them.

It has become the largest sporting event in the country. In 2023, 480,000 fans streamed through the gates over the weekend at the home of British motorsport, an increase of 80,000 from the year before and the biggest attendance in its 74-year history. In 2024 they achieved the same total, including 164,000 on the Sunday, which was a new single-day record. It is undoubtedly a jewel in the national sporting calendar.

The end of the Second World War left Britain with no race tracks but plenty of airfields. In October 1948 the Royal Automobile Club hosted the British Grand Prix at one of those airfields that straddled the border of Northamptonshire, Buckinghamshire and Oxfordshire, at a place called Silverstone. It was the first British Grand Prix since 1938, and more than 100,000 people turned up to see Luigi Villoresi lift the trophy in his Maserati. In 1950 the venue hosted the first ever Formula One world championship race. Attended by King George VI and Queen Elizabeth, it was won by Giuseppe Farina in an Alfa Romeo. Two years later the British Racing Drivers' Club (BRDC) took over the lease for Silverstone and they have remained owners and operators ever since they purchased the freehold in 1971.

The BRDC is an exclusive, invitation-only members' club for drivers from Britain and the Commonwealth who are judged to have achieved success in the upper echelons of motorsport over a number of seasons. It was started by Dr J. Dudley Benjafield in 1928. He was one of an informal group of racers known as the 'Bentley Boys' who set it up mainly as a socialising club. From an initial membership of 25 people it set out an agenda to celebrate success in motorsport and further the interests of British drivers racing overseas. Membership now sits at around 850 people, including most of my esteemed colleagues, and while the British Grand Prix had spells at Aintree and Brands Hatch, since 1987 Silverstone has been the permanent home of the race, recently securing another ten-year contract meaning it can plan forward until 2034.

The job of running the circuit and the Grand Prix falls to the CEO of Silverstone, Stuart Pringle, and his team. Delivering a sporting event of this scale is a huge responsibility, but Pringle has broad shoulders. An impeccably spoken former tank commander and motorbike enthusiast, he began his career in motorsport at the age of 28, fresh out of the army, as secretary of the vintage sports car club. He went on to run track days and events for Jonathan Palmer out of Brands Hatch before becoming club secretary of the BRDC in December 2006. Having spent eight years getting to know the club inside out he then moved across to the circuit side of the business, becoming managing director of Silverstone in 2016.

Due to 40 years of chronic underinvestment, Silverstone was all but out of cash. Bernie Ecclestone had had a fractious relationship with the circuit and the BRDC, frequently squeezing them and threatening to take the race elsewhere.

Pringle – 'It was creaking and groaning. In a good year the Grand Prix would make a small profit but in a bad year, a loss. There was simply no cash to reinvest in improving the facility. It was like a game of snakes and ladders: one step forward, another back. Now I'm pleased to say that the owners take the sensible view that it's not in their interests to crush the promoter and recognise that the BRDC invests all its money back into the facilities.'

Pringle took on a mammoth task in trying to turn Silverstone's fortunes around but, since doing so, the circuit has gradually started to become profitable. When he started, morale was on the floor and the pain of decades of making do had become debilitating for the organisation. It needed a cultural reset and a rebrand and he slowly prioritised the areas that needed investment.

'There's never enough to do everything at once, you just have to concentrate on cutting the elephant up and eating it one bite at a time. Plus, the people who came on board said to me, "Stuart, with the greatest respect, we've never seen you wearing anything other than a collared shirt and deck shoes, this isn't really where the business needs to be, we are not talking to people like you." There's now a whole new world of Formula One fans so I just had to shut up and listen to people that knew better than me.'

The Grand Prix is just the largest commercial piece of the annual jigsaw puzzle for Silverstone, a disproportionately important part of the business but a puzzle that has been a lot easier to fit together in the years post-Ecclestone.

'There is only one difference that has mattered and that is the profile and active promotion of the product, centrally, by the commercial rights holder. In the old days Formula One was always popular. It was always high profile, always had a large fanbase but it wasn't bringing in truckloads of new fans. Sean Bratches, former CMO of Liberty, the owners of Formula One, had the vision for *Drive to Survive* and then followed it up with social media diversification. They've done a great job of making it a better product for the promoters to sell. We're paying a lot more

money than ever before for that product, but we're now getting more value in return.'

It also helps to have a circuit that Pringle believes, as do most of the rest of us, is the best in the world. I've been lucky enough to have been driven around Silverstone in a number of cars, and I even (somehow) managed to secure my racing licence there (it has since lapsed). The most memorable experience, though, was ripping around the circuit with Paul di Resta at the wheel in the old two-seater V10 Formula One car. The forces on your body as you change direction through Copse and then Maggotts, Becketts and Chapel are indescribable and you can sense the history in every corner.

'We've got a heritage that you can't make up, coupled with a modern, world-class facility and a layout that wasn't designed by computers or CAD; it was an old airfield perimeter road with some pencil lines on a chart that set out where the corners were going to be. But it's a layout that's fast and speed has always won out in motor racing. A fast course is a good course.'

What is unique about Silverstone is that unlike Wimbledon, where you can't have a knock-up on Centre Court, or Wembley, where you can't go for a kick about with your mates, here the grassroots competitor can race in the wheel tracks of Sir Lewis Hamilton, George Russell or Lando Norris within a couple of weeks of the Grand Prix taking place.

Each year when we arrive at Silverstone something new seems to have been added; most recently a hotel has been erected on the start/finish line of the main straight. This has been hugely important for the circuit. When Pringle took over it was clear that the business had too much of a reliance on Formula One, so one of the biggest challenges was to get the circuit making money all year round. The 'Wing' at Silverstone opened in 2011. Built at a cost of £27 million, the new pit and paddock complex is world class, but it left a massive dent in the finances.

'We decided to sell off an acre of land to a guy who builds hotels for a living. One of the biggest reasons that the business was struggling was because of the lack of on-site accommodation. We needed the accommodation to power the 'Wing' because its overheads were enormous. When the hotel opened in September 2022 we doubled the revenues on conferences and exhibitions simply because we now had a place where people could stay.'

These days there are things to do at Silverstone seven days a week, 52 weeks a year, and being slap bang in the middle of England means that it is accessible for a large proportion of the UK population. More than 22 million people are within a two-hour drive of the circuit.

'We want to get people to a point where they don't want to rush off at the end of the day. Make it a two-day visit, stay longer, spend more money with us, have reasons to come back again within the same year, to come and try different things. Essentially, though, we are sweating the track asset as hard as we can. If there is a harderworking piece of asphalt at any top-line motor-racing circuit in the world, I would be very surprised. I doubt anybody's got cars going round [their track] as often as we do.'

So among all the other activity at Silverstone, how much planning does it take to deliver an event of the size and scale of the British Grand Prix?

'The cliché is that we start preparing for the next one the day after we've delivered the Grand Prix. Much of our learnings are taken as part of the debrief. We have decades of retained knowledge but the process is constantly evolving. Last year, for example, we had the second-biggest stage in the UK, one that's graced the best festivals in the country, and we'd not done that before. That, in itself, was a massive logistical challenge but now that we've locked down the ten-year contract we can plan three years ahead rather than from one year to the next.'

Over the last few years, since the *Drive to Survive* phenomenon, there has, for the first time in the history of the sport, been an increased, sustained interest in Formula One in one of its biggest markets, North America. There are now five Grands Prix on the continent, including Mexico and Canada, and Pringle and his team are ever watchful of how these newer kids on the block go about selling their own events.

'Where America leads in sport, Europe and the UK follows. America has always been better at entertainment. We now second staff into other people's businesses to learn from them. We've just had someone from our marketing department spend six weeks in Melbourne to understand how they put the Australian GP together and we'll have an Aussie come and spend six weeks with us in the build-up to our race. The promoters getting to know each other has been actively encouraged by Liberty. The old days of divide and conquer don't exist anymore, where if Bernie thought you were talking to other promoters he'd chop you off at the knees. But we fundamentally aren't competing; there is just a huge amount we can learn from each other.'

It is clear though that Formula One don't want a homogenous product. In fact, in a crowded market as a promoter, it's about standing out from the crowd and developing an identity. In the last few years the offering from Silverstone has increasingly moved towards a British festival vibe. Silverstone is second only to Glastonbury in the UK in terms of number of people in one place at any one time. On any given day of the Grand Prix there can be up to 160,000 at Silverstone, compared to 230,000 at Glastonbury.

'Fundamentally, Formula One absolutely encourages every round to have its own unique international identity. I look on with immense admiration at Wimbledon, which has done a great job of commercialising its brand without putting stickers everywhere. It's still green and purple with strawberries and cream and Pimm's and it is still quintessentially British. For us, because we are a four-day event, we couldn't get all of our current audience in and out every day if they all commuted, so having people camp greatly helps with the traffic challenges. It also helps having people on site because they buy their pints of beer off us!'

Every year the acts playing Silverstone get bigger. In 2024 they had the Kings of Leon and Stormzy. In 2025 Sam Fender and Fatboy Slim took to the stages. The vision that Pringle has set out is becoming engrained into the offering. It makes sense to tap into the psyche of the British people, who have always enjoyed the collective euphoria of sport and music. Silverstone, the festival, is about as British as you can get. They have definitely found their identity.

Over the course of the British GP and the Moto GP weekends, more than £100 million is spent in the local economy, benefiting the whole area, but one thing that doesn't serve the local area well is the resultant traffic. As a greenfield site in the middle of the country, one of the issues for Silverstone has always been that it is not well served by public transport. Despite renting 280 double-decker buses to bring people into the circuit from park-and-rides and renting extra trains to bring people into Banbury and Milton Keynes, the problem has always been road access. Anyone who has tried to get out of the circuit on race day knows that they can be stuck in queues for hours. It can leave a bitter taste in the mouth for spectators and has been a perpetual headache for Pringle, who ultimately has to wear the criticism. He is acutely aware that these challenges are part of his job, though, and is constantly looking for solutions that have included making the dual carriageway into and out of the circuit a one-way system. In the future he hopes that the HS2 high-speed rail link will stop for one day a year near to Silverstone to give a viable alternative to the roads.

Every year there are a different set of issues to address and Pringle's job is to stay one step ahead of everything that is thrown at him and his team. Those pressures and challenges that Silverstone face, though, are entirely different to other Grands Prix on the calendar, the most recent of which, in Vegas, Pringle feels would have been altogether on a different scale.

'Between myself, our COO, Alex Lacey, and our circuit manager, Lee Howkins, we have worked on over 80 Grands Prix. The Las Vegas team had worked on absolutely none. To come in and run a race on a street circuit, in a city that's not done one since the 1980s, to do it at night, to close the roads, deal with the commercial implications and to do it in such short order, I think they did an absolutely stellar job. From an operational, promotional and delivery point of view, I thought it was an incredible first effort.'

Watching the sport grow exponentially and begin to thrive in the US and beyond has been one of the genuine joys of my broadcasting career. When we started with Sky Sports F1 back in 2012, the grandstands weren't always full and many of the promoters were struggling to make ends meet. That is not the case now.

It has taken a long time for Formula One to get a foothold in the States, a country with its own particular sporting ecosystem. Over the years 12 US venues have hosted Grands Prix, but interest waxed and waned until recently. A lot of credit for the sport's resurgence across the pond must go to Austin and the Circuit of the Americas. Austin came on board in 2012 and has become one of the most popular events on the calendar, certainly with the Sky Sports F1 team. Its unique charm and 'Keep Austin Weird' motto struck a chord with some of the more esoteric members of our travelling community, and for those that haven't ventured to this particular corner of Texas, I highly recommend it. The track is fast, has a good mix of corners and often produces great racing, there is live music playing in every bar you set foot in, the barbecue is unparalleled (just ask our commentator, Crofty) and if you set foot on 6th Street after sunset, literally anything might happen – and frequently does.

There are now three US races on the calendar, all with a very different feel. The owners know that it is THE key territory for growth and commercialisation.

Tyler Epp is Pringle's equivalent for one of the newest US races on the calendar, as chief operating officer of the Miami Grand Prix. He began his marketing and operations career in motorsport in NASCAR and IndyCar before a period in major league baseball with the San Diego Padres and the NFL with the Kansas City Chiefs. While Silverstone provides its own unique challenges for the promoter, the same can also be said for Miami, where Epp's team is tasked annually with putting together a temporary circuit in one of the busiest cities in the States.

Like Silverstone, the Miami Grand Prix is privately owned, privately funded and privately operated. There is no governmental support but that also means no governmental bureaucracy. It also means there is no safety net if you fail to make ends meet. The first Miami Grand Prix took place in 2022, piggybacking on the burgeoning interest in North America. Florida has always been the home to many successful winter series because of the year-round climate and tracks such as Daytona, Homestead and Sebring are staples of these.

There are a number of hurdles for potential promoters to over-come to have a chance of hosting a race, but there also has to be a tangible reason for Liberty to want to stage a race in any particular location. The battle to get the Miami bid off the ground faced several setbacks, including intense objections from locals when the initial proposal was to race downtown as early as 2019. But when Steve Ross, the owner of the Miami Dolphins NFL franchise, threw his weight behind a plan to relocate the race around his Hard Rock Stadium to the north of the city, the dream started to become a reality. With a promise to invest $5 million into the local community, including internships for city residents, the mayor of Miami Gardens then also rallied behind the project and, in 2022, a second US race was born.

'From the very beginning, it was decided that we were going to be all about the experience of coming to Miami. Somebody should be able to fly here, come to the circuit for three days and feel like they have experienced the city. Building that brand promise while selling it to the different segments of the local population has been the core challenge. It's about bringing the greatest form of motor-sport in the world to the greatest sports entertainment market in the world and putting on a spectacle like no other.'

And putting on a spectacle like the Miami Grand Prix is no small challenge. The pit building and paddock club are permanent but everything else is temporary and needs to be built up and torn down every single year. The circuit in its Grand Prix form currently exists for only four days a year, but that's about to change. As with Silverstone, or any modern privately owned circuit, you have to make your key assets work for you, and Epp has a target of making different configurations of the track operational for 50 days a year. They are cutting in an inner loop that can morph into different shapes depending on what else is being hosted on site at the Hard Rock Stadium in any given week. And any given week can mean a totally different proposition; 2024 was an extremely busy year. They hosted Copa América football games and various concerts in the spring and summer before the Miami Dolphins training camp began in August. In the autumn they hosted 20 NFL and college football games for the Dolphins and the Miami Hurricanes as well as three nights of Taylor Swift's Eras tour. As soon as the Dolphins were eliminated from the NFL playoffs the build began for the Grand Prix. That meant starting preparations around late January, with eight or nine weeks of heavy building before they had to back off while the Miami Open tennis tournament took centre stage for two weeks in late March.

'As they are taking pictures of the men's singles final winner, the trucks are moving in, dropping materials and starting to remove the courts. This happens over a ten-day period. We have to tear down the grandstand court in the centre of the football stadium and build the entire Formula One team village. So April is our busiest time as we are all systems go getting everything erected for the Grand Prix at the start of May.'

On top of all that, in June 2026 they have the football World Cup games to host. It is a never-ending annual cycle at the Hard Rock Stadium as they attempt not only to find their place in the Formula One landscape but also to nurture the foundations of something that will last.

'In the short term, it's not really about making money. We certainly want to be profitable but it's really about building an environment here so people know that the Miami International Autodrome is a place that does more than just host Formula One.

This is about creating a South Floridian car culture, similar to the Californian car scene that is centred around Long Beach. We've met with 70 different car clubs around the world and they all want what we have: a core event that brings people to them. We have that with Formula One now and it's about using the Grand Prix to create other ways for people to engage with and experience our track.'

And that is the challenge for every promoter at present. As the global fanbase continues to grow and the revenues get ever larger, more and more sponsors come on board and everyone wants a slice of the pie. Historic circuits are facing a greater challenge to their status and presence on the calendar than ever before. You can no longer rely on history alone. Spa, Monaco, Monza and Zandvoort all have contracts to negotiate beyond 2025, and with countries in the Middle East paying upwards of $50 million per year to secure their right to stage an event, those that pay less, and with no state support, have to ensure their offering consistently provides a grand spectacle with no empty seats. If the product on track remains interesting, their job is made easier, but that is not always the case and therefore promoters like Pringle and Epp need to stay creative to stay afloat, especially with the pressure of so many other countries wanting their own slot on the calendar. Now with 24 races spread across 5 continents, the task of ensuring all the teams' equipment gets from event to event is becoming even harder. In the next chapter we will show you how it's done.

CHAPTER 3
THE LOGISTICS TEAM

I n terms of scale, there is no greater logistical challenge in sport than Formula One. Moving everything from country to country, often from week to week, with the amount of equipment and personnel that needs to be transported is an unparalleled endeavour. Mistakes just can't happen, and that is a specific kind of pressure for those whose job it is to keep the show on the road.

Danny Lowe joined the army at 16. For the next 27 years it was to be his life, completing six tours of Iraq, three of Afghanistan and several more that he can't talk about. Lowe joined the Royal Corps of Transport straight from school, thus beginning his career in military logistics. Specialising in aviation, his job was to move equipment around either by parachute or underslung beneath Chinook helicopters. He later moved on to the massive Hercules cargo planes, where 80 per cent of his time was spent ensuring Britain's special forces were well supplied.

When he first joined the army, like many youngsters, Lowe lacked the guidance he needed at that point in his life, but he counts himself incredibly lucky to have had a corporal who looked out for him.

'He taught me everything about life, even how to talk to girls. This is how you do it, this is how you speak, this is how you act, this is how you brush your boots, how you do your job. Don't do this! Don't do that! It was hard. If I messed up, I was punished and made to do whatever task it was over and over again. It's a cliché but that's what happens in the army. It taught me some very valuable lessons which I hold true today. It was only in my late teens that I learnt how to act, react and conduct myself properly.'

That discipline was put to good use in war zones around the world, where he had to work closely with the pilots and crew of the Royal Air Force, in his role as an air dispatcher for the 47th Air Despatch Squadron, the same squadron that has recently been deployed to parachute aid packages into Gaza. Still employing the same methods today as they did in Lowe's time, the 47th take raw supplies, food, water and ammunition and rig it into nets. They then attach parachutes, fix them to static lines running the length of the Hercules and deploy the packages over specific drop zones, often under intense enemy fire.

'It wasn't always just rations and ammunition we had to drop. I remember once I had to sign for a million dollars in cash on the Afghan border. I have no idea why it was needed, and I didn't ask questions, but I saw it disappear out the back of my Hercules with my own eyes! I hope it was put to good use!'

By the time he left the army, Lowe had worked his way up to the rank of regimental sergeant major. He had come a long way from the young, wide-eyed private he'd been when he enlisted – seven ranks to be precise – and, by the end of his military career, he was responsible for more than 550 soldiers. He was offered a commission to become an officer, but respectfully declined and decided to take his chances on 'civvy street'.

'I took a year off and cut grass for some of the older folk in the village where I live in Oxfordshire. I did some hazel-weaving for fences, felled some trees and just generally decompressed. I did receive some job offers but, no disrespect to companies like DHL, Amazon or Eddie Stobbart, I just couldn't work for them. How could they offer the same exhilaration and excitement that I had felt for the past 30-odd years?'

But in 2017, a job popped up on LinkedIn as logistical support for the Williams Formula One racing team, and Lowe decided to come out of his career sabbatical.

'I applied and got an interview, which was promptly followed by a second, and relatively quickly I was offered the job. Obviously, I was delighted, but they said you need to pass the Claire Williams test.* So I was flown out to Budapest on a Monday morning and I met Claire on the Thursday before the Hungarian Grand Prix. It was like the Roman empress giving me a thumbs up or a thumbs down. Thankfully I got the thumbs up and here I am today.'

Within 18 months, Lowe had become responsible for all trackside logistics at Williams. It is his responsibility that everything, outside of the car and garage equipment itself, is moved on time and without a hitch around all 24 race locations across the globe. Even for a man with Lowe's experience, it is a massive task. There is always a mountain of work to get through and the planning for the following season begins as soon as the calendar is confirmed. When the team lands after the last race in Abu Dhabi, their logistics department get to work.

'As soon as the sea freight arrives back in the UK it needs to be stripped out, cleaned, washed and serviced. All the electrical appliances need to be PAT tested, and any breakages replaced. Any rebranding needs to be done and the equipment is packed back in to start the whole process all over again. We have six sets of sea freight, and all will do different routes, depending on changes to the calendar. Each set contains five shipping containers: four for the garage and one for the marketing and catering teams. Four of those six sets need to be sent on their way by the end of January, so there is always huge time pressure. There are specific things that we need to be careful of. I need to make sure the electrical equipment is compatible for each region. I know, for example, that I need a lot of electrical cables in Mexico, whereas in Saudi I don't. All of the races in the States are now massive, so we need much more equipment for them, and it all needs to be packed specifically for the requirements of each individual race.'

---

* Claire Williams was team principal at the time and daughter of the late Sir Frank Williams, founder of the team.

On top of the usual headaches, with so much geo-political instability in recent years, Formula One planning teams need to factor in that certain routes may be impossible.

'Let me give you a perfect example. One set of sea freight is destined this year to cover Bahrain, Singapore and Abu Dhabi, and it is not coming home in between. But, because of what is happening in the Middle East, we can't use the Suez Canal and so we've had to reroute around the Horn of Africa. It's a long way and adds a great deal in transport costs to what is already extremely expensive. We've had to send sea freight the wrong way around the world. It's hugely disruptive. In Bahrain, because of the issue with the Suez Canal, the freight didn't arrive at the track until the Tuesday of the race and it usually arrives the week before.'

There is a balance to strike between the difference in costs of what can be transported by sea, and what needs to be transported by air. In this day and age, the Formula One calendar is so dense and far reaching that most of the race essential items, i.e. the car and the garage equipment, has to be air-freighted at a cost of around $550/kilo, which is astronomical but is so high because the cargo is so precious and fragile in the form of the F1 cars and includes handling fees and specific chartered flights, which are top priority, so the air freighters (DHL) and agents know they can charge top dollar. The teams need to transport roughly 18 tonnes by this manner but, obviously, any tonnage they can shave off has to be weighed up against the cost of buying six of the specific items, if they are to be moved in ships.

'We try to move as much as we can by sea. It is cheaper to buy six front-end jacks and ship them by sea than it is to transport one around the world by air for the year, but the same can't be said for the IT stacks, which are super expensive so we just have to suck up the air-freight costs for them. There's so much to think about but, when the sea freight is done and it's out the way, it's a huge weight off the mind, because when it's gone there's nothing you can do about it.'

That's January and that's the organisation and logistics done for the flyaways.

There's obviously another huge part to Lowe's job and that's the logistics surrounding the team's motorhome. Motorhomes are the beating heart of each team and take pride of place in the paddock at all of the European races. They go into hibernation for the winter but, once all the sea freight has been dealt with, Lowe and his team need to get theirs into shape for a long spring and summer on the road. It needs to be serviced, rebranded, refurbished and made ready in a matter of weeks. It was often a struggle to get it turned around for European winter testing in Barcelona or Jerez but, now that testing takes place in Bahrain, it gives the teams more time to do the necessary work. With five flyaway races before the first European race in Imola, in 2023 it meant it could be sent on its way in early May, rather than mid-February.

The Williams motorhome is impressive. When it is erected, it has three floors and incorporates offices for senior management and the communications department, a kitchen, two bathrooms, the drivers' rooms, two open-plan areas for entertaining VIP guests and a roof terrace with a fully functioning bar that many of us have been prone to decamp to, particularly when there is a big football match on. The motorhome gets built and de-rigged 20 times a year, all told. It is driven 20,000km over a season and uses over 8km of cables to keep it working.

The home is transported on 15 trucks around the nine current European locations. Lowe and his logistics partner for Williams, Graham Clayton, need to firstly make sure that they have recruited 15 capable drivers who are prepared to spend all summer away from their families, sometimes for 20 concurrent weeks. They are then put through a training programme to teach them how to fit the motorhome together. Ten pods make up the home, with two or three support trucks, a truck that houses a 16-tonne telehandler and a refrigerated truck to transport all the perishables.

As Clayton says, 'In layman's terms, the motorhome is effectively two levels of five containers, plonked on top of each other. Each truck converts into a pod. They are put on a laser-levelled metal framework and the pods are dropped in and connected one at a time like a massive Lego construction. The pods are 13m wide and 2.5m deep. So the width of the motorhome is the length of a truck, and it is 5 [trucks] deep.'

The difficulty these days with the congested calendar for the European leg of the world tour, is that double and triple headers have become more commonplace and, unlike the long hauls, there is only one motorhome and it simply has to get to each race on time, or the team would have to be working and entertaining out of a few gazebos. In my time in the sport, I've never seen that happen, but I have witnessed some pretty close calls, with some teams still putting everything together as the media day arrives.

'If I start building on Tuesday night prior to a race, I find that we will have the paddock to ourselves,' Clayton says. 'A lot of teams don't like doing it but it means that I can move a lot quicker. From start to finish, landing a pod takes 25 minutes. If I do it overnight it will take me roughly 15 hours to build and connect the whole motorhome. Sometimes, though, Williams will have a roof terrace on top of the motorhome. If they want that put on, it will take us an extra nine hours or so. If we are on back-to-back races, I will try and convince them not to put it on as it takes so much longer to pack down. The tightest it's ever been was in Monaco in 2024. I was pretty much awake for 48 hours.'

If you've ever been to Monaco you can understand just how hard it would be to co-ordinate the arrival of the ten teams plus Pirelli, the FIA and Formula One Management (FOM) into such a tiny space. The paddock runs along a narrow strip to the right-hand side of the harbour as you look out onto the waters of the Mediterranean. As if the confusing tunnelling and one-way systems of the principality weren't enough to deal with, roughly 200 trucks each have to be individually manoeuvred before being unloaded. It is a round-the-clock job, as Lowe describes.

'Our 15 trucks need to be parked out of Monaco in FOM-designated car parks. I will position them in three different countries, Italy, France and just outside of Monaco on the border. We call them down two at a time to park on the swimming pool road, and then we wait our turn. Each truck has to be reversed into the paddock, one by one, whilst battling with all the other teams and their respective agendas. The elbows inevitably come out and I'm fighting fires and sorting problems constantly for 48 hours. You just have to push through. I've had the chief of police's wife reprimanding me at four in the morning because my forklift was beeping. Thankfully FOM will help me get it sorted, but you wouldn't believe some of the things I've had to deal with.'

Once the motorhome is built they need to clean the whole thing and ensure there is power and water on for the Tuesday, ready to hand over to the catering team on Wednesday. Then it is just about managing any issues as they arise, while the race team focus on getting the best possible result.

Pack-down occurs on Sunday and starts usually before the race has ended. You will often see my colleague, pit-lane reporter Ted Kravitz, manoeuvring between forklifts during his *Notebook*. We have to keep an eye out while we're on air at the end of the programme as well, as things get loaded onto pallets and backed onto the trucks to transport to the next event. The cars are stripped bare and packaged into trucks or air-freight boxes, to go back to base or the next race depending on where that is.

It takes approximately as long as the build to get everything de-rigged and, on back-to-back weekends, they need to get it finished by Tuesday morning at the latest because they have to drive to the next venue. There is a knock-on effect and set-up will therefore start on a Wednesday and the motorhome needs to be built and ready to go again by Thursday morning for the next race. This is when it becomes exceptionally tight. It means that Lowe and Clayton have to have their logistics watertight. The trucks need to be manned correctly, so that nobody exceeds legal working hours; a minibus will send some of the truckies ahead to a point on the route to the next race to take over from the first set of drivers and the team have to be raring to go at the next venue. They only stop to refuel or change the drivers.

The logistics involved in Formula One is some of the most complex in sport. Ensuring that everything looks spick and span and works perfectly so that the team can go racing falls to logistics experts like Lowe and Clayton. They must deal with headache after headache and are a couple of the unsung heroes that keep everything on course with military precision. They are also among the first to arrive ahead of a race, along with the mechanics.

CHAPTER 4
THE NUMBER ONE MECHANIC

Leaders in Formula One come in many different shapes and sizes but the number one mechanic is one of the most important. With Formula One teams now, in many cases, numbering more than a thousand people, ultimately the responsibility for getting the car out on track rests on the shoulders of one individual. The build of the car to the specifications required, the running of the team of mechanics on their of the garage and the decision that the car is ready to hit the track is down to them. There is a lot at stake.

Mikey Brown grew up in the same village that I did, East Horsley in Surrey. A keen karter, his dad was a second-hand car dealer. Being more practical than academic, he left school at 16 and went straight to work for Barwell Motorsport in nearby Bookham. Barwell's racing history dates back to the 1960s and they have competed in GT classes all around the globe. Brown started off at the bottom, washing the wheels and sweeping the floors, and trained to be a mechanic on the job. Gathering experience, he then spent eight years with Gulf Racing, working his way up to chief mechanic on their World Endurance team, including the Le Mans programme, but in the back of his mind there was always the niggling feeling that he had to have a taste of the top series and see what all the fuss was about with Formula One. He knew a couple of people in the paddock, and when a job came up as a front-end mechanic on Sergio Pérez's car at Force India (the team that later became Racing Point and then Aston Martin), he jumped at the chance.

'I was 28 before I got into Formula One. I had served my apprenticeship and after a few races the job of number one mechanic came up. Even though I had only been there five minutes, I knew I was qualified to do the job. I was desperate to run a car crew.'

The number one mechanic reports into the performance and race engineers, and is in charge of a team of around 9 or 10 people, which is one side of the garage:

» The front-end mechanic who, funnily enough, looks after the front end of the car, the cockpit and anything driver related, from the steering wheel to the pedals. They are also responsible for the front suspension.

» The rear-end mechanic is responsible for the back end of the car, including the gearbox.

» The senior number two mechanic is the number one mechanic's right-hand man and will step in when required to run the crew if the number one is ill, injured or required elsewhere, for example while communicating with any of the engineering team.

» The floating or support mechanic acts as a spare pair of hands to help out anywhere on the car.

» The hydraulics specialist works on the lifelines relating to the functionality of the car including DRS, the gearbox and power-steering.

» Another mechanic deals with the electronics and the wiring of the car.

» Two people, who often double up as the truckies, will run the tyres for the weekend as well as two more who solely look after the fuel.

» The systems engineer is perhaps the most pivotal member of the crew. They run all the electrical data for the car and without them the car simply wouldn't work. They provide the link between the extremely complex electronic control units and the mechanical part of the car. And, while they are considered part of the engineering team, when they are at the track they need to work hand in hand with the mechanics and also the engine supplier. In the case of Aston Martin that is Mercedes until they switch to Honda in 2026. The systems engineer will ensure everything talks to each other, and that includes the driver communicating with the pit wall and the systems on the car relaying data back to the factory and the engineering office.

All these people have dreamt of working in Formula One from a very young age, but over the years the age profile of mechanics entering the sport has changed.

'When I entered the sport, I was almost overqualified for the role but now there are kids coming in at 19 or 20 who have done nothing but apply for a role in a Formula One garage. I push back on having very fresh people in my crew, I prefer people with experience. The average age of our crew is slightly higher, around early thirties. It's brought up by Towey. He's our electronics guy, from Essex, he's 56, and Jim, our tyre guy, he's 61. Both old bastards but they've been there, done it and their experience is invaluable.'

Nowadays if you came into the team at the base level in Formula One, you would most likely come in as a support mechanic or in the hydraulics role. That is the channel that new crew go down but not Brown, who arrived as a front-end mechanic and moved straight to number one, which isn't normal and put a few people's noses out of joint. Such is the politics of the garage.

His personality was big enough to cope though.

Having known several mechanics over my time in Formula One, it would be fair to say that there are some big characters in every garage up and down the pit lane. In the good old days the phrase 'work hard, play hard' could very much be applied to the life of a travelling Formula One mechanic, fixing cars by day and terrorising city centres by night. But these days, as the sport has grown and become more and more professional – and with so much money at stake – there is simply not enough time for any of the evening antics. Some nights they don't even leave the track until closing time. Mechanics are some of the hardest workers in the sport and their job is increasingly a young person's game because of the long hours and the time spent away from home.

Unlike the engineers and most of the travelling media, the mechanics are some of the first to arrive at the track. As a general rule they tend to get to the circuit on the Monday before a race. Tuesday is about setting up the garage with the main equipment that has been air-freighted. This includes the chassis shacks that carry the cars, all the shacks that carry the wings, and the engine kit. The working day on Tuesday starts around nine and finishes close to four. It's on the Wednesday when the hard work begins and the first major job is to build the entire car.

A modern Formula One car is made up of around 14,500 individual components, although they don't all have to be put together from scratch every time.

'On a Wednesday the job begins with getting the chassis, the bit where the driver sits, up onto high stands in the garage. I will then receive a build specification which is issued from the factory with instructions of how they want to run the car that week, with various test items or whatever. The first thing that I would do is get the fuel cell built because on a Wednesday we will be waiting for the engine. Also, the gearbox will be being built out the back as a separate unit. The only thing that is being done as I'm building the fuel cell is the front end of the car, so all the front suspension, the front uprights, the wiring and the harness for the driver. All these areas are being constructed independently and we bring it together at the end of the day. So the aim by the close of Wednesday is to have the engine and gearbox on, and that is basically a good day for us. You then have what looks like a car with no floor and no bodywork on it.'

Curfew starts on Wednesday at about 8pm and continues until 8am the next day to ensure that the teams can only work up until a certain point, to stop them working all hours of the day and night, but also to put extra time pressure on the build.

'On Thursday it feels like the weekend begins properly. It's when the engineers and team principals roll in. In the morning you get into all your bleeds. So by that I mean the hydraulic bleeds, brake bleeds, system checks for the fuel cell, running fluid through them and checking the clutch before the gearbox goes on. Bleeding the brakes on a Formula One car is much the same as doing it on a road car. We push the air out of the hydraulic system. Then you fit the ERS (energy recovery system) pack. You can't fit that without the engineers because they have to program stuff up.'

The energy recovery systems on modern Formula One cars, since 2014, consist of two motor generator units that harness waste heat energy from the turbo charger and waste kinetic energy from the braking system. This energy is then stored and subsequently used to propel the car. The ERS can provide an extra 120kw of power or 160bhp for approximately 33 seconds per lap.

Once all this is done the number one mechanic and his team set the car up.

'I get the set-up from the race engineer for the particular circuit and I tend to do this without the floor of the car on because it is easier to work around it. You can now only fire up the car 24 hours before the start of free practice one. They do this because if there is an engine issue for example you are then up against the clock.'

Thursday is the first point in the week that the team in the garage have any contact with the driver, who is also having to balance his media and engineering commitments. For the number one mechanic it's about liaising with the race engineer to work out when the driver will have time to get into the cockpit and do things like clutch practice, pedal and seat adjustments while trying to work around pit stop rehearsals. This communication between the pair continues all the way through the weekend.

'The time between third practice and qualifying is one of the busiest times for a mechanic because when the light goes green for qualifying you can't change anything, really, apart from the front wing angle on the car. So the chat between myself and my race engineer between those sessions is relentless. It's just me badgering him constantly. If it was any other industry I think you'd be promptly told to fuck off. I'm trying to get the ballast correct and any geometry changes that take time plus anything to do with legality, as this is the time that we have to get it right.'

The number one mechanic has to understand the car better than anyone. It's something Brown prides himself on.

'In my honest opinion I probably know how to fix 90 per cent of the car off the top of my head, because there are now so many bits on it. If you said to me, "Go and build the front end," I could do it but it would probably take me twice as long as my front-end mechanic because he knows it like the back of his hand and I don't do it every day. But fundamentally how the car runs, works, is set up, how it goes together, how it comes apart, I know inside out and upside down. Even though the cars are brand new every year, fundamentally they don't really change. If I have a wishbone from a suspension system, it might be a different shape and [might] bolt on to the chassis differently but it's still, fundamentally, a wishbone. If we had to put the car together from scratch, and we had all the bits lying out on a bench separately, we could put it all together I reckon in about 12 hours.'

Like any team, they are only as good as the sum of their parts.

'There is an enormous amount of trust that must run through every part of the garage. It has to be perfect every time. Because of the forces being generated by these cars, any part of the car that is not put together correctly could fail and that cannot afford to happen at 200mph. Just look at what happened to Felipe Massa back in Hungary in 2009. That's a good example of what can go wrong when something loose falls off the car, in that case a spring. It nearly killed him, so there is a responsibility to get it right. I say to my guys to go to the swimming pool section when we are in Monaco to see first hand how aggressive these cars are when cornering. It's a stark reminder of the loads that they generate and therefore how careful we need to be when putting the cars together.'

The bulk of the work on the race weekend is done by the mechanics prior to qualifying. As soon as the light goes green for the first part of qualifying the cars are deemed to be in parc fermé conditions. Under these conditions mechanics are only allowed to replace parts like for like and they are not allowed to modify any part of the car or adjust suspension set-up. There are 20 specific jobs that can be done and these include bleeding the brakes, changing or rebalancing tyres, adjusting the front wing angle, mirrors, pedals and seatbelts. They are also allowed to repair accident damage and replace anything that is a safety concern but, compared to the volume of work carried out earlier in the week, the amount that can be done is minimal.

And then it's on to the best part, the bit in which the bulk of the mechanics are actively involved in the race and that gets the adrenaline coursing through the veins: the pit stops.

'I have never walked out onto the pitch in a stadium in front of 40,000 people and I never will, but I have walked out into a pit stop when you are leading the race and it's fucking mental. You are in your own little mind, you've got your helmet on, you are hot, you are tired because of the weekend and you are thinking, *Everything has got to go right here*, but you are just this tiny little cog. You need to get it right but you need the other 21 people to get it right as well. It's a great feeling when we do, it really is, I love it.'

In general in a standard 300km Formula One race there are usually one or two pit stops, depending on the surface and the degradation of the tyres. There are often more in changeable conditions, but the crews train all year to ensure that they get these consistently fast and like the drivers they are constantly striving to improve the time it takes to change all four wheels on the car under pressure. It is also the point of the weekend where the crews from both sides of the garage come together. There are only 22 spots available and therefore there is intense competition, as not everyone will be selected. It also doesn't follow that, for example, a front-end mechanic will be changing one of the front wheels.

A pit stop crew is generally made up of the following:

» Three people on each corner: wheel off, wheel gun operator, wheel on.
» A front and rear jack man or woman to jack the car the inch and a half off the ground needed to get the wheels on and off cleanly. There are also two reserve jacks standing by in case there are any issues.
» Two car steadies that brace the car from side to side to stop it rocking. These two grab the halo and the roll hoop in the middle of the car.
» A stop-board guy and a side jack man in case there is a nose change and the car needs to be elevated higher.
» Two people on fans to cool the car during a longer stop.

'We work through things in the winter and select responsibilities depending on the build and abilities of the individuals. I'm not hugely muscly and I'm also quite tall, so putting a wheel on is just a silly idea because I'm not low enough and I'm a bit too gangly. So I'm on a wheel gun because firstly I've done it for a long time and secondly it just suits my movements better. We generally put the more experienced mechanics on the wheel guns, because it's usually our fault if it goes wrong. Generally the wheel-on guys are low to the ground and stocky, with good upper-body strength because it's a bit like a rugby scrum really, whereas the wheel-off guys are a bit taller with a longer reach so they can lift the wheel out of the way and get it gone. Front and rear jack it's generally who wants to have a go and who's good at it.'

The teams do between 30 and 40 pit-stop practices per weekend. Usually they will do some on a Thursday, some on Friday morning, including live ones in practice, none on Saturday due to the schedule and four or five before the race on Sunday. There is plenty of time for the crew to get their eye in but repetition is key in order to perform under pressure. The best teams are aiming to get stops under two seconds and while that is still rare, anything below three seconds is considered a good regulation stop.

'It's about getting the choreography right and the team work hard at it. There is data for everything. If you have an issue on the gun someone will pick you up on it. Did you pull the trigger for too long or not long enough? Everything is measured. The guys on the corners have so much data to go through. We get a pit stop report and there is tonnes of information in it. It's like being a driver. You can sit there for an hour in the evening and you can picture what you are doing physically through the data. Because of this we can adapt what we are doing and ultimately if you are not good enough you will be taken off the pit crew.'

Bad stops happen though and Brown has made errors himself in the past.

'I had a wheel loose with Checo Pérez in 2017. We were having an issue with wheel nuts back then as the technology on the guns wasn't as good as it is now. It was all done through feel and a button. We did a stop, it felt good, the wheel went home, I put the gun up and sent the car on its way. It did three quarters of a lap and I thought *Happy days*, and then on the onboard camera I saw the front left pop off. And you just have that horrible feeling come over you.

'One, you are going to be hated, two you are going to be reamed by everyone in the garage and thirdly you think, *How the fuck did that happen?* That was probably my worst mistake and it was there for all the world to see.'

But it's not just in the pit stops where there is a constant quest for improvement. Good mechanics add value to the team by making the car more reliable, faulting things, identifying potential future issues ahead of time and using their experience to flag good ideas and report them up the chain.

There is constant dialogue with the designers, the people back at the factory and the specialist faults engineer who will be able to get anything that doesn't work redesigned and re-machined. The feedback never stops in order to increase efficiency at every level from build to track and it helps if you have a driver in your car who can inspire the crew.

'I've been blessed in that I have had world champions in the car. What you get with a world champion is something that you don't get from other drivers. The dedication and the focus that you get from these guys is a different league. They're all good in their own ways. Sebastian [Vettel] is obviously a four-time world champion and extremely quick … But Fernando [Alonso] is just a fucking machine. The way he is in the briefings, the way he talks to the engineers, how he gets the team to work for him, his driver feedback, his feel is just incredible. Everything he says you just trust and you just want a driver who's going to get every last tenth out of what you give him so there's nothing left on the table. He's more reserved than Seb Vettel or Checo, who I am still very close to, but he extracts everything out of everybody. He comes in, has a laugh and a joke with the guys, knows what they are all up to on Instagram and gets everyone working with him. With Fernando there's just that aura of *I'm fucking good at what I do*, and that is what the crew wants from a driver.'

Car crews are a team within a team. They are at the coalface, ensuring that the car is faultless and hits the track able to perform at the peak of its design capabilities. The number one mechanic is the skipper of that team and requires the respect of everyone in the garage including the driver. It's clear that Mikey Brown has both.

CHAPTER 5

THE TEAM COMMUNICATIONS DIRECTOR

nternal communication is vitally important in any team, from the garage to the pit wall and everybody operating back at base, but so too is the messaging externally. It is common when working in the media within Formula One to get fed a narrative that you simply don't believe at all. If you were to take everything that you get told in the sport at face value you would either be extremely naive or incredibly stupid. The concept of communications within Formula One has one aim and that is to ensure that the team's brand and their partners are talked and written about as positively as possible. So long as the sponsors are happy, the team is happy because ultimately more money means better performance and this is why a good communications department is so important.

Matt Bishop was born in Highbury and Islington in north London to Catholic parents who split up when he was two. He and his brother were brought up by his mother Bernardine, a teacher, writer, psychotherapist and an author who wrote five novels. She is the reason that Bishop first fell in love with books. Growing up in the seventies, Formula One wasn't really on the TV or the radio all that often but he discovered it one day, when he was walking past the local newsagent's and spotted a magazine called *Autosport* on one of the shelves in the window. At that point, aged nine, as captain of his school football team and a keen subscriber to *Shoot* magazine, for just ten pence Matt was able to sate his thirst for Arsenal every week within the budget of his pocket money. However, upon seeing Sir

Jackie Stewart's 1972 light blue Tyrrell glistening on the front cover of that particular edition of *Autosport*, Matt went back to his mother and immediately lobbied for a two-and-a-half-pence raise, for it had been love at first sight.

'I opened up the magazine and thought I've never seen anything so beautiful. I was used to Morris Oxfords and Ford Cortinas parked on the street, I didn't know you could have a thing that looked like that and I was thrilled to bits, transfixed and have never looked back.'

It was a while though before he managed to turn his passion into a career. Like many of us he took an unconventional route into Formula One.

'I didn't do well in my A levels so I actually started working at a factory in Willesden in north-west London which made yoghurt and cream. That was supposed to be a filling-in job before going to university but because I didn't do well enough in my A levels I didn't go to university, so I stayed at the factory. I would get up at 6am to work in the raw reception, where the 4,000-gallon tankers full of cream and skimmed milk would arrive. It was my job to attach the pumps to the trucks to get the product into the holding tanks in the factory. When the tanks were emptied, we would climb on top of them and lower a rope ladder into their depths. We'd then climb down into where the milk or cream had been and, armed with a high temperature, high pressure hose, some caustic soda and a broom, scrub them clean. You couldn't see anything as it was dark and full of steam and if you kinked a hose you could burn yourself badly but it was an occupational hazard. If I'd said at that point that one day I would be director of communications at a Formula One team, I would have been shipped off to the funny farm.'

Bishop moved seamlessly from the glamour of urban dairy work to the shadier environs of the north London gambling scene, where he took a job as a betting shop manager. It was during this period that he became interested in the 'dogs'. In the mid-eighties, men in porkpie hats and Burberry trench coats would gather in their tens at the multitude of greyhound racing venues scattered around the capital. From White City to Wimbledon, Romford to (ironically) Catford, these meetings were places where, as the urban myth went, the last to take a crap would bring home the bacon. It was while attending one of these meets at the old Wembley stadium that he met a man by the name Jim Cremin. Cremin was the greyhound editor of the *Racing Post* and he recognised that Bishop had the gift of the gab, gave him the chance to write a column for the *Post* and, as simply as that, Bishop's journalistic career had begun. After a few months a vacancy as a sub-editor came up on *Car* magazine. Armed with a love of motors, a quick wit and a decent turn of phrase, Bishop got the job and swiftly progressed to features editor.

'Back then the whole world of car and motorsport journalism was quite incestuous and when Haymarket [the magazine publisher] wanted to launch a monthly magazine called *F1 Racing* I was brought in as permanent editor. At that time, it was thought that Formula One wouldn't sustain 12 monthly editions but it did and in the 11 years while I was there from 1996 until 2007 we grew the readership from a UK-only reach in English to being on sale in 34 languages across 110 countries. It had become the world's bestselling motorsport magazine. It was great fun and a great privilege to do.'

It was also to provide his path into Formula One communications.

McLaren's *annus horribilis* was 2007, when they were fined $100 million because of the 'Spygate' scandal. Their owner at the time, Ron Dennis, had led McLaren to become the second most successful team in the history of the sport.

'Ron used to phone me up. I'd befriended him, I don't know why because we were very different types. We used to go to the same barbers and that was about it. But we'd often go for dinners while I was editing *F1 Racing* and Ron was great company after a couple of glasses of red. It was at the Turkish Grand Prix in 2007 that he said, "Look, Matt, I'm in the shit! Max Mosley [then president of the FIA who had imposed the crippling fine] and his communications man, Richard Woods, are making my life a misery in the press and I need someone to help rehabilitate McLaren's image because it's been severely damaged." So he wanted someone he could trust as his strategic communications director to help get the McLaren brand back on track.'

Dennis wanted a person who understood the landscape of Formula One, who knew the journalists and was also on good terms with both Bernie Ecclestone and Mosley. He believed, quite rightly, based on the evidence of what had happened, that Mosley had a personal vendetta against him.

'I once asked Max at the end of an interview when I was still editor of *F1 Racing* why he disliked Ron so much, and he said, "I don't dislike him, I pity him."

'He spat the word pity with such venom. I thought *Pity, PITY?!* Ron Dennis is the boss and majority owner of the second most successful team in the history of motorsport. He is as rich as you could possibly want to be. He has a lovely wife and three kids, how could you possibly pity him? Why would you pity him? Actually what Max meant was pure snobbery. Ron started as a mechanic and had had a normal education, leaving school in his teens, and he didn't go to university. Whereas Max was fantastically and expensively educated and as posh as anything. I think he minded that Ron was more successful and richer by an order of magnitude than him. It used to stick in the back of his throat. I think he thought, *Who is this fucking guttersnipe that is trying to rain on my parade and fuck me and Bernie*, and he used the term pity but actually it was a mixture of hatred and envy because it was a more derisive term.'

So against this heavy backdrop, how did Bishop begin to go about the job of rehabilitating the McLaren image? It was about using all the tools at his disposal to reshape the perception of the brand through a mixture of clever PR, media and communications. At that point there was an atmosphere of defensive pessimism within the team and although respect for them was at an all-time low, it wasn't completely trashed.

'We needed to move the needle from the point it was at, through admiration and eventually towards encompassing love. Love is an odd word to use in the context of a brand that produces high-tech racing cars, but I thought it was appropriate because we were still a sports team that had won so much in the past and retained a loyal fanbase.'

The first thing that Bishop set about doing was engaging the press in a more friendly manner. Whereas previously the default tones from McLaren when it came to interviews with Ron Dennis or his drivers had been 'No', the default answer was changed to 'Yes'. On the front door of the brand centre, the McLaren motorhome in the paddock, where it had previously said 'For VIPs and invited guests only', it now read, 'Welcome'. Two very simple changes but changes that led to journalists and broadcasters entering the motorhome whereas previously they had been reluctant. On top of that, they would be served food and warm drinks. Bonus!

'Martin Whitmarsh, Ron's deputy, used to moan about it. He would ask, "Why is that scruffy oik having bacon and eggs in here for breakfast?" And I would counter with, "That scruffy oik works for the *News of the World* and they sell about 5 million copies every Sunday. It's probably read by about 20 million people and I think if we costed what he's got on his plate, that's about £2.50. So I reckon that's good value, what do you reckon?" I used to have arguments about it because this is some of the easiest and cheapest comms you will ever do. If a journalist came in and said I'm going to write this about you and I said, "You don't want to write that, because it's inaccurate, and by the way why don't you write this instead about Michael Schumacher or someone else? I'll give you a nice little story," it plants a seed in their head because, subconsciously, really all they are thinking about is who gives them breakfast. And Ferrari would give them fuck all!'

Praise is in short supply in Formula One, but blame is a daily currency. Anything and everything that is written, broadcast and posted on social media about the team and the sponsors is the responsibility of the communications department. That is a very broad canvas which means that it is a 24/7 job. If anything goes wrong, these days it will be all over social media in an instant and it is the communications director that gets the blame. There is always an element of fire-fighting and with a never-ending news cycle for a truly global sport, there is no let up.

'You can't wave a magic wand and make everything happen as you'd like but you can create a strategy where you use the media. And this is totally mutual, by the way, because the media use you. Although you won't be able to tell journalists how to write a particular story, there is an element of quid pro quo, which is, *Look, I will give you your interview with Lewis Hamilton but don't screw me over because I'm giving you an exclusive.* Honestly, the gin and tonic and prawn cocktail offensive is a good one in comms, it always will be. You want to make sure that you know the journalists, that there is mutual trust and you have given them things. If you do that, they are more likely to play ball. There's a large degree of horse trading at play.'

It's one thing keeping the media sweet and using everything in your armoury to maintain positivity around the brand, but you've also got to manage what comes out of the drivers' mouths and often that can be difficult when things haven't gone their way on the track.

'I've got the most enormous respect for Lewis Hamilton. Brilliant driver on the track. Brilliant guy off it, whatever anyone tells you, but Lewis was a challenge. He was a problem because they all are. A genius, one of the best at doing what he does that we've ever seen, but they are all extremely driven and therefore they are not easy.'

For Bishop, one particular moment starkly illustrates this point and how he had to employ crisis comms to manage a difficult situation. It came after the Monaco Grand Prix in 2011 when Hamilton had been penalised by the stewards for a couple of incidents, one with Felipe Massa and another with Pastor Maldonado. When asked by BBC reporter Lee McKenzie why he was so magnetic to the stewards and whether he felt he was being unnecessarily targeted, Hamilton replied with the Ali G phrase that was common vernacular at the time, 'Maybe it's 'coz I'm Black.'

'The chief steward that weekend was the former president of the Swedish motorsport federation and experienced politician, Lars

Osterlind. He was a Christian Democrat and a very liberal guy who had all the right attitudes but he had read Lewis's comments and was understandably furious and, more than that, he was hurt. It was after the Grand Prix and all the senior management at McLaren had gone home on Ron's private jet. Lewis had gone back to his apartment in Monaco, extremely pissed off, when I got wind that the FIA was coming to see me. They said, in no uncertain terms, that it would be helpful if Lewis went to see Lars to apologise. Anthony Hamilton [Lewis's dad] was also there and said his son had got a point. I finally got hold of Lewis on the phone and urged him to come back and apologise, but Lewis was adamant he wasn't going to say sorry. So I was in a really difficult position, as there was a chance that the FIA were going to throw the book at us and race bans were a distinct possibility. I remember thinking, what can I do? I was having to think on my feet to avoid this escalating any further.

'Eventually, I said to Lewis, "I will come up with a form of an apology that is not an apology, but it will feel like an apology to them." It was something along the lines of, "It was not my intention to offend and I hold all officials in high regard etc." but it didn't contain the word sorry. He came back from his Monaco flat to the track and was still unsure about it all. I remember saying to him, "You're furious, Lewis, I understand that, but imagine waking up tomorrow and seeing that there is a fax that says you have brought the sport into disrepute and that you are going to be facing a race ban. Would you regret not trotting down to the stewards and talking some bollocks to them that isn't an apology, but that gets you out of jail?" And he eventually agreed. We went down there, and he repeated my statement almost verbatim. All the bollocks that I had written, and we got away with it. We still got a stiff letter from the FIA and Jean Todt, who was furious on behalf of Lars Osterlind, but it could have grown into something much bigger.'

It demonstrates that there is a perpetual game of cat and mouse in the sport on almost every front. While designers and engineers look for loopholes in the regulations to exploit, the communications department need to constantly paint a positive narrative for the good of the teams and sponsors. Isn't it therefore naive to believe that they are always telling the truth?

'I don't lie as a comms person because it does not work. These relationships are important. If you've known a journalist for a number of years and you tell him a big fat porky, why should he ever believe you again? Just for the sake of getting one monkey off your back, which might be a difficult story, you've closed down that avenue. I've had to say to senior people who told me what to say, if that's not true I'm not going to say it. Sometimes I've been lied to. And if you find out you've been lied to by a senior colleague then you have internal trust issues. Lies just don't work.'

But does that mean that you have to tell the whole truth?

'No, you don't. Why would you? If you don't want to give the complete answer to a difficult question in a comms capacity, you simply don't give the journalist everything. And I think that's totally legitimate. You don't have to say everything, but you shouldn't say anything that is untrue because, as in life, it will inevitably come back to bite you. However, I think people repeat lies that they have been told. I always thought that it's not the comms people that are the originators of the lies, it's at the team principal level. I remember at McLaren, the senior management used to say, oh, we won't tell anyone this, we'll just keep it. Only the senior people will know this and that way it won't leak.

'I'd say to Ron, "The only way it will leak IS from the senior people! When I was a journalist, if I wanted to find out something about McLaren, do you think I'd ask a junior marketeer or a mechanic? No, I'd ask you, Ron, and you'd tell me. And I might even slightly tease you into telling me something. So I might say, 'We think you've got a dual clutch gearbox? Oh, I shouldn't ask you, you probably don't know, you're not really involved in the tech, are you? So I'll go and ask someone else,'" and he'd go, "No, no, I know all about that," because the ego would kick in. So as a journalist you could trick someone into saying things. But you couldn't trick junior people because they're perfectly happy to say either "I don't know" or "I can't talk about that". Senior management's egos prevent them saying either of those things. It was the same with the lies, they would often catch themselves out.'

Good communication can make the car go faster in a couple of ways. Formula One machines are extraordinarily expensive to design, build and develop. The budget must come from a number of sources and one of the prime sources is commercial sponsorship. Time was, 30 years ago, when Marlboro, for example, would want their logo plastered on the side of the car and the rear wing and they would add up the minutes and seconds their logo was on screen per race, to measure the advertising value. On top of that, the sponsors would get a certain amount of driver appearances and other rights that they could use to leverage that sponsorship. Nowadays, the logo on the car isn't what they derive their benefit from. They derive value from activation, which is a posh term for communications. All the communications and PR across every platform add up to how a sponsor is perceived by its desired customer and if you get it right it can be extremely beneficial for the team.

'When it's time to renew and the sponsor was expecting a four-to-one return on their sponsorship, but they've had an independent auditor look at it and determined that it was an eight-to-one return, that drives the price up, and you have contributed to the car going faster. Money makes the car go faster and comms makes money.

'There's another way. And I'm talking about drivers here, lovely, brilliant people. I choose my words carefully. They are brilliant, but they are nervy. They're nervous because they're doing something that is actually dangerous and daunting. But also, if they make a mistake – you know, clip the wall – fuck me, what a disaster. It means I'm gonna score no points today. It means that everybody's going to give me a hard time. It means that I'm not going to win the world championship, or I've fallen behind in the championship chase. So they are nervously brilliant. And by nature, they are highly strung geniuses and they worry. Because they google themselves.

Imagine if you were Lewis Hamilton, of course you google yourself. Max Verstappen googles himself. They all do. And not only do they google themselves, they put their names into Twitter to have a little look at what's being said. And even if they claim they don't mind out of bravado, they might say, I don't give a shit what's written about me, but of course they do. The only person who really didn't was Kimi Räikkönen. But everybody else does. And if something nasty has been written in the *Daily Mail* or been broadcast on Sky about a driver, or if there's been a Twitter pile-on, it affects him badly. It means that when he's sitting in an engineering briefing talking about where he can be faster, he's not dialled into that conversation. He's still thinking about what is being said about him. So if I do my job and help smooth out the negativity, there is lap time in that. I can help get the driver back to focusing on his day job and not on the unnecessary noise.'

Matt Bishop spent almost a decade at McLaren, leaving in 2017 to become communications director for the W Series. In January 2021 he moved to Aston Martin to become chief communications officer and remained in the position for a couple of years. Now freelance, he continues to advise in a field that he knows and loves. Communications is constantly evolving, with new platforms springing up all the time. It means that teams are having to grow to keep up with the ever-changing media landscape and this is only going to continue.

We live in a post-truth world where not everything can be taken as read and the challenges facing the communications departments from sports teams to governments have never been greater. Managing the message is still one of the most important tasks within Formula One and that is why good communications departments are central to the success of any team. Those teams take their lead from their director and Bishop was undoubtedly one of the best.

CHAPTER 6

THE FORMULA ONE COMMUNICATIONS OFFICER

Whereas Matt Bishop's job focused on promoting and protecting the image of a specific team, the Formula One communications officer is responsible for managing the global image and media strategy of the entire sport. That responsibility lies with Liam Parker, who arrived with a big reputation from the world of politics, but when you look at how much politics there is, and always has been, in Formula One, it was probably inevitable that one would lead to the other.

The son of a roofer and a care worker, Parker was brought up in Bromley, south-east London. He was the first in his family to attend university and almost as soon as he had finished his further education, he got a job at the special advisers' office in the Treasury. Initially an office assistant, within eight months he had moved to their communications team and was thrown straight into the melee of the 2008 financial crisis when Alistair Darling was the chancellor. Talk about a tough paper round as a junior press officer. Fighting fires of that magnitude was inevitably going to be a huge challenge for anyone but Parker excelled and quickly moved through the ranks. He looked after David Laws, the chief secretary to the Treasury for a week, until he resigned over an expenses scandal, and then Danny Alexander, the man who replaced him, before working under George Osborne and moving across to Number Ten.

In high demand, he was then lured by the Labour Party, defected and worked for Ed Miliband, but that didn't last long and

Parker found himself at a crossroads. He made the decision to move out of the main cut and thrust of the front lines of politics and to the Financial Conduct Authority (the UK's regulatory body for the financial services industry), running the campaign for Adair Turner to become the governor of the Bank of England. Turner's campaign wasn't successful but Parker transferred to the bank itself, where he eventually became press secretary for then governor Mark Carney, who is now the prime minister of Canada.

'I remember having a conversation with Laura Kuenssberg from the BBC who asked me, "When are you coming back to politics?"

'"I dunno," I replied.

'"You should meet Boris [Johnson]," she said, "Go and talk to his people."

'So I met Boris in the Foreign Office. I wasn't the biggest fan, but we kind of connected and got on and within a couple of weeks I was appointed as his special advisor for communications and strategy whilst he was foreign secretary.'

Parker rattles through his past life in politics and it is easy to see why he has excelled in his field. Like all good communications directors he is extremely articulate and can get to the crux of a story immediately. His is quite the CV and, in career terms, quite the rise.

'You just never rest. There wasn't a fire I wasn't going to run through, a river I wasn't going to swim across. I didn't care what time of night it was. I wanted to be the first one to respond, to come up with an idea, the first one to do something, I just had an insatiable desire to be in the fight. I will take the financial crisis as an example. The banking sector was collapsing. The whole system was going under. There is the type of person who says, "I will just follow someone else's lead on this," and there is the type that says, "Fuck it, I wanna be in it." I want to be advising and I want to be in the room, no matter how bad the story is. It was a relentless work schedule. I mean for the past 20 years, I've never turned my phone off once. It's just an inbuilt thing, that I am always on.'

It is interesting to understand the level of influence that communications directors, special advisers and press secretaries have over their 'bosses'. People's minds will probably flick back to Dominic Cummings, Alastair Campbell and Peter Mandelson, those figures within politics that operate in the shadows and, despite being unelected, have a front-row seat and a say within the corridors of power.

'For someone like Boris, you knew where the red line was. You knew you had no ability to influence beyond that red line. His view was solid. The government's view was this, no matter if you disagree, your opinion will be heard, but never used. So I knew when to keep my powder dry and when to push. But there were different types of advice. There were situations where they might say, "Let's get the comms person in the room and see how it plays out," others where you might be in from the very beginning advising them what to be careful of, and then there were the times where you were invited into the room after something had happened and it's all turned to shit and they want you to fix it. So, basically, in crisis comms, there's a kind of influence, a guide and a fix. You couldn't really influence Boris because he was a strong-willed person who knew who he was. It was just a question of trying to guide him down narrow channels every now and then and balancing a negative headline versus what I wanted the outcome to be, which was actually, he was doing quite a job as foreign secretary and wasn't just this gaffe-prone guy who, at that stage, most people loved.'

He remained with Johnson for a couple of years but Parker's route into Formula One came while at the agency Pagefield, which he joined straight out of the Foreign Office as a partner and head of their sports arm. His first job was advising McLaren's CEO, Zak Brown, and then head of comms, Tim Bampton, while they were getting rid of racing director Éric Boullier.

'I remember thinking, this is quite interesting, there's a lot of politics here, there's lots of personal wealth involved, which makes it even more political. And there was an attraction that I hadn't felt in the two years since I'd left politics. The challenge is the global nature of it, the issues the sport faces and the personalities. It is full of big, dominant characters. I said to Tim, if there's ever a job, I'd be interested in a discussion. It never came to anything, but Tim referred me to Formula One and it ended up in an interview.'

Inevitably, he got the job.

For the first couple of years Parker was head of corporate and consumer communications while Luca Colajanni (former Ferrari head of comms) looked after the motorsport side for Formula One. But Parker really came into his own and started forging a reputation in the paddock during Covid, where he helped get the sport going again by securing an elite sport exemption.

'Because of my relationship with Boris [who was by that stage prime minister], with the cabinet ministers and certain civil servants, I was able to hammer it home that, unless we go racing again, Formula One is finished. The teams would not survive. The sport would not survive. It was more or less two or three weeks of relentlessly showing them our protocols and procedures so that we could safely restart.'

It was this influence that made the then CEO and chairman of Formula One, Chase Carey, sit up and take notice. It was obvious that Parker had plenty of strings to his bow and from that point on their relationship changed.

'I think for the first time there was a trust that I could do certain things that could help the business. Although it was exhausting, it had been the first fight that I had been involved with that had got my juices flowing in the same way as they had during my time in Westminster. I had to deliver something and it invigorated me.'

Formula One is hugely important to the UK economy. It's worth around £10 billion. The sector employs 4,000 people directly and 40,000 indirectly. Three of the UK-based teams were in serious danger of going under as a result of the pandemic and it is a testament to the will of those that forced the hand of government that they got racing going again before any other global sport.

'I got a message from someone at *The Times* saying they were about to run a front-page story about football, cricket and Formula

One being granted the exemption. I just stopped what I was doing and messaged Boris and the secretary of state asking whether it was true. One of them came back to me and said please don't comment, the legislation will be published shortly, but the relief was immense. It was one of the proudest moments of my career, but it wasn't just me. Chase was hugely involved, as was Ross Brawn [former MD of Formula One] and Steve Nielsen [Formula One sporting director] but it was from this point on that I started to get into the sport more and into the political side of the decisions that were being made across Formula One, providing an input and advising on matters. It was just a great thing to be a small part of, in such a bleak time.'

Since Covid his job has involved advising the current CEO Stefano Domenicali – he is effectively his right-hand man – but also the rest of the team at Liberty, when necessary. He has put himself in a position where he is once again at the heart of the decision-making processes. He advised on the decision not to race in Russia after their invasion of Ukraine and also when the floods affected Imola.

In summer 2023 all of the teams and many of us in broadcasting were invited to Number Ten to meet with ministers to underscore to MPs the importance of the sport as an industry. Parker is trying to replicate this in all the territories we visit. He spends much of his time lobbying foreign governments and ambassadors, in much the same way he did in the UK, to recognise Formula One as a vital presence and a business card, not just for Britain, but all the countries it now visits, as well as for those who seek races in the future. He is also trusted to liaise with all the teams and the president's department at the FIA to ensure that the relationship, which has sometimes been fractious, stays in the right place so that the strategic aims of the three parties are aligned.

'Liberty is very much a company that looks a long way ahead. When it comes to future planning, about where Formula One wants to be in the world, we tend to look five years ahead and work back from there. Not everything can be purely a business decision when you look at developing the calendar.'

If Formula One were to get rid of a load of historic tracks there would be uproar. It would upset the fanbase and the drivers, so Liberty operate within a sensible framework, constantly assessing the market potential. Africa is a good example.

'We could probably turn up and do something in Africa whenever we wanted but if the fanbase isn't there, ultimately it will just be a load of very wealthy businessmen that fly in for the race. If the local community are not engaged and no one is watching on TV then the sponsors will not waste their money. What you end up with is racing somewhere for a couple of years and then leaving. So we have to future-proof. We need to understand whether the market will sustain us for a long period of time. Is it a government-backed race? Is it privately funded? What is the best mechanism for this? What is the TV rights deal – is it free to air or pay to view? Is this country even interested in Formula One? Are we going to turn up and from day one will we be fighting a losing battle? So you can't just dive in, you need to understand exactly what you are getting into.'

For those of us that have been in the paddock for a while, you could now describe Formula one as pre-*Drive to Survive* (PDTS) – careful with the lettering there – or post-*Drive to Survive* (also PDTS – let's go with 'after': ADTS). The Netflix series has detonated an explosion of interest in the younger demographic. The ADTS years, since 2019, have kept Parker and his team busier than ever.

'In terms of growing the sport, the opportunity it has created has been huge. When I first joined in 2018 (PDTS) trying to get *GQ*, *Cosmopolitan* and *Grazia* interested in doing something about a race wasn't easy. Now you can go to all these global, diverse publications and reach a brand-new audience. We've gone from talking about how the drivers race around a track to what they wear and who they are. You see it on our social platforms. We've gone from not having a platform in 2016 to 90 million-plus followers, and growing.'

But ADTS, to keep spreading and growing the gospel of Formula One, the sport's communication strategy has had to morph, simply because of the breadth of audience now interested. Previously, the viewership was massively skewed toward middle-aged white men, but that isn't the case nowadays.

'Our approach is that you can't throw everything out and focus on one core demographic or market. You have your core fanbase, who read *Autosport* and *Racer* and are interested in the regulations and the technical aspects of the sport that you need to continue to serve. Then you have the audience that have watched *Drive to Survive* and are starting to follow it a bit, but not avidly, and whose interests differ from the core audience. How do we provide them with content, access and information that actually means something to them and gets them excited? And then there is this whole new group who have never watched it. And my comms strategy with them is don't wait for them to come to us, let's get into their news feeds, tell the stories and understand what those audiences are interested in. An audience member in the USA will be interested in something totally different from an audience member in Australia, so you have to understand what that market is and what the barriers are to engagement. What do they like? What are they passionate about? We are very lucky that Formula One encompasses technology, sport, speed, travel, personalities, culture and hospitality. With such diverse elements, there is usually something that appeals to most people. In PR terms, you can tailor this model to the right audience and the right outlet for the maximum effect.'

If you are not learning something new in Formula One every day, then you are wasting your time. I have been involved with Sky and in televised sport for the past 28 years. Never have I been a part of something that has grown so sharply or has so many layers. It is a rich ecosystem that, although sometimes can be a bit of a bubble, is a microcosm of life. As Formula One's chief communications and corporate relations officer, Parker must deal with and have extensive knowledge of every one of those layers, because they all interact. Liaising and ensuring that all of them work together for the benefit of the sport is a thankless task because altruism between competing teams is always in short supply. Ultimately, what is good for the show, is good for Formula One, a wise man called Martin Brundle once told me. Parker's job is to make sure the audience keeps growing and the messaging remains positive. The 12-year-old who dreamt of working in politics is now swimming with Formula One's big fish in the 'piranha club', but does it still excite him as much as being in the fight in Westminster?

'I don't want to return to politics. There's still so much to do here, so much to learn and so many challenges. For now I've just got to do this properly.'

For a man who has worked for Boris Johnson, that says a lot about Formula One!

CHAPTER 7

THE CHIEF COMMERCIAL OFFICER

' $\bigvee$ in on Sunday, sell on Monday!' is a phrase that still holds true in motorsport and while it was coined by a Ford dealer called Bob Tasca in the 1960s, it is still relevant in the sponsorship world of Formula One. And if championships were handed out to sponsorship teams, then in the last couple of years, McLaren would have added to their 2024 constructors' title, on that side of the business as well. That year they had 53 partners in all and, with a CEO in Zak Brown who previously ran his own extremely successful marketing agency, the team have an inherent understanding from the top down about the importance of creating a brand that others want to partner with.

Nick Martin is one of a strong trio that run McLaren's commercial department at the executive level. Martin is the co-chief commercial officer, responsible for securing new partnership revenue globally. He and his team work on developing sponsorships as well as licensing and merchandising collaborations. Nick's co-chief commercial officers are Matt Dennington, who nurtures and retains the partnerships across all the team's racing platforms, and Louise McEwen, the chief marketing officer who looks after the strategy of the brand and oversees their creative visual identity. I stole those bio's from the McLaren website and bear with me if the next two chapters sound overly corporate, but the language of business is the language of money and money makes the cars go round faster, so it is a hugely important part of the puzzle.

Growing up in Santa Barbara in California, Martin was sports mad. He realised early on that he wasn't going to make it as a professional athlete so, inspired by the film *Jerry Maguire*, he studied sports management and marketing at Syracuse University and, following that, found a job with a small boutique basketball agency, representing NBA players.

'There is so much luck in life and I was really fortunate that my first client was a gentleman named Jimmy Butler, then an unknown player, who was looking unlikely to get drafted, but ended up being the last pick in the first round. Anyway, fast forward to now and he's a six-time NBA All Star, who's played for the Chicago Bulls, Miami Heat and Golden State Warriors. He's won an Olympic gold medal and signed multiple hundred-million-dollar contracts. He's what started it all for me.'

Before long, the agency was looking after 350 athletes, including top players from the NBA, the NFL and major league baseball. He stayed there for the first eight years of his career but in 2016, when Butler left, Martin had a decision to make.

'It was either follow Jimmy and be his guy or do something else. At that time I met Zak Brown in New York. He had just joined McLaren and he talked to me about the state of the business that he was coming into and that he was really looking to solidify the shape of the marketing and commercial team at McLaren.'

So Brown invited Martin over to the UK and after meeting the top brass told him there and then that he would have an offer waiting when he returned to his family in New York. After talking to his wife, he quickly decided it was the right move.

'Initially I was running the agency side of the business, because 50–70 per cent of McLaren's sponsorship deals were coming in through third-party sales agents and representatives. I was responsible for co-ordinating them all, whilst we started to build our own internal sales team.'

McLaren runs a different sponsorship model from other teams. They don't have any exclusive relationships. Red Bull, for example, are represented exclusively by the agency CAA. When Martin joined there were 20–40 agencies that they would use to bring partners to the table, including the likes of CSM, Wasserman, Octagon or Right Formula. They still operate in the same way today, but are less pro-active in outsourcing, because they now drive a lot of new business themselves. And now that there are more partners than ever, how they organise their brand categories is extremely important. It avoids having crossovers and means that the commercial department can be creative in order to boost revenues.

'A good example is in the beverage category, which is quite broad. We have Coca-Cola as a sponsor, Jack Daniel's, Estrella Galicia, Monster Energy and Optimum Nutrition. That covers off soda, spirits, beer, energy and protein and wellness drinks but we still have space for a water brand, for example, depending on how we structure the deals.'

The McLaren commercial and marketing team sits at around 140 staff. Their attendance at races rises and falls depending on the activity of the particular brands within the region.

'We operate a hub and spoke model with partnerships at the core. Around that we have a digital and social team, a content team, a brand experience team, a communications team, a strategy team, a brand creative team and all of them support the commercial and marketing apparatus inside McLaren. We then report into Zak and service all the different racing series that we have.'

For McLaren, Formula One is obviously the core racing series but they also have representation in Formula E, Extreme E, IndyCar, e-sports and in 2027 they will be entering the World Endurance Championship. They have a base in Indianapolis with a commercial and marketing presence that look after things state-side and a base in Bicester with their own team looking after their Extreme E and Formula E requirements. But their decision to branch out obviously had strong commercial reasons behind it. McLaren have a deep history in IndyCar, having competed in the series in the 1970s, winning the Indy 500 three times – first with

Mark Donohue for Team Penske with a McLaren chassis in 1972 and then Johnny Rutherford in 1974 and again in 1976 for the McLaren factory team. They rejoined the series full-time in 2020 partnering with Arrow Schmidt Peterson Motorsports to form Arrow McLaren.

'At that point there was only one Formula One race in the States, and it was absolutely the right decision for us to move back into IndyCar, because we wanted visibility, we wanted to dominate that American market and to become America's favourite Formula One team. It paid dividends for us as Formula One expanded in the region, allowing us to tap into the Silicon Valley and technology sector for Formula One. It also opened up opportunities for part-nerships across multiple racing series.'

McLaren have run studies, brand-perception surveys, that have confirmed that they have achieved that status as America's favourite racing team. Formula One also run their own survey called F1 Fan Voice that has backed up McLaren's research.

In marketing terms it has been quite a turnaround for McLaren, since the dark days of 2015 in Suzuka, Japan, when Fernando Alonso was so dismayed with the performance of the car and the state of the team that he called the engine a GP2 engine on team radio at Honda's home race. At that point, there were virtually no sponsors on the car and things had never been so bad. That year they finished ninth, their lowest position since 1980. Brown arrived the following year and began to gradually bring the sponsors back.

'Zak is an unbelievably driven and passionate individual and it's been incredible learning from someone who has probably the most brilliant commercial mind the sport has ever seen. What I think is unique is that he will never ask you to do anything that he is not willing to do himself, and that goes for the time and energy that he puts in. He works harder than anyone in the organisation. He leads by example, gets into the trenches and does whatever it takes. He is also incredibly brave in his decision-making. It was not the easy option to divorce from Honda. It was a lucrative deal and to walk away from that for performance reasons was bold considering where the business was at that stage.'

Brown and his commercial team, like everyone competing in Formula One, set themselves one specific goal, and that was to work towards winning the world championship. In the pursuit of that goal, sponsorship played a huge role.

'Ultimately investment drives performance, performance drives profitability and profitability drives investment. It is a virtuous cycle.'

But Martin cannot underestimate the importance of the arrival of *Drive to Survive* in helping to boost that cycle.

'I remember when I first joined I was having conversations with prospective partners and I would ask them what they knew about Formula One. By and large I would have to educate them about the sport and then tell them about McLaren. But after season two or three, *Drive to Survive* circumvented the need for those introductions. It also created huge demand from a sponsorship perspective and opened up new race markets that were needed to keep the sport fresh.'

Commercially, the last three years have been some of the most successful in the McLaren brand's history. They dispensed with a title sponsor a while back, and now have a few primary sponsors, a handful of principal partners and a number of other official partners. They set ambitious targets but, ultimately, the positioning of sponsors' logos on cars is a finite resource and therefore the team are always pursuing other ways to help generate more cash, particularly through the licensing of the brand.

'Our model now absolutely works, and I do think there is an opportunity to re-introduce a title sponsor in the next couple of years but licensing allows us to expand into new markets and demographics. Our partnerships with Reiss, Abercrombie and Levi's enable us to reach a new audience – the younger generation who are going into Abercrombie and Fitch wanting to buy a vintage McLaren T-shirt, for example.'

And Martin and the commercial team are constantly exploring new avenues. No sector is off the table.

'We know that McLaren is a brand that is extremely sophisticated in lightweight, durable materials such as carbon fibre. Therefore, could we expand the brand into golf or tennis? We look at other companies like Porsche designs that have built the Porsche Tower in Miami. Aston Martin have come up with Aston Martin Residences. Do we look to go into maritime like Lamborghini, who make a yacht? There are so many areas that we haven't tested yet. But if we do go into a specific market we know we need to do it authentically and resonate with the audience that we are trying to sell into.'

But how do their partners measure the value of their sponsorship and gauge whether it is worth it for their own purposes?

'Every sponsor is different. Some of them would like to enhance their own brand perception. Some of them might want to be associated with X, Y or Z in terms of demographics, and want to work out how they can use the McLaren partnership to drive those associations forward.

'They will then measure the success of our partnership when they run brand campaigns after they've been with us for a certain period of time. Some measure the impact from brand awareness and some measure success from the business that they are generating off the back of the partnership.'

Ultimately one of the strengths of McLaren's resurgence in partners is the fact that a good proportion of them are Fortune 100 and Fortune 500 brands. These are some of the biggest companies in the world and they are all keen to be involved with the 2024 world champions.

'One of the main reasons that we have some of the best partners in the world is because they seek to do business with each other, and we facilitate and support those connections. We've been able to show that we have driven $100 million in new business in a single season and that's directly linked to the people we have looked after at races. This shows a clear return on investment.'

Some of McLaren's partners host high-net-worth individuals who want to give their clients a money-can't-buy experience, like a hot lap, paddock club access and a garage tour. On the other hand they might be a technology partner involved with McLaren because they want to show that their product is supporting the team's performance or a marketing technology tool that can help grow and support the business off the track. What is common, though, is that each of these partnerships needs to be symbiotic to achieve their potential.

There are a multitude of different ways that brands can leverage their sponsorships when they are tied in with a Formula One team. Sponsors come and go, they move teams and are fickle when it comes to success. Ultimately, people like Martin are competing with others up and down the 100-metre stretch of concrete that is the paddock. Success breeds money and money breeds success, even in a cost-cap era, where the team spend is limited to a certain amount on performance. However, it is clear that the commercial department, as in any business, is a cornerstone of that success and a barometer of the health of the team. McLaren were at rock bottom when Zak Brown joined. In eight years they've become the constructors' champions and are hoping to stay that way. The commercial team have done an outstanding job bringing in and retaining their partners, but they couldn't have done it without the brand refresh that was executed by Lou McEwen and her team.

CHAPTER 8
THE CHIEF MARKETING OFFICER

Ron Dennis took over McLaren in 1980. Despite having already won two championships, in 1974 with Emerson Fittipaldi and 1976 with James Hunt, by the late seventies the team were struggling. Under Dennis's leadership, however, they were transformed and during the 1980s and 1990s became one of the dominant forces in Formula One. In 2004 they moved premises to the McLaren Technology Centre, a building that has been described as a real-life Bond villain's lair. Designed by Sir Norman Foster and situated just outside Woking, it is, nevertheless, an architectural masterpiece that was opened by Queen Elizabeth II.

The foyer of the MTC is nicknamed 'The Boulevard' and on its perfectly tiled floor are housed many of McLaren's Formula One championship-winning cars, Can-Am machines, Indy 500 winners and road cars. It serves as a showcase of the team's rich racing history. But McLaren had suffered a drought of titles since Lewis Hamilton pipped Felipe Massa to the post in 2008 at Interlagos and when their disastrous 2015 performance was repeated in 2017, it spelt the end of Dennis's tenure. After a boardroom coup he sold his remaining shares and officially ended his four-decade reign.

Zak Brown had already been appointed executive director of the McLaren technology group in late 2016 and was now overseeing the business side of McLaren's operations including marketing, sponsorships and commercial partnerships, helping to turn the company's ailing fortunes around. McLaren fans will remember the last few years before Dennis left as dark days, as I mentioned in the last chapter, with an uninspiring grey car, bereft of sponsors, floundering at the back of the grid.

It was time for a refresh and a rebrand.

'We had hit rock bottom. Zak was here and at the helm. When he arrived he knew it was bad, but he didn't realise exactly how bad. I pull it up in presentations sometimes, this grey car with a red line on it, DNF [did not finish] with smoke billowing out the back and very few partners on it. That was where we were and it was quite a poignant moment because [if you] compare that to where we are now, you wouldn't even recognise it as the same team.'

Louise McEwen graduated from Loughborough University having studied sports science and psychology. She started her marketing career at the agency Octagon where she was put onto the Vodafone account at the time when they were moving into Formula One.

'I hadn't got a clue about Formula One when I started and to be quite frank it was a miracle that I stayed on the account. But Vodafone took off and were sponsoring Ferrari. As a young 22-year-old I was travelling the world, staying in amazing places, getting helicopters everywhere and briefing Michael Schumacher. I was ridiculously naive, when I look back, but it was an incredible start to my career. After a couple of years I worked in-house for Vodafone. I had moved from the agency to the client, who were also sponsoring Manchester United and who then switched their allegiances from Ferrari to McLaren when they became their title partner.'

It gave McEwen a 360-degree view of how sponsorship worked within Formula One, but when mobile phone companies started to pull their budgets and sponsorship within the sport dried up, she left and entered the freelance world. It was when Zak Brown took over that she got the opportunity to work for McLaren directly, eventually taking over as the group brand director in 2017. One of her first tasks was to take responsibility for the refresh.

I was lucky enough to travel to Navarre in northern Spain in 2018 to host the launch of the MCL33. They even stuck me in a

McLaren road car and I was driven round on cold tyres by Fernando Alonso early that February morning, an experience I will never forget. But that is not the point. I was there to have a look at their new car, which was unveiled via a digital launch. It was low key; McLaren had decided not to make a massive deal about the rebrand because of their lack of success the previous year but, when it was revealed that day, it undoubtedly felt like the dawn of a new era. It had been decided that the team would return to the iconic papaya-coloured livery that had adorned Bruce McLaren's Formula One cars from 1968, their Can-Am entrants and the Indy 500 winners of Johnny Rutherford in 1974 and 1976. It was a bold statement.

'We had run the car in papaya when we returned to the Indy 500 with Fernando Alonso in 2017 and the feedback we got was that the fans were responding really well to it. It gave us the confidence to go for it with our Formula One car. Zak and the shareholders were very much behind this drive to defrost the brand, and papaya gave us this tangible thing to hold on to. Big brands would pay a fortune to have amazing provenance and we knew that we could play it back. We knew where it came from. It wasn't something that we just made up on a whim. It was the colour that Bruce McLaren had chosen.'

Now as chief marketing officer at McLaren, McEwen is responsible for the narrative and the strategy of the brand and for overseeing the creative visual identity of the team's entire racing programme. The shift to papaya was inevitable given its heritage.

'When you are not winning, as we weren't back then, you have to have a greater purpose and create stuff to talk about from a marketing perspective, and I remember looking into this treasure trove of all these amazing heritage stories that we had never told as a brand. So, whether it was the Senna campaign that we did in 2024 to mark the 30th anniversary of his passing or the 60 years of McLaren that we celebrated a couple of years ago, there was all this incredible history around our past drivers, and by going back to papaya, we were embracing that. Its association with Bruce and all these stories still felt as true to the brand today as they did a long time ago.'

However, in that fallow period when they weren't winning and bringing in sponsorship, things were looking bleak for McLaren. In fact, it got worse before it got better. While results on the track began to improve the year after the rebrand, in early 2020 Covid struck. As a result, a year later, they were forced to sell the MTC in a sale and leaseback deal worth £170 million, to free up capital for the business. In financial terms, it gave them the breathing space to continue into the cost-cap era that started in 2021 and which provided the stability the teams required to become profitable. McLaren came out of Covid swinging, and determined to scrap their way back to the top in every department.

These days marketing is more than just a badging exercise and, as we've already mentioned, there is only so much room on the car, but since the rebrand the sponsors have started filtering back to McLaren. Dell came on board in 2018 and British American Tobacco a year later under their Vuse e-cigarette brand, then Gulf Oil in 2020 before fintech and crypto giant OKX in 2022 and Google at the same time. The Google deal was huge for the team.

'We call it the commercial flywheel. First of all, you have to have a great brand that people want to buy into. Ultimately, we were selling our brand with more than just performance, but with rich storytelling and the values that we have as a team. So people could see an upward trajectory ahead, even though we hadn't delivered on it yet. The companies that came to us in the last five years brought in the dollars, that in turn gave us the upgrades on the car to keep pushing the boundaries and move to the front of the grid.'

As the number of sponsors grew, so too did the requirement to be able to fit all their logos on the car without affecting performance.

'Everything we do has to make that car go faster. I can't tell you how much, but a few weeks ago, Piers Thynne [McLaren's operations director] came to me and said we need to save X number of grams on the car. We managed it. I can now tell you the weight of every single sticker on that car. It was the same when we moved to papaya. The car used to be fully painted, adding kilos of weight, but when we transitioned we decided to vinyl the car instead because it was easier to do and it saved weight and man hours. That was in my remit. We had to get the whole team on board with wrapping the car rather than painting it, as they had done for 20 years.'

Once they had got the car looking good, McEwen had to convince the mechanics and engineers to come round to wearing papaya as well. She wanted the team to look cohesive. But that can be hard with group of fashion-conscious mechanics.

'They simply didn't want to wear papaya. But if you want to sell more merchandise you need it to represent what people see on TV. If we take 2016, we were a cold, steely brand and no one really knew what we stood for because we were constantly changing power units and sponsors and we were always pivoting from one thing to another. So eventually we got the entire team to believe in papaya. I won't be changing from that colour in the time I have left here. If you look around at the Premier League teams who do this well, they are consistent. My goal is to instil that in our team, make sure our colour is a fan favourite and that we stand out.'

At the launch of the 2025 season at the O2 in February, McLaren, as the reigning constructors' champions, were the last on stage to showcase their livery for the new season. It was the first time that this kind of spectacle had been attempted by the sport and it featured every team and every driver on the grid. With an allocated slot of seven minutes each, you can imagine that, competitive as they are, the teams all tried to outdo each other with their launches – and some fared better than others.

Ultimately it was a showcase for their brands and partners and so, to some extent, it could have been viewed as a marketing competition, something that was not lost on McEwen. When we spoke for this book the next day, the adrenaline was still working its way out of her system. She and the team had used the event and the scale of it to launch their new campaign, entitled 'Never stop racing'.

'When you are at the pointy end of it and you've been so involved in the planning it is incredibly tense. As I was watching it,

I was keeping everything crossed. I thought, *I think this is playing out all right*. And today I've been reading the sentiment and the polls and I've just seen an article in *F1 Racing* rating all the presentations and we pipped Ferrari to the top. They were talking about the authenticity and the heritage coming through the cars. It felt like a team up there on stage with Lando [Norris] and Oscar [Piastri], Zak and Andrea [Stella, team principal] interacting, all skilfully held together by Martin Brundle. So I'm pleased.'

'Never stop racing' is a two-year marketing campaign that recognises the heritage of the brand and charts its origins right through to the modern day and their first constructors' title since 1998.

The campaign was developed in-house with an eye on the next generation of fans, who are consuming Formula One content in a vastly different way from traditional audiences. This means that the marketeers are having to adjust their strategies to keep up with the insatiable demand within the youth market, who can't necessarily afford tickets or TV subscriptions. One in three fans have discovered the sport within the last four years.

'Only one per cent of Formula One fans will attend a race in their lifetime. So, where we want to be in the future is showing up in their lives as a lifestyle brand. They might not sit down and watch the race on a Sunday. but they might buy a T-shirt, so we need to take our brand to them rather than expecting them to consume traditional Formula One as it is presented on TV. Where we get most cut through is sometimes away from the Grand Prix weekends.'

In 2025 McLaren will be on the track in 70 races across the different series that they compete in. It affords them a great opportunity as well.

'Somewhere on the planet nearly every weekend of the year we are rocking up in papaya to race, so with "Never stop racing" we wanted a broader campaign. That's the point. It is designed to encompass all the racing series and it's a good way of creating cohesion and connectivity between the series that we race in.'

The expansion has meant more work for McEwen, who is busier than ever co-ordinating them all to fit the brief she set out in Formula One. McLaren set themselves up for success by expanding the brand into these new territories and racing series, so that there is more opportunity for fans to get to know them.

'When I started I had one car and Zak has added a further series every year that I've been in this job! I'm not sure what else he can come up with that we can race. We try and keep the strength of the brand together as we roll out. My day-to-day has changed from a small team of 30 to 110 now. So it keeps growing, just like our sport.'

They are undoubtedly one of the great commercial success stories since Covid. Their move from the back of the grid early on in 2023 to constructors' champions was one of the greatest turn-arounds in the sport's history. It was a monumental team effort that involved McEwen's strong rebrand, Nick Martin bringing in the new sponsors and Matt Dennington retaining them. The three pillars within McLaren's commercial and marketing department were doing their job and it allowed the engineers and designers to do theirs. When it works in harmony it produces results. And in this case, a championship.

CHAPTER 9
THE FLEET STREET JOURNALIST

'By all the laws of humanity, I should not be the motor-racing champion of the world.'

In 1976, after that most storied of seasons, James Hunt lifted his first and only drivers' championship. He emerged from the monsoon at Mount Fuji and, with the help of Ian Wooldridge, penned a story in his own words that was plastered on the front page of the *Daily Mail*. It was the first race to be televised live by satellite in the middle of the European night and it precipitated an interest in Formula One in the UK like never before.

'In the earlier days it might have been a news story about a death but it's my view that after that race, and in the early years of Bernie's involvement, the BBC and Fleet Street did more to spread the word of Formula One than any other organisations, probably up until the Netflix growth of the last few years.'

Jonathan McEvoy has been the *Daily Mail*'s chief Formula One correspondent since 2006.

'Journalistically, I believe we are in the midst of a huge revival of the sport at the moment. Yes because of Netflix and the younger generation who are now watching but also, slightly paradoxically, as the physical papers decline there has been a massively increased online consumption. You can now, of course, measure the volume of readers digitally and the Formula One numbers stack up well. It's now impossible for sports editors, who might have been reluctant in the past to run Formula One stories, to ignore the facts.'

When I first arrived in Formula One, I was lucky enough to meet and get to know some of the great names of motorsport journalism. People like Maurice Hamilton, Nigel Roebuck, David Tremayne and Bob McKenzie had been attending races since the 1970s and had lived through, and reported on, some of the great eras of the sport. They had borne witness to tragedy and triumph and laid it all out in print. Most have retired and while new faces have moved into replace them, in the 14 years that I have been involved, the media landscape has changed beyond all recognition. In the days of Bernie Ecclestone, entrance to the paddock was sacrosanct and reserved for the teams, their sponsors and guests, officials and paying broadcasters. If you were a journalist you had to belong to an accredited publication, be it a newspaper or a magazine, and every single daily newspaper had a dedicated journalist on site.

In the last decade or so, as the way people consume their media has changed, so too has the number of 'journalists' allowed to enter the paddock. Quite rightly, the owners want to spread the gospel of Formula One as far and wide as possible but it has created as many problems as it has solved, particularly for the Fleet Street journalists that operate within the sport. Now chief writer for Motorsport Network, Ben Hunt was the Formula One correspondent for the *Sun* from 2012 until 2024.

'Nothing these days has an embargo. I mean, back in the old days, there would always be a print-first mentality. Unfortunately we don't have that now. Everyone's tweeting everything or worse still there's a practice where people who aren't actually journalists but audio file distributors who are getting into the paddock. They record interviews and send them around the world to various different people or their own websites to transcribe and write up. I frequently find that I'll be in an interview and by the time I've got back to my desk in the media centre that interview is running on a website written by a journalist who wasn't even at the session or even in the same country and that's hugely frustrating. That's where I feel Formula One needs to stop and rethink, because soon you'll have a situation where nobody will be needing to go to the race. You'll have one journalist, one question and one audio file sent all around the world, and that's just dumbing the sport down.'

McEvoy agrees: 'I've always believed that to do journalism, you need to be there. That is where you start from as a journalist.'

You can understand their frustration but we live in a world where people want information immediately. It's why most publications these days are digital first. It's the only way to keep up with the pace and spread of the stories. Tom Cary has been the *Telegraph's* correspondent for Formula One on and off since 2009.

'When stories break, they are put up immediately online and then at the end of the day you'll judge what the best and most up-to-date lines are and they will be the ones that make the following day's paper. We've been digital first for a while now but it's taken a long time for people's mentalities to change. I think a lot of people who work within newspapers have an old-school view where there's still the buzz of seeing your words laid out in print. But now that most people are consuming their news online, we've had to change our approach. When I first started, the previous generation of journalists would go and play rounds of golf and find a story a day to file, enjoy a few glasses of wine and then go to bed and no one would be able to get hold of them or would even think to pester them. I remember Australia in 2010 when Lewis Hamilton got pulled over for hooning [performing tyre burnouts] outside Albert Park and we were up all night because of the time difference. The desk wanted updates until he was out of the police station. It's just a totally different world now.'

There are a couple of types of journalist in Formula One. The Fleet Street journalists who endeavour to bring the excitement of the sport to the casual fans on the back pages of the dailies and break stories, and the pure motorsport journalists who dive deep into the technical side of the sport. In Britain, where football dominates, Formula One must fight hard for column inches and sometimes, in periods where one team or one driver is winning all the time, that can be hard. Selling a narrative that doesn't change from week to week and year to year has been one of the biggest problems that Formula One has to face. When a team gets ahead, more often than not, within the confines of that set of regulations, it stays ahead. Thankfully the pack have bunched up as the current set of regulations have matured and some feel it is a shame that, with the racing now better than ever, they have to be reset in 2026. But Formula One, according to Hunt, has so much more to offer than simply who is winning,

'It's sports, entertainment, history and business. It's got all those four hooks to it. It also has that mystique. Anyone can go and play football, tennis or golf, whereas Formula One is unattainable for most people on the planet. Even karting isn't accessible for a lot of people. It's people risking their lives every time they get behind the wheel of a Formula One car, and then there's the politics. We call it the Piranha Club for a reason. Everyone is out to get each other and when one driver is winning all the time there is always an off-track story to get your teeth into, because it never stops.'

As we began the season in 2024 with Max Verstappen looking to continue the domination he had enjoyed the previous year, one of those stories hit the headlines. It was one of the most difficult stories that I've ever had to cover as a broadcast journalist and it was the same for everyone reporting on the sport, not least those on Fleet Street, who were following it every minute of the day. When Christian Horner was accused of inappropriate and coercive behaviour by a female member of staff, which he has consistently denied, it started a chain of events where, as a journalist, you had to be meticulous about your reporting. It was such shaky legal ground for all media outlets because of the injunctions that had been put in place by those involved, as Cary explains.

'You'd be on deadlines and then you'd have to check it with the lawyers as well and that adds another layer to the filing process. And our job is to try and get ahead of it and move the story along in any way we can, but this one was particularly tricky because libel and

Dr Ian Roberts pulling Grosjean out of the flames in Bahrain, 2020. As soon as the driver was clear of the car, Roberts worked quickly to treat his burns.

Hamilton celebrates winning at the 2024 British Grand Prix. 164,000 people attended Silverstone that Sunday, setting a new single-day record.

Mikey Brown and his team changing the wheels of Alonso's car during a pit stop at the Red Bull Ring in Austria.

Hamilton celebrating his 2008 world championship with Matt Bishop after the race in Brazil.

In 2016, the McLaren car driven by Alonso was uninspiring and bereft of sponsors.

Less than ten years on, the iconic papaya-orange livery is full of sponsors and embraces Bruce McLaren's legacy.

Damon Hill wins the 1996 world championship title at the Japanese Grand Prix after a disastrous previous season. It was announced 15 days later that he would be leaving Williams.

Mark Thompson's photograph of Alonso's crash with Leclerc, which won sports picture of the year in 2018 at the British Sports Journalism Awards.

Thompson's favourite shot: Schumacher driving onto the grid at the Indianapolis Motor Speedway in 2002.

Giorgio Piola working on Prost's McLaren MP4/2 car in 1984.

Piola's poster for the 1975 Ferrari 312T. The car was driven by Lauda who won the first of his three world championships that year.

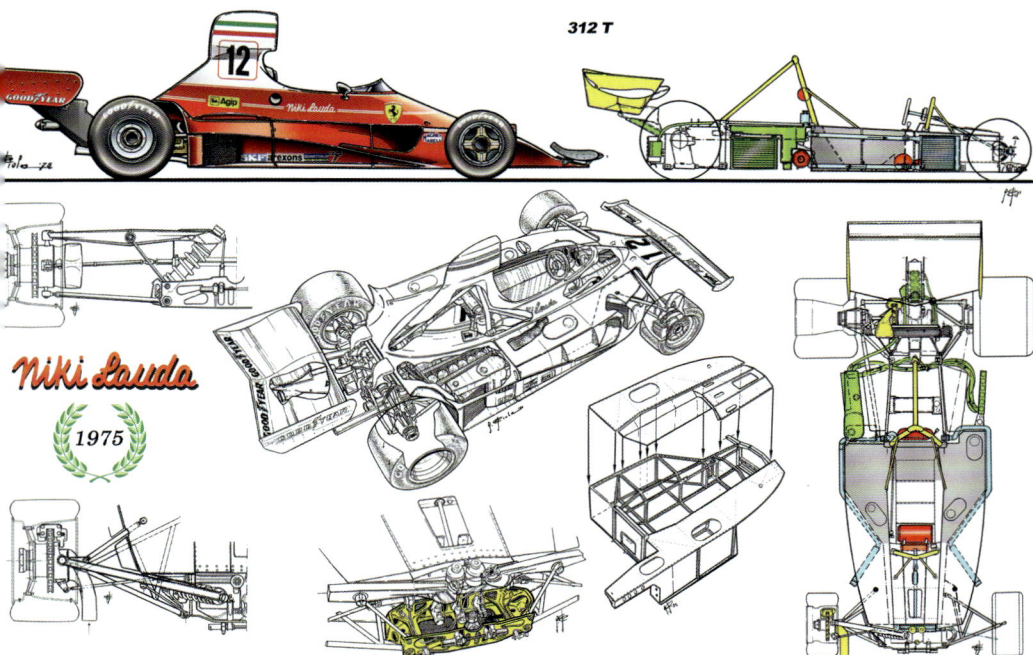

A technical drawing by Piola from 2017.
The Ferrari SF70H was driven by Vettel and Räikkönen.

media laws vary from country to country and because the story was breaking in multiple territories at once. Certain countries could say things that we couldn't in the UK. In Holland and Germany it is different and certain parts of the case could be published, whereas we couldn't. Things like the content of messages and naming of certain parties. *De Telegraaf* in Holland broke the story about the grievance. They also published the leak of the messages but we couldn't touch those. We weren't allowed to mention them, you couldn't even follow it up, let alone break the story. So it was sort of developing at different speeds in different places.'

It was front as well as back-page news and that's one of the unique things about Formula One. All of a sudden everyone is interested, everyone has an opinion and the story becomes global. It also means that, as journalists working within the paddock, you might not just be reporting the facts and trying to move the story on, you might get dragged into the debate yourself. Hunt was doing a book about Red Bull at the time, a book that Horner was central to, and as a result was fielding lots of requests for interviews about his thoughts on the matter.

'You had to stay on your toes and stick to the script. I thought, *Are you looking to trip me up?* We are not political journalists, we are sports journalists and we are not out to get anyone. But of course the people interviewing you are out for the story and yes it was a case, I suppose, of poacher turned gamekeeper but in that situation I didn't want to say anything wrong, so I turned down a lot of interviews. There was an information vacuum and with the 24-hour news cycle people thirst for an update every day, and between the independent investigation and the publishing of the report there simply wasn't anything new to say.'

'It was a story that had everything,' says McEvoy. 'It had Formula One glamour, it had a Spice Girl [Horner's wife, Geri, was Ginger Spice in the 1990s pop group], it had sex, it had unknowns and it had many layers. So every voyeur in the land was drawn in by it. It worked brilliantly for numbers but it wasn't easy to write. You felt you had to honour the story and be down the line with it rather than go with one end of the argument or the other.'

. . .

There is one man in Formula One, though, who is a gift for journalists everywhere and who has helped sell more newspapers than anyone else in the history of the sport: Sir Lewis Hamilton. There is not a Lewis-related pun that Hunt hasn't heard – in fact he's crafted most of them himself in inimitable *Sun* style. B-Lew-it, Lew-King Up, No thank Lew and Lew-Roll are just a taste of some of these powerful headlines, but your average Joe will always be drawn in by an article about Hamilton because there is never a dull moment: he is always up to something.

Hunt explains: 'He's an enigma. I've never met or known any sports star to generate as many stories on such a regular basis, every single day there's something new with Lewis. It really is 24/7 and I have, at times, lived my life studying his life. Certainly during the years when he was winning at Mercedes. There were some quite extreme moments where I'd be charting which country he was in and figuring out the number of miles he'd done, the time differences and trying to work out who he was with. I needed to study his lifestyle and keep a diary of where he was. He was travelling and doing so much, it made it easier with a private jet because on flight websites, you could see where the jet was going. Oh, he's in China now! It was almost sleuth levels of investigation, but it was also knowing your subject. At least that's what I told myself!'

Hamilton remains the only star to have transcended the sport, and that universal appeal is what sells newspapers.

'You know, I've always been a little bit hamstrung on this. Part of the reason I left the *Sun* was to write about other subjects, because there is so much demand for Lewis Hamilton that it prevented me from doing pieces with other drivers; he is just so newsworthy. He's so important for our audience, more so than Lando [Norris] and George [Russell] and any other British driver that has come and gone, The focus, the attention has always been on Lewis. I've had conversations about Max winning. And the question put to me is, "What does Lewis think about Max winning?" It's like, hang on a minute, Lewis isn't the story on this one. But people want to know what Lewis thinks. So it constantly circles back around to him. And it would be nice to write about someone different for once. But that said, I really do enjoy everything that he's done for Formula One.'

McEvoy is in agreement that Hamilton has been the dominant star of this era and perhaps any era, but he remains optimistic that the baton of superstardom will pass on. There is a conveyer belt of talent coming through and some of the faces will look just as good on billboards and generate just as many column inches, especially if their talent matches their marketability. There is always another big story just around the corner, like the last race of the season in Abu Dhabi 2021.

'I've never seen anything like it. It was the biggest weekend we've ever had on the *Telegraph* website,' says Cary. 'The numbers were through the roof, stratospheric, and it felt like the epicentre of global sport.'

The allure of Formula One to journalists and fans alike is that it keeps you waiting. People are always more engaged when the drama takes time to unfold and the story builds to a crescendo. In the 75-year history of the sport, the championship has rarely come down to the last race of the season but in 2021 it did. For those of us that were there and reporting on it, whether in print or on live television, it is a night we will never forget, and we'll return to it later, in detail. And now there is this wonderful addendum to the story, after Hamilton decided to switch allegiances to Ferrari for the start of 2025. The coming together of arguably the two biggest brands in Formula One was simply massive. As the popularity of the sport has grown, this was that next big story, the narrative that will attract even more eyeballs. In 2026 there is a new set of regulations, Hamilton has made the move to Ferrari, something his hero, Ayrton Senna, never managed after his life was so tragically cut short. The possibility of redemption after the pain of 2021 is almost too good to be true. If Hamilton were to win in a red car, after denying Felipe Massa in another for his first title in 2008, it would be the ultimate bookend to his career. The fairytale would be complete and Hollywood would undoubtedly come calling. This is a script yet to be written but if it did happen it would provide journalists like Cary, Hunt and McEvoy with enough copy to last a lifetime. Or at least, until the next big story comes along.

CHAPTER 10
THE BBC CORRESPONDENT

mentioned in the last chapter that there are two types of Formula One journalist, those from Fleet Street and the more technical types. That's not strictly true because Andrew Benson straddles both disciplines and over the years has broken some major stories himself, but also the BBC has its own set of guidelines to adhere to and that makes his role unique. As a BBC writer, Benson is not allowed to convey an opinion because objectivity and impartiality is absolutely sacrosanct, and this must run through everything he does.

'You are only allowed to express an opinion if it is backed up by fact. That's not the same as saying something is good or bad for Formula One. If you wanted to express the opinion that Max Verstappen was having a better season than Lando Norris, you'd have to point out the fact that he's hardly made any mistakes at all and that Norris has left some points on the table. But where there is an opinion that is just a matter of opinion then, as far as the BBC is concerned, that is straying too far.'

Benson has been the chief Formula One correspondent for the BBC since 2000. Like many of us, he entered his last year of university not having a clue what he was going to do with his life. I remember the different potential employers coming to Durham, where I was at university, and feeling exactly the same. I hadn't once thought about what I wanted to be when I grew up, because I hadn't grown up! It would've been quite easy to drift into a job that you hadn't given much thought to and that is exactly what happened to me when I became a trader. Benson was at least putting his student time to good use though and was writing for the university paper, whereas I'm pretty sure I was either on a sports field or in the college bar.

'I remember seeing an interview with comedian and broadcaster Michael Palin describing his careers advice sessions at school. He was brought up in Sheffield, where I went to university, and he was reminiscing about the teacher asking him what he was interested in. "Theatre and the arts," he remarked, and the teacher immediately responded, "It's Pilkington Glass for you!" The next kid walked in and was asked the same question, "Engineering," he said. "Well, it's Pilkington Glass for you!"

'And it felt like that to me. I was expected to be a lawyer or a doctor or an accountant and I didn't want to be one of those. It had never really occurred to me that I could become a Formula One journalist but I had been following the sport since the age of nine and I loved writing, so I sent an on-spec article [a piece written without a commission] to *Autosport* about the lack of environmentalism in Formula One and to my surprise they published it.'

When he came back from travelling after university, Benson saw an advert for a job as an editorial assistant at the magazine.

'I only really knew about Formula One. This job entailed editing club reports about Formula Ford races and all the stuff that goes on around the UK at Snetterton, Donington and Cadwell Park for example. If they'd asked me who the reigning Vauxhall Lotus champion was at the time I wouldn't have known, but they just chatted to me about Formula One for an hour. It was the weirdest, easiest interview I've ever done, and thankfully I got the job.'

After joining *Autosport*, Benson quickly became assistant news editor. It was 1992, the year that Nigel Mansell won his Formula One title. James Allen, who later became ITV's lead Formula One commentator, was the news editor at the time, and when Mansell decided to move to IndyCar in 1993 Allen went with him, as his press officer. Benson was promoted into James's role. He stayed as news editor for a couple of years until he was promoted again to Grand Prix editor at the start of 1996.

'My first Grand Prix was in Melbourne and I had a really unpleasant start. There was a guy there by the name of Mark Skewis, who was working for *Motoring News* at the time. He was much more experienced than me and knew a lot more people in the paddock. Anyway there was a sniff that Tom Walkinshaw was going to buy the Arrows team. I kind of got most of the way there with the story and went and asked Walkinshaw on the Sunday morning if it was true. Walkinshaw told me it wasn't and then Skewy went to see him and he must have said yes to him. So Tom had lied to me. Anyway, I had a story that said it looked like it was happening but Walkinshaw denied it whereas *Motoring News* had run a story saying that it was true and confirmed. So I got hauled over the coals by the publisher of *Autosport* for not completely getting the story right and I didn't like that feeling at all. I vowed that it wouldn't happen again.'

And therein lies the nuance in paddock journalism. Everyone wants to be the first to break a story but more often than not it is the more experienced writers who have developed the connections who are the ones that get the scoop. Benson has always been tenacious though, and in that same year he broke a story about Damon Hill that was arguably his biggest scoop even to this day.

• • •

In 2025, my production company, Sylver Entertainment, released *Hill*, a documentary film about 1996 championship winner, and my former broadcasting colleague, Damon Hill. As producer, I spent much of the preceding seven years trying to get it financed and made. It is such an incredible family story. Hill's father, two-time Formula One world champion Graham, was killed when piloting his plane back from testing in France along with the other five passengers on board. With the insurance papers not in place, Damon, his mother Bette and two sisters were left with nothing. Damon had had to fight his way into Formula One and, in an eerie parallel with his father's career, helped pull the Williams team together after the death of his team-mate Ayrton Senna in 1994, much as his father did with Lotus, after the death of Jim Clark in 1968. Following this, Michael Schumacher had controversially cost Hill the chance of winning the title in the last race at Adelaide after he 'deliberately' crashed into him. 1995 had been a disaster for Hill, his form and confidence had suffered and so 1996 was to be his year to try to right all the wrongs that he had suffered in attempting to emulate his father and become a world champion. But halfway through that season, Benson broke his story.

'Someone tipped me off that Williams were going to get rid of Damon at the end of 1996 and replace him with Heinz-Harald Frentzen. We agonised over it because it was a really good source. I spent a bit of time doing some background work on it and it got to the point where I just thought there is just too much to this story to not run it. And so we published and it went out on the Thursday of the German Grand Prix weekend.'

At that stage Hill was leading the championship by 21 points from his team-mate Jacques Villeneuve, with six rounds remaining.

'I knew it was going to be massive. I woke up that morning, was having my breakfast and was about to go to the airport when I put on the breakfast news. Simon Taylor, who was the Radio 2 Formula One commentator and also the chairman of Haymarket, which owned *Autosport* at the time, was on the telly saying that the story wasn't true and was by a naive young journalist who had been led up the garden path by the darker forces in Formula One.'

Benson was understandably perplexed and more than a little worried.

'I was pretty sure that it was true but I thought, *God, what is going to happen when I get to Hockenheim?* I decided not to go to Damon's British media session because I thought I wasn't going to be very popular.'

Instead he waited to the end of the day to go to Hill's motor-home and explain to him personally why he had run the story.

'In those days, they didn't have the fancy motorhomes that they do now. It was basically a bus with a three-metre awning off it that you could zip up. I hadn't even taken a step into the awning when I saw Damon sitting with his wife Georgie and his manager Michael Breen at the far end.

'Get out, Andrew,' he said, 'you've made yourself look very stupid.'

It was at that point that Benson had to endure the purgatory of waiting to find out if the story that he had run would turn out to be true.

'I knew it was going to be an uncomfortable few weeks. We'd been quite careful about the story and our sources, but it wasn't 100 per cent definitive that it was happening.'

Hill went on to win the world championship at the last race in Suzuka in a tearful finale that drew the immortal line, 'And I've got to stop because I've got a lump in my throat,' from legendary commentator Murray Walker, in reference to the journey Damon had been on in the aftermath of the tragedy of his father's death. Just 15 days later Williams announced that Hill would be leaving to be replaced by Frentzen. Benson had been vindicated.

Formula One is the most political of sports and there were multiple rumoured reasons for Frank Williams's decision to sign Frentzen. Yes, Damon hadn't performed well in 1995, but to this day Hill believes it was linked to Williams's desire to run BMW engines in the future and that having a German driver in the team would strengthen their negotiating hand. That deal was announced at the Frankfurt Motor Show after the Italian Grand Prix in 1997, 18 months after Hill had left. For journalists like Benson there is always so much subtext to think about when trying to be the first to report a big story in the paddock.

'I revisited the story for *F1 Racing* magazine ten years after the event and I talked to Damon and to Frank Williams and co-founder Patrick Head and not once did BMW come up in those conversations. It was always presented that they had decided to get rid of him on the basis of his performance in 1995.

'Head and Williams had a huge amount of respect for Damon, after what he did for the team following the death of Senna, but they didn't see his performances in the dominant car as justification enough that he could take on Schumacher and Ferrari on a consistent basis.'

There had always been speculation about whether Frentzen had signed that contract with Williams at the end of 1995 or in 1996, and Benson pushed Head on this during the interviews for the piece a decade on.

'I asked Head when exactly it was that Frentzen signed for Williams. Was it at the end of 1995, as everybody thought, or was it in 1996? He said, "I'm absolutely sure it was 1996," and he went off to get the contract. He was gone for about ten minutes but when he came back he wouldn't show me the contract and said, "It was definitely the summer of 1996!" In the end, Damon got a column in the magazine and he asked me to write it for him. I asked his friend and photographer Jon Nicholson why on earth he'd wanted me to do it, and he said, "That's Damon's way of saying sorry!"'

By the end of the 1990s Benson was freelancing for the *Guardian* as well as continuing his work for *Autosport* but a confluence of circumstances made him realise that he needed a change.

'I was in Australia at the start of 2000 writing a piece about the Sauber engine supply when I had a massive déjà vu moment. I was sure I'd written exactly the same story before. I checked back on my computer and it turned out I had. I could have taken the same story from 1998 and run it word for word and I took it as a sign that I had to get away from this level of minutiae. I thought, *I'm not interested in Sauber's engine supplier or whatever, I'm interested in the big picture stuff.*'

Benson had grown disillusioned with the sport and was considering moving to a newspaper as a general sports writer.

'I felt I was losing trust in what I was watching and that there was manipulation going on at times. For instance, there were all those stories about Max Mosley and Ferrari. Obviously there is no proof of these things but, in 1999, five days after Ferrari had been thrown out of the Malaysian Grand Prix for having illegal barge-boards, confirming Mika Häkkinen as champion, the FIA contrived a way to miraculously make them legal again, allowing the championship to still be alive going into the last race. I thought, *What actually is going on here? Is this real?*'

So when the BBC started their sports website in spring 2000, Benson jumped at the chance. It gave him the opportunity to write about other sports as well as Formula One.

'I was running the desk the night that Marco Pantani, the Italian cyclist, was found dead in his hotel room [as a result of acute cocaine poisoning]. I got to work on the Sydney Olympics and wrote an article on the importance of Cathy Freeman, an aboriginal Australian, lighting the flame at the opening ceremony, as well as numerous football articles. It was also the Lance Armstrong era so it was a really interesting time. But when the BBC won the Formula One contract back in 2009 I was asked to go across and set up the website to go alongside the TV coverage and had a fair amount of input in the editorial as a person who was breaking stories and writing about the sport.'

Much as the Fleet Street journalists have explained, the world of journalism has changed dramatically in recent years. Benson shares their frustrations with the audio file sharers that run quote pieces on the basis of what they see broadcast live on TV from their bedrooms. But for him that doesn't threaten the core of what he does.

'The people that break the stories are still the people that travel to the races and have the contacts. That is always going to be the case.'

But how much time and effort goes in to getting an exclusive?

'It can take ages but it can also happen very quickly. You just have to keep talking to the right people. The more you talk to them, the more they trust you and the more little bits of information will slip out. And then it's a question of knowing which bits of information are important and which aren't, which people you can trust on which topics and which you can't. Who can back up that bit of information until you get to a point where you can be as confident as you can be that something's true, but then you still have to be careful about how you present it.'

Benson has had his fair share of exclusives down the years and is one of the first people I will look to talk to when a story is breaking because he is always across all the gossip and has an inside track to virtually everyone in the paddock.

'One news story I was quite proud of breaking was when Ross Brawn [then team principal] was getting replaced at Mercedes. I broke that in early 2013 before the season started and I had been working on it for months. Someone had let something slip in a conversation in autumn 2012 about him but it was a bit nebulous and quite frustrating because I would get somewhere and I would hit a brick wall. I would let it lie for a while and then I'd go back to the person who had originally said it and someone else who might have known. Suddenly, one day that winter, it all fell into place and I knew Brawn was out. So I phoned Bradley Lord, who is the Mercedes communications director, and told him what I knew and he said he didn't think it was true so he went away to check, came back and his position had changed on it. And I got so wrapped up in it and the excitement of finally nailing this story and running it that I'd completely forgotten that the next day I was going to Mercedes for a press conference with Ross. I was in his office with the rest of the British journalists and I've never seen him more nervous or upset than on that day.'

Benson's story made for a tense atmosphere but the official announcement of Brawn leaving the team didn't happen until much later, in November 2013, after the end of the season. It was part of a restructuring by the incoming head of Mercedes-Benz motorsport, Toto Wolff. A case of too many chiefs at the top of their Formula One programme, which ultimately hadn't yielded immediate success under Brawn's leadership since his eponymous team was bought by the German automotive giants at the end of 2009.

Benson was also part of the BBC team that broke the story about Lewis Hamilton moving to the Mercedes works team from

McLaren, a story that Eddie Jordan had got wind of first. But he also enjoys challenging the perceived narratives that have become gospel in the closed environment of the paddock.

'What happens in Formula One is that there is an accepted truth that emerges about an event. The problem is that quite often the accepted truth isn't quite the full truth at all but people haven't troubled to look into it properly. The accepted truth about Fernando Alonso leaving Ferrari at the end of 2014 was that he had been tricked into signing a release from his contract and that he had never intended to leave. And that was simply not true. He'd always wanted to leave. Whether it was wise for him to leave is a different question but it was his decision. I spoke to literally everybody to get to the core of what had happened and I realised that it's not possible to tell the definitive truth. People that were in the same room at the same time will tell you different stories.'

Benson's scoop highlighted the power struggle and tensions between the management and Ferrari's short-lived team principal Marco Mattiacci, and once again he correctly predicted the end of Alonso's time there and the identity of his replacement, Sebastian Vettel, before any other major outlets had announced official confirmation.

'In the period that I've been covering Formula One, everything has become so much more structured. When I started, if you wanted to speak to a driver, you just hung around and waited for them. Now you're pretty much expected to only speak to them in these formalised events, like press conferences or pen interviews. Once you've built a relationship with people, when you see them in the paddock, they will talk to you, but the default position these days is that they don't speak to the media unless it is formally arranged through a press officer. Part of journalism and breaking stories is that you don't want to go to a press officer and say, well I've heard this, can I go and ask such and such, because you don't want the press officer to know, but as long as you are well connected you can usually work around that.'

The BBC covers things slightly differently from both the specialist journalists from *Autosport* and other motorsport-focused publications, and the Fleet Street journalists.

There are certain journalists in the paddock who are incessant in peeling back the layers of spin to get to the essence of the story. These are the ones that invariably get the exclusives and spend their entire weekends talking to people up and down the paddock to work out what is actually going on. It takes time and effort to uncover the truth in this cloak and dagger sport. Andrew Benson puts in both.

CHAPTER 11
THE PHOTOGRAPHER

While the journalists paint pictures with words, the job of the Formula One photographer is to capture the moment. Whether on track or in the paddock, that moment could be a smart overtake, a massive shunt, a team principal courting a driver's signature, the elation of victory or the despair of a lost championship. It could be a political, competitive or deeply personal moment because Formula One has so many layers and to be a good photographer in this sport requires experience.

'It was the early 1990s and I was staying in some shitty hotel in Harare, covering a World Cup qualifier for Zimbabwe, when I got a call from my agent, who told me that Princess Di was in the country visiting a leper colony. I mean I didn't even think they still existed. Anyway, he says, go to the British consulate, pick up a pass and get down there ASAP and to make sure I got a fucking good picture!

'I sorted the pass and jumped in a filthy taxi to this Red Cross event. When I arrived there's all these royal photographers who followed them all around the world: Kent Gavin, all the Fleet Street lot. I was late and they're all grouchy and crammed into this pen that I'm pointed to, but I thought, *Fuck that, I ain't gonna get a picture from in there with that lot 'cos it's side on and it'd be shit.*

'I had to think quickly so I said to one of the organisers that I was the official photographer for the Red Cross, which was total bullshit, but they bought it.

'"Oh, OK, we'll give you a special pass then!"

'Imagine that with the security these days. I couldn't believe they fell for it! I marched round to the front where Di was doing her thing, and I was literally ten foot in front of her and she looked at me straight down the barrel with this beautiful light on her. All the royal snappers start shouting, "Who's that geezer? Why's he over there?"

'They were livid because they'd never seen me before, they hadn't got a good shot and I'm the only photographer that's not in the pen. Well, I just started taking pictures, happy as Larry, with everyone yelling and screaming at me ... surrounded by these poor lepers.

'Anyway, I got the shot and a few years later, you know that bloke Andrew Morton, who did her official biography, he picked my picture of Di at the leper colony, to go on the front cover of his book!'

Mark 'Thommo' Thompson is a mod. He's the drummer the Style Council could've had if they'd ever met him, and as a teenager he aspired to be a professional musician. Instead, he now channels that 'Wellerian' spirit into his work as one of the pre-eminent Formula One photographers of his age, an art form in its own right. He's also a veteran of more than 500 Grands Prix. He doesn't count Donington 1993 though, his first race and one of Senna's greatest drives, because he blagged his way into that one too!

Thompson was born in Northampton, a couple of hundred metres from Franklin's Gardens, home of Northampton Saints rugby club. By his own admission he wasn't particularly academic at school and describes himself as a bit of a rogue. When he was 15, he and his mother, Alice, who had given birth to Thompson when she was 43, were summoned to the headmaster's office of the secondary school that he attended. The headmaster, a disciplinarian who apparently resembled the Yorkshire Ripper, sternly informed them that although young Mark was a talented boy, he made too many mistakes and his life was heading in the wrong direction.

Clearly irritated by these comments, Thompson's mother curtly replied, 'Well that's probably about right because Mark WAS a mistake. Weren't you, darling?'

She took Mark by the hand and marched him out of the office. He left school shortly after.

At the age of 16, Thompson went to work in a local shoe factory, hand-cutting leather. It served as an apprenticeship, although he kept slicing the tops of his fingers off, so unfortunately it didn't last. He navigated his way through a succession of mundane jobs until he eventually hooked up with a girlfriend who generously bought him a camera and paid for him to attend an evening course in photography, as Thompson was skint. Now, 40 years later, this girlfriend, Cath, is still his wife. It was the best gift he could ever have received because it was during this course, shooting black-and-white film, that his instructor said he had a natural eye and the potential to make a career as a professional photographer.

'At first I laughed, but I was never gonna make it as a pop star. I tried but I was sick of waiting to be discovered, so the guy who was running the course put me in touch with the local newspaper and I began picking up shifts covering the Saints rugby club, who back then were lounging in the second division. But it was good money and I could earn the same as I was doing in the factory, without cutting my fingers off.'

His work in the paper was spotted by Bob Thomas, a successful football photographer who ran his own agency. He offered Thompson a six-month trial on his books. In those days it was all manual focus and shot on film so a good photo was harder to take but easier to spot. Thompson passed this trial with flying colours and had his foot in the door.

'All of a sudden I was going to places like Old Trafford, Anfield and FA Cup finals. It was insane. To this day I can't believe that I'm still doing this because I didn't really have much training. I just learnt on the job. Bob had a lot of deals with FIFA so that's why I ended up in Zimbabwe with Princess Diana, but I was all over the place in 1992 and 1993 doing World Cup qualifiers. I travelled to Cameroon, the Ivory Coast, Ghana, I even went to Peru during a military coup. I remember coming out of the hotel to go and shoot the players training and there was a fucking tank outside. I said to the doorman, "What's going on?"

"'It's a military coup," he replied.

"'Do you think the players will still be training?"

"'Yeah, it's OK … we have one every week!"

'I just couldn't believe that people were actually paying me to do this. I used to go and see my mum after these trips and she just didn't understand why they didn't get local photographers to get the picture rather than flying me all the way round the world for a football match. She said to me one day, whilst smoking a fag and stroking her chin, "I know what you are up to. You're smuggling drugs? You'd better not be, I'm not coming to see you when you get locked up."

'She just couldn't get her head round it, until she saw my shot of Princess Di in the local paper!'

After these gallivanting escapades, Thompson began freelancing for the largest photographic agency in the world at the time, Allsport. When one of their Formula One photographers fell ill suddenly in 1996, Thompson got his first (legitimate) opportunity to capture a Grand Prix up close. Almost immediately he was hooked.

On any given race weekend a stills photographer has to wear many hats. Capturing images in such a fast-paced sport requires not just technical prowess but an understanding of the sport, a keen eye for detail and an acute sense of timing. When Allsport were bought by Getty Images, Thompson was taken onto their staff. The first contract he secured was with the Benetton race team.

'It was just after Michael Schumacher left, so when they turned shit basically! This was around 1998 and I've been to every race since. In those days we obviously shot on film and used to take a small processing kit and have someone developing our pictures on site. A lot of the tracks back then had small, purpose-made darkrooms. The major press agencies would share them: Getty, Reuters, AFP. We'd shoot about five or six rolls of colour negative film a day, with 36 exposures, which would be processed on Sunday and sent across for the papers. But the rest was shot on colour transparency, or what people would call slide film. That was where the quality was. Straight after the podium, we would leg it over to the airport to get onto the first flight back to London. [The photographs] would be processed overnight, and at about half five on the Monday morning we would be going through the sets of film to get the images to the sponsors as soon as possible. If we couldn't make the flight, we'd give bags of film to anyone who could get it back for us. DC [David Coulthard] used to be a good mule for me because he was often going back on his private jet, or JB's [Jenson Button's] dad. They knew what was at stake for us.'

Of course it is a totally different world now. When the first digital cameras came out, the file sizes weren't big enough to be practical and they weighed a tonne so most of the photographers persisted with film until the second or third generation of digitals arrived around 2007.

'There are photographers working at the circuits these days who have never shot on film. Take the race scenario, when you had 36 exposures. You'd be on the grid shooting away, taking photos of celebrities and drivers before they got into their cars. Then you'd run up to the first corner, rewind that first film that you've just shot, take it out, rip it, so that you know it's been used, put it in your jacket pocket and then put another one in for the start of the race. Bear in mind, you've only got 36 frames and that can go pretty quickly in a motor-driven camera, as they were, five maybe six frames per second. So, in those days, and I sound like a pompous old twat when I say this, there was a lot more skill to what we did. It was a lot more manual focus. You had to time what you did and almost predict what was going to happen. And that's the skill; pictures had to be correctly exposed, in focus and the composition had to look great. It was hard.'

When Thompson started there were only basic scanners and you could not alter photos as you can today with Photoshop. If you didn't get it right in the camera, there was no saving it. Even today, while Photoshop is fine for sponsors or the arty stuff, as a press photographer, Thompson must abide by a set of rules known as editorial integrity. No press photographers are allowed to digitally alter a picture. They can lighten or darken it, and crop it, but they are not allowed to take anything out or put anything into a picture via Photoshop.

'I employed a guy once in Austria who had a really good portfolio. I sent him out on track and there's a lovely shot at the Red Bull Ring on turn two, where you can crouch down behind the Armco barrier and you can't see any advertising boards. It's just the car on track with the trees and the mountain behind it. It's a pretty straightforward shot for any sports photographer on a long lens. But he came back and it was terrible. Nothing was sharp. He'd cut off the tops of the trees and the car was in the centre of the frame. He had used a thing called autofocus, which is always in the centre of the frame. He should have pre-focused, but he had no idea. I asked him why and he said in his portfolio he just used Photoshop to layer cars and backgrounds on top of each other so that everything was in focus. You can't do that as a press photographer. I sacked him on the spot.'

At the British Sports Journalism awards in 2018, Thompson won sports photographer of the year, specialist portfolio of the year and sports picture of the year for his image of Fernando Alonso's crash with Charles Leclerc at the first corner at Spa during the Belgian Grand Prix. It's an astonishing shot and required split-second timing because even with today's technology the one thing that can't be saved is an out of focus image.

'There were around 30 photographers there that day and only five or six got the shot. When you have 20 cars coming towards you at 80 to 100mph into the first corner, everyone follows the big drivers at the front and stay on them round La Source, because it's a hairpin. Those of us that had been doing it a while almost saw it before it happened because you can hear the brakes. So I swung back and took it. Most of the crashes that occur are in the middle of the pack because it's so congested, but I was looking through the viewfinder. It hasn't changed on that front. I was in the moment. You can't do that if you are staring at the screen on the back of the camera, it's not the same. I did the treble that year at the sports journalism awards and no one's done that before!'

Nowadays a decent camera for a professional sports photographer costs around £7–10,000 but it is the lenses that quickly make things mount up. They can cost anything up to £20,000. They include telephoto lenses that are essential for capturing cars from a distance, wide-angle lenses for broader scenes like the start of the race or crowd shots, to give scale and context. And there are also the prime lenses that are favoured for their sharpness and ability to create a shallow depth of field, often used for portraiture or finer detail. It's a lot cheaper to be a photographer in the digital age, simply because they don't have to pay for rolls and rolls of film and the associated processing costs. Formula One photographers work their equipment hard, taking around 10,000 images per weekend. If they capture an important moment these can be sent anywhere, almost instantaneously, from trackside. The snappers use dongles containing SIM cards and, having viewed a decent image on the screen on the back of the camera, if the connectivity allows, they can be sent to the picture editors at the various agencies with voice notes attached explaining the context of each shot.

'We have four picture editors at Getty and I'm not the only Getty photographer on site at any race. Within seconds of the picture landing, they will caption it and say you were the *Telegraph* or the *New York Times* – or anyone who subscribes to us – you could receive that image a couple of minutes after it was taken and use it for publication.'

So where are the best places on the current calendar to get the ultimate shots of a racing car in action, and how much preparation goes into understanding how to get the best possible photograph?

'I get a massive buzz in Monaco. Everywhere you look there's great pictures. The first time I went there I walked the track and there are all the classic shots you see every year, the chicane out of the tunnel, coming through the swimming pool section and up the hill with the casino in the background. I used to go round knocking on doors and asking if I could use people's apartments, so that I could get some elevation with the harbour as the backdrop. Every year I would take them a copy of the shot from their apartment, signed by one of the drivers so that they'd let me use their place again. Another amazing spot was as the cars climb up out of Eau Rouge in Spa and over the top into Raidillon. It was blind for the drivers and you could really capture a car unsettled coming over the brow of the hill. To get that speed wobble in focus with the Ardennes Forest in the background was epic. But we can't stand there now because of all the accidents that have happened. It was really dangerous just being there.'

Conversely, Silverstone is one of the hardest places to take a good photograph.

'It looks so great on television from the helicopter nestled in England's countryside but it's really difficult for us because it's so flat, and you are miles away from the cars as it's a massive circuit with huge run-off areas. All the grandstands look like scaffolding poles and often there's bad weather. Rain can make for great photographs but not when it's grey and dull and flat light. It does nothing for the colour palette of the cars and the occasion.'

Thompson is adamant that one of the first things that a Formula One photographer has to get to grips with is the geography of the circuits and how to get from A to B while the race is happening, Their accreditation can get them to places that the general public can't access but a race only lasts between 90 minutes and two hours and there are a lot of good vantage points that you need to know your way to and from instinctively. It's the city circuits that are the hardest to navigate.

'The Singapore Grand Prix looks spectacular but the circuit weaves through a maze of hotels and shopping centres. If you haven't done your homework as a photographer on the quickest way to get around, you are just missing opportunities. In Monaco, to get over one particular bridge we used to have to cut through a restaurant whilst posh people were eating their lunch. It's like cabbies doing the knowledge.'

Like all good Formula One photographers, Thompson has gone to great lengths to capture the perfect image.

'My favourite picture is Schumacher going to the grid at Indianapolis in 2002. I'd noticed that whenever he was on pole position, he was always last onto the grid, about a minute behind everyone. It was obviously the way he operated: "I'm on pole, I'm going to drive through the whole lot of them."

'You can't get that shot from the ground. It doesn't quite work. But at Indy there was this thing called the crow's nest. Because Indianapolis is an oval, you can get up onto a roof and down through a hatch and you harness yourself into this tiny little cage. It's really dodgy. I went up and there was this massive American already strapped in. I've no idea how he squeezed in there! But it was worth it. I got Schumacher in his Ferrari slowly making his way to pole through the throng of the whole grid like Moses parting the Red Sea. It's not, technically, a brilliant picture but it tells you everything about the way Schumacher's brain worked. Always mind games. If the picture tells a story, you've done your job. We had the Shell contract with Getty at the time and I'd go to Fiorano [the Ferrari test track] with him and Michael was super cool. He'd stand there for hours doing photos with different bottles of oil and then at the end I'd ask if I could do a couple of nice portrait shots of him and he would always oblige. Not many would do that. He knew exactly what people wanted. He was ruthless on the track, but a gentleman off it.'

Thompson still feels privileged to do what he does, 500 races in. He's undoubtedly one of the biggest characters in the sport, but at the age of 60 he's now contemplating slowing down and dropping the number of races that he attends. Last year he had an operation to remove his kneecap and the meniscus; 40 years of kneeling down to get to the eye level of the drivers in the cars has taken its toll. The fact that he has the option to pick and choose the races he attends in the future speaks volumes for his talent and standing within the paddock. For the past 17 years he has been Red Bull's trusted photographer, and they have looked after him well. When he talks about this he gets quite emotional. To celebrate his 500th race they flew his daughter out to Imola to celebrate with him and put together a presentation with past and present Red Bull drivers and management who all said extremely nice things about him. How did that make him feel?

'They're all just fucking bad liars.'

CHAPTER 12

THE FORMULA ONE ARTIST

'I was good at drawing as a child and loved making cartoons like Snoopy, but when I was about 12 I started to draw racing cars. I was very quiet at school and got ten out of ten for behaviour because I was always concentrating on my sketching. I trained myself to be able to sketch whilst looking at the teacher, so that they never thought that I was drawing in class.'

Giorgio Piola was born in Genoa three years after the end of the Second World War. He has dedicated his life to the sport that he loves and has produced technical drawings of Formula One cars for publications and broadcasters that are adored the world over.

He will be 77 in November and this will be his seventh decade following Formula One; 2025 will be the last year that he travels around the globe. No one has attended more races, with his tally standing at more than 900. While discovering how he does his job was fascinating, it was also a pleasure to pick his brains about some of his favourite stories and characters as he prepares for the next chapter of his life.

It all started in his late teens, when Piola had a bet with one of his brothers. They each sketched a Formula One car and sent it to a couple of Italian motorsport magazines to judge which was better. It was 1969 and he was studying engineering at university. One of the publications replied to Piola declaring him the winner and offering him the opportunity to travel to the Monaco Grand Prix to do a technical report for them. He has never looked back.

'I was so proud because it was the dream of a boy becoming a reality. Really I invented my own job because there was nobody before me. There were photographers and journalists but there was never a guy doing drawings in the pit lane, so I was really emotional when I arrived in Monaco. What started as a joke became a profession. I never returned to university.'

In the beginning Piola created larger, more artistic drawings of the cars that would take him 40 days to complete. They would be hugely detailed, two-metre-wide sketches done on tracing paper with the Rapidograph pens that are common in technical drawing. In those days he couldn't afford to make mistakes because the only way to correct them was to use a razor blade and shave the paper, which would damage it. As an illustrator he likened it to driving the streets of the principality, where any sort of error spells the end. He completed about 20 of these, which he still considers his masterpieces; many of them are now housed in museums around the world. Since then he has drawn more than 10,000 smaller sketches that have become his business and that will also be his legacy.

'First of all it is important to say that I am not that technical but I do have an ability to spot even the smallest differences on the cars. So I will walk up and down the pit lane and when I see something that has changed I will stop and take a photograph to sketch later. These days it's a bit annoying because the teams are required to give a list of upgrades on their cars, which means the tiny modifications are there for everyone to see!'

Piola was in heaven in the late sixties and early seventies. This was the start of the aerodynamic era, when the cars were incredibly varied. It was Lotus founder and engineer Colin Chapman who pioneered the use of wings to create downforce. The Lotus 49B had a wing mounted directly on the suspension and it significantly improved cornering speeds and overall grip. It led to all sorts of imitations over the next few years as the aerodynamic innovation within Formula One became an arms race.

'If you think of the Tyrrell six-wheeler, the Brabham fan car, the Ligier "teapot". There were many that were weird and wonderful but some cars, like the Lotus 72, were the starting point for a lot of others: milestone cars. I really loved the Tyrrell six-wheeler, though, because when we were flying to Brazil, Ken Tyrrell himself asked me to do a sketch of the car for their "Elf" brochure. They were one of the biggest teams in Formula One then, so it was a huge moment for me.'

It was at this stage that engineers and paddock insiders were really beginning to acknowledge and respect the uniqueness of Piola's work. He was also beginning to gain their trust.

'We were in Monza the year before the Lotus 78, the first wing car, and an English journalist went to Chapman and told him that I had done a drawing of his new car. I had a very good relationship with Colin, so he called me and asked whether it was true.

'"Yes, I've done the drawing," I said, "with the wing, the side-pods and the skirt."

'He said, "If you do publish this, it will ruin the launch with the sponsor, John Player Special, and I'm afraid it will damage our relationship." I told him, "Listen, the magazines will pay me this much for my sketch but my relationship with you is much more important." So I took my drawing and ripped it up in front of him. As a result he invited me to the assembly of the car the day before the launch. I was without my camera, but I saw everything and I was accurate with the drawing that I had ripped up. It was worth it.

'Something similar happened with Alan Jenkins with the first Stewart Ford, much later, in 1997. They used my sketch, rather than the car itself, for the launch. This was special because they called me over to England in November, but it wasn't launched until January. It was a car full of new solutions, like the central oil tank and carbon brakes. It was so revolutionary. I was a journalist, as well, and I had to keep it all to myself. It showed that they trusted me.'

When the fax machine arrived commercially in the late 1970s, Piola's job changed. No one could wait 40 days for his drawings; he needed to commercialise.

'The quality of the first fax machines were very poor, so instead of doing very complex drawings, I had to make them much simpler. I was working for *La Gazzetta dello Sport*, and a few other publications, and it caused me a problem because always, in the back of my mind, I wanted to do a book at the end of my career, and those drawings for the fax-machine era I had to redo, because they were very poor. The fax machine made everything I did more immediately relevant for the publications, but it compromised my quality.'

In 1998, Piola started to use the computer, because he realised that colour gave his drawings much more impact, although his techniques have remained largely the same. If he is not at a race, he employs a photographer to take the photos for him with exactly the same parameters.

'When I do the front wing, the rear wing, the side pods, I am always in the same position, so that you can compare everything. For example, for the front wing I will always take the picture from one metre in front of the front tyre, and then another perfectly from the side. I will take a photo of each car from every position at every race and always focus on the ones that have changed from the previous weekend.'

The teams don't always want to help Piola, because of the secretive nature of upgrades up and down the paddock. It's then that he has to get creative to make sure he gets the right picture, so that he can create his sketch.

'Last year I was trying to get a photo of the back of the McLaren's steering wheel. The engineer wasn't being very helpful when I asked if I could get a picture of it. So I went on the starting grid and set myself quite far away with my 300mm lens, and when the mechanics took out the steering wheel at a certain point it was in the perfect position and I got the shot that I needed from afar. I had to wait 20 minutes for this. I will wait for as long as it takes. If there is something I need, I can be very patient!'

Piola is utterly committed to his art and still works every hour that God sends.

'I am 76 but I still have a very strong work ethic, because this is a passion as much as it is a job. I get to the track at seven in the morning. I do my work and in the press room I will talk with my boss in Italy. We will create the features and perhaps I will do a video of the major upgrade. Then I will go back to the hotel and eat alone. I will go to bed early and wake up at two or three in the morning and sit down at my little A4 portable drawing table. I will print the picture that I want to sketch in the press room. My tracing paper goes on top of it and I will do the tracings of the photos that I have taken. I am still the only one to do this freehand. Then I will scan the tracing onto the computer and we will colour it on there. So I will do three or four drawings each weekend, as each sketch takes about four hours.'

These days Piola has a couple of assistants to help him with the back end of his work, including the colouration. When he is back at his studio in Italy he will do his tracings on an A2 drawing table, which allows him to sketch in more detail. Before the arrival of the internet, Piola sold his work to 14 publications around the world, but when Bernie Ecclestone launched his *Formula One* magazine back in 2001, Piola got the opportunity to work with one of his heroes, the legendary McLaren and Ferrari designer John Barnard. Together they produced the in-depth technical articles within its pages.

'I was so embarrassed when I had to make the telephone calls to John, to give him instructions on my drawings, and he would explain how things worked. He was like Jesus to me. I was like a stupid rat giving information to an elephant and a great genius! But I loved doing it.'

And that is the special part of the job for Piola. Many of the best designers have loved talking to him over the years because his passion and knowledge course through his work. Ultimately, he is a huge fan of the sport, whose talents led him down the path of illustration, rather than engineering, but he remains fascinated by it and in awe of the greats in the field. Adrian Newey, technical director of Aston Martin, who has been technical director of McLaren, chief designer of Williams and chief technical officer of Red Bull, is right at the top of that field, and famously sketches all of his designs by hand.

'He is wonderful. I tell you he is one hundred times better than me! It's very funny because his handwriting isn't very good, but he has a very special skill, artistically. For example, if I was to do a sketch of you, I would start with your head and then work down to your shoulders and body, whereas Adrian could do just as good a sketch starting from any point of your body. And it's the same with his cars. That is very hard. There are very few engineers who can make beautiful drawings like Adrian.'

And some designers can draw better than others.

'I was working for the Italian television company Rai. It was 1998, the year that Adrian Newey introduced the chimneys into the sidepods of the MP4/13 [a novel aero solution to improve cooling while minimising the impact on performance]. I got Adrian to sketch them for me live on TV, and in two minutes he did a wonderful drawing. Ross [Brawn] was the chief engineer of Ferrari at the time, so the Italian TV producers thought it would be a great idea to get him to do the same thing the following week, and he agreed to do it for a specific part of the Ferrari that we were focusing on. As soon as he started drawing on the piece of paper, I realised he couldn't sketch in three dimensions. So I nodded to the cameraman to show his face instead of the paper, whilst I quickly sketched it myself. When the cameraman panned down I substituted mine in for Ross's, because his was horrible and it would have been embarrassing for him. Ross was a wonderful engineer but he couldn't draw at all!'

If Piola were to rank his favourite engineers in order they would look like this.

1. Patrick Head
2. Adrian Newey
3. Gordon Murray
4. Mauro Forghieri
5. John Barnard

An impressive list with 33 constructors' and 32 drivers' champion-ships between them – but why does he rate Patrick Head above the rest?

'You would pop in for a 20-minute interview with Patrick, and we would often still be there a couple of hours later. It was a chat between two people who had an unending passion for Formula One. That is what stood out for me about Patrick, and that I believe was the key to his success. When you speak to people like him you realised you were talking to someone like yourself, who had wanted to be in the sport almost from the day he was born.'

While some see beauty in a Caravaggio or a Hockney, people like Piola and Head take their aesthetic pleasure from the individual parts that make up a Formula One car and their unique intricacies. Unlike most, they have an eye trained to understand what the tiny differences mean.

'I was often asked to cover IndyCar and Le Mans but I never did because the bodywork covers everything. Whereas in Formula One, everything is so pure, so extreme. One of my favourite parts of the car to draw are the brake callipers, the materials that they are built of and the way they are designed, they are so beautiful. I have one in my sitting room so that everyone can see that it is a piece of art. It's the same with the upright on a suspension arm. Gorgeous!'

One of the busiest and most exciting times of the season for Piola is pre-season testing. It is here where he comes into his own and makes his first sketches of the new season. While teams are often sandbagging and unwilling to reveal their true pace during these few days, Piola has learnt over the years to understand the signals from the garage.

'I'm often asked at the end of testing which team I think looks in the best shape. More than from the timing screens, I will make my judgement by the way the mechanics are working. I spend a lot of time in the pit lane and I can tell by the way the garage is operat-ing who is looking good. I don't like to get much information from the team principals because they are very diplomatic people and they just lie! I was a very good friend of Frank Williams because I was in Formula One before they started, so I followed their journey from the beginning. And whilst you had to be careful when Patrick was angry, he never lied to me in his life. Whereas Frank was much nicer, because he had a touch of the Italian in his behaviour, but he was always lying, so when he said to me, "Giorgio, honestly ..." I knew he wasn't telling the truth!'

Very few have spent more time in the Formula One pit lane than Giorgio Piola. And while the cars were always his focus, his love for the sport drew him close to many of the drivers.

'I was extremely tight with Carlos Reutemann, Riccardo Patrese and Alain Prost, but also Niki Lauda. Niki was just a remarkable human being. The man who was born twice, once naturally and once after his accident [his near-fatal shunt at the Nürburgring in 1976]. When I was at *La Gazzetta dello Sport* I used to interview him every day at the races. Before his accident he was a man of few words, incredibly technical and would only really speak about the cars. There was no real human side to him. But after his accident, he was a totally different man. He would really open up. His humanity shone through and he would never lie. He could always spot bullshit and would call it out.'

Of all the people that I have met and had the pleasure to interview in Formula One, I would say that Niki Lauda was my favourite for exactly those reasons. He had an aura about him that few possess. He survived that accident, but it left him with horrific burns and unable to regulate his body temperature because of the damage to his skin. He would always be wearing his trademark red cap, a sweater and usually a coat, even in warm conditions. But he had a wicked sense of humour and was one of the most grounded men that I have ever met. He worked as an analyst for the German TV station RTL alongside my presenting equivalent, Florian König, and standing next to them on the grid and getting Niki's take on what was really going on was one of the best moments of any week-end. As Piola mentioned, he would always tell it to you straight and always knew what was happening, right to the core of the sport. It was Niki, along with Toto Wolff, who persuaded Lewis Hamilton to go to Mercedes in 2013, because he knew just how good that car was going to be and Lewis trusted him. If Niki were around today I am sure he would have approved of his move to Ferrari, the team where Niki won all three of his championships. People always say that Lewis wanted to see out his career at Ferrari because his hero Ayrton Senna died before he got the chance. I imagine Niki was also in his thoughts when he made that decision.

When Niki passed away in 2019 the paddock shed tears; Piola has witnessed more than his fair share of tragedy during his time in the sport.

'I was working informally as an interpreter for Tom Pryce in 1977 when he was with the Shadow Formula One team. They had another driver, Renzo Zorzi, who was Italian, and I helped them communicate because Zorzi couldn't speak any English. I was very close to the team, but also to Tom and his wife. We used to ride horses and spent several evenings together. When Tom died at Kyalami, I was really lost.'

Pryce, who was just 27 at the time, died tragically when he hit a fire marshal on the track who was attempting to get to a burning vehicle. The marshal was killed instantly, as was Pryce, when the fire extinguisher the marshal was carrying flew into Pryce's head and caused a fatal collision.

'I didn't see the race, or the incident. I went back to the ranch where I was staying and couldn't stop crying because I was really part of the family. The only other time I cried when we lost a driver was with Jochen Rindt in Monza in 1970. I saw Bernie Ecclestone come into the pit lane with Jochen's helmet. I just left instantly. I was responsible for a monthly magazine at the time and was due to do the race report but because I left, they fired me. I didn't care. That day when a driver dies it is like some part of your body leaves you. Also because there is always some stupid reason why they shouldn't have died. With Jochen, he had asked Colin Chapman not to drive the Lotus 72 that weekend. He wanted to drive the Lotus 49 and Colin said no. He drove the 72 and the brake shaft broke because it was not stiff enough. If he had been in the Lotus 49, this would not have happened.'

Pryce's death spelt an end to Piola forging close relationships with other drivers. He no longer comes to races to socialise and is very much a lone wolf.

'It evolved naturally over time. I just couldn't take any more of the loss. Who knows what it was like for the wives and girlfriends. Back then, we were all much tighter, like one big family. In those days we were always staying at the same hotels, dining in the same restaurants, so there was plenty of fun and, of course, girls. Today, I think drivers only want to be friends with journalists when it benefits them, and vice versa.'

He has been there and seen it all. When he hangs up his pens and puts the sketchpad down, it will be the end of an incredible career. Piola is a paddock lifer, someone who has dedicated his life to improving people's understanding, through his unique passion and skills. His is an opinion that everyone up and down the pit lane respects, but who does he think is the greatest driver of all time?

'Hamilton, Senna, Verstappen and Schumacher, in that order. For me, the others were better than Schumacher. When Senna was winning, he was fighting with Prost, Mansell, Berger and Alesi, and now Verstappen is doing it with a lot of drivers. When Schumi won there was nearly nobody. He was number one at Ferrari and his team-mate couldn't win. He had to fight with Damon Hill and look what he did to him in Adelaide in 1994. I like Hamilton the most because of his human side as well as his ability. In Abu Dhabi in 2021, he went straight over to congratulate Verstappen. Can you imagine what would have happened if it was the other way round?'

He also feels like the sport is in rude health at the moment and is not one to claim it was better in his day!

'I think that 2024 was my favourite season in all my time in the sport, in terms of fights, competition and drivers. There were at least seven very good drivers and four teams capable of winning. The racing was also spectacular. I always considered these hybrid cars the best because of the amount of overtaking they do. And I know that DRS [drag reduction system] plays a huge part, but if you consider the old days at somewhere like Hungary, there would be one overtake on the first lap and that would be it. It's the electric part of the engine that produces the difference and allows for more overtaking, as well as the DRS. It has really helped the on-track action.'

And so back to his favourite subject: in Piola's view, what are the best cars in the six decades in the sport that he has enjoyed drawing and reporting on the most?

1 - LOTUS 72

Created by Colin Chapman. It was a revolutionary car with a wedge shape and innovative aerodynamics, but it remains associated with Formula One's first and only driver to win the world championship posthumously, Jochen Rindt. Emerson Fittipaldi went on to win the 1972 world championship in the 72D.

'It was a wonderful car because it was groundbreaking but from a moral perspective, the brake shafts at the front were terribly dangerous, and were believed to have caused the crash that killed Jochen. I loved the shape and it was an extreme version of Forghieri's Ferrari 312 B3.'

2 - FERRARI 640

Piloted by Nigel Mansell and Gerhard Berger. They won three races between them but it was the first Ferrari Formula One car powered by a V12 engine for 20 years and the first Ferrari that John Barnard ever designed.

'This was the first with the semi-automatic gearbox. Barnard introduced the torsion bar at the place of the spring and the damper and now every car has a torsion bar at the front and the back.

'At the rear the springs and the dampers were mounted horizontally rather than vertically and I have always enjoyed sketching different suspension arms. Unfortunately Barnard was a difficult character and so he found it difficult to work with the Ferrari people. But he was a genius and I admired him greatly. It's a shame he retired early because he could have carried on for years.'

3 – LOTUS 78/79

This was the car in which Mario Andretti won the world championship, in 1978. The John Player Special black livery is often argued to be the greatest livery of all time and the car was the first of its kind to fully utilise ground–effect aerodynamics. It was the last Lotus car to win a world title.

'It was the wing car and Chapman used to let his team of engineers get on with innovation. Colin was on holiday. His aerodynamicist Peter Wright was in the wind tunnel and when the side pods and wings worked together to produce downforce, he is claimed to have said, "The mosquito flies." It paved the way for the next era of wing cars, like the Williams car that Alan Jones won the championship with in 1980.'

4 – MCLAREN MP4/4

Perhaps THE iconic car, it won 15 of the 16 races of the 1988 season, the last of the original turbo–charged era that saw Senna and Prost racing against each other at the peak of their powers. Senna prevailed to win the first of his three titles.

'There is always a big dispute about who designed it. Gordon Murray or Steve Nichols and Neil Oatley. Steve Nichols was working with John Barnard on previous McLaren cars before Barnard left for Ferrari in 1986 and they followed the concept of the Brabham BT55 that Gordon designed but it was a dynamic evolution of the MP/3 from the previous year which Nichols created. So you could say, Nichols designed it, Gordon influenced it with his low-slung concept from the BT55 and Oatley refined it. The centre of gravity was so low and the engine so good that it became one of the most dominant of all time.'

5 – RED BULL RB5

The car that gave Red Bull their first pole position, first win and first ever one-two finish at the Chinese Grand Prix in 2009. Designed by Adrian Newey, it paved the way for the RB6 that won the championship.

'Another milestone car. It had the exhaust-blown rear suspension which laid the ground work for the blown diffuser. It also had an unconventional pull-rod system and was the starting point for all the other Red Bulls. It was revolutionary in every way: aerodynamics, suspension, engine layout and gearbox. I congratulated Newey when it first launched as it gave me great emotion. I am nothing compared to the great man, but I think he was happy to receive this comment from me because he knew just how good the car was.'

Formula One will miss Giorgio Piola when he goes. There have been others who have tried to imitate him but none have endured as long or seen so much. I am told that one day soon he will release his memoirs; he has a thousand stories to tell and the photos and sketches to accompany them. It looks like his final tally will fall just short of 1,000 races, but his is a lifetime dedicated to the sport and what he leaves behind will outlive him, a body of work that beautifully records the progress of technological innovation within Formula One.

CHAPTER 13
THE JOCK OF ALL TRADES

Someone who has been hands on in that technological innovation throughout his career is Jock Clear. But he is not your typical engineer. While, like most who have made it into the Formula One paddock, he was pretty damn good at physics and maths at school, his first love and real passion as a youngster was rugby.

'If you've ever been on a rugby field there is a uniqueness to it and a mentality that still exists today. There's not a rugby player in the world that will ever disagree with a referee and it's that level of respect that I enjoyed. I think a lot of my formative experiences were impacted by my time on the rugby field rather than in the classroom. What I wanted to seek from my career was the adrenaline of Saturday and Sunday because ultimately I see Formula One as a sport, not an engineering exercise, although, of course, it is both.'

It's this attitude that makes Clear different.

'Some people would argue that it's not really a sport, it's a multi-million-pound business that is all about the car and engineering. The fact that there's 1,200 people at Ferrari and 1,197 of them are looking at the car and about three at the driver suggests that it is hugely biased in that regard, but that allowed me to carve out a niche. I knew early on that I wasn't a great engineer. I didn't get the best degree and I wasn't the cleverest guy. You meet people like Ciaron Pilbeam [chief race engineer at Alpine] or Andrew Shovlin [Mercedes trackside engineering director] and you think, *Fucking hell, these people are clever.* I'm not as smart as them. I knew that I wasn't going to be the next Adrian Newey but I soon found that the drivers enjoyed working with me because I talked their language quite well.'

One of the things that it is difficult to ignore, having spent a number of years around them, is just how different drivers are from engineers. While most engineers would give anything to swap places (and potentially lives) with the drivers, I'm not completely convinced that the opposite is true. It's what makes the paddock such a peculiar environment, this blend of some of the brightest people on the planet all working every hour God sends to produce a piece of machinery that can elevate the chosen few to a higher plane. Having conversed with both, it's clear to see that not everyone can simplify engineering language to a level that us mere mortals can understand.

'A lot of these engineers that are sharp with facts and figures, numbers and calculations tend to be on the spectrum, and some of them feel that the driver is a bit of a hindrance. In fact, some of them think life would be easier if we didn't have one. Whereas I always viewed it from the point of view that the driver is what it's all about. It doesn't matter how fussy or complicated he is, you know your challenge is to get him to drive the car as fast as he can and, to do that, you need to be able to have some empathy with his situation and talk his language, because he isn't an engineer and you don't want him to be one.'

Nico Rosberg, the 2016 world champion, famously turned down an offer of a place at Imperial College in London to study aeronautical engineering and, prior to signing to them in 2006, scored the highest ever marks in the Williams team's engineering aptitude test, but he is a rare example of a driver who could communicate with engineers on their level.

'Nico is a very bright guy, but he wasn't a faster driver because of it. No one within a team is ever thinking, *We need to find a clever engineer who can drive a car.* All you want is someone who can drive fast and then we will adapt what we do to enable them to go faster.'

For Clear, this first became critical when Jacques Villeneuve arrived at Williams in 1996 from IndyCar in the States. He was the son of the late Formula One legend Gilles Villeneuve, who died in an accident during qualifying for the Belgian Grand Prix at the age of 32. Clear was to be his race engineer.

'When I first met him, he was extremely bright but an outspoken, Marmite character. There were certain social norms that he didn't seem to have. It brought a very different dynamic to conversations. He would say some things on the engineering side about how he felt the car was working and it was counterintuitive to the extent that it would prickle Patrick Head. Patrick would tell Jacques that he had no idea what he was talking about and that he should just concentrate on driving. And then literally seconds later Adrian Newey would tell Patrick that actually what Jacques was saying made sense but he was just using the wrong words! I think between myself and Adrian we managed to get a lot out of Jacques because we just tried to understand how to talk his language.'

It was a relationship that bore fruit just one year later when Villeneuve won the 1997 drivers' title.

In 1997 there were only three men on the pit wall: one engineer on vehicle dynamics and two race engineers. The race engineer back then was a jack of all trades. He would set the car up, decide upon strategy, what tyres they were going to run and at what pressures. Race engineers were largely autonomous. These days Formula One has evolved to the point where there is a master of each trade and 'jacks' are extinct, but Jock Clear is as close to one as you can get.

Clear began his career as a design engineer for Lola, working on F2000, F3000, IndyCar and the group C cars that they designed for Nissan for their 1989 Le Mans attempt, before moving on to their Formula One project. In the late 1980s Lola made cars for the French Larousse & Calmels team. Clear stayed with them for a year before applying for a job with Benetton. It was here that he got to learn from some of Formula One's most storied names. Rory Byrne was the chief designer, Pat Symonds was on the engineering team and Nigel Stepney was the chief mechanic.

'The design office at Benetton in those days employed a total of seven people. I was the only one using computer-aided design (CAD), whereas these days the drawing office at Ferrari amounts to nearly 500 people, plus 200 in the wind tunnel.'

Clear was able to draw upon a deep well of knowledge in his early years in the sport but he also had an object lesson in the politics of Formula One when John Barnard, another legendary designer, arrived and squeezed Rory Byrne out.

'I was very much a Rory man. He was a lovely guy, but I didn't get on with John Barnard at all. I found him ignorant, rude and arrogant and I couldn't find anything likeable about him at all. But he did bring a few decent people with him from Ferrari, including Pat Fry and Giorgio Ascanelli. Both had brilliant minds. So I was learning from some very good people.'

Design engineers put into place what the chief designer decides is the best direction to go in.

'The clever thing about Formula One is that you can't just copy other cars. When people say why don't you copy the Red Bull as it's the fastest car? You can't, because there is no optimum design, there are just compromises. The great skill in the technical directors is to understand which route to take and where to go with that compromise. The James Allisons [technical director at Mercedes], Adrian Neweys and Rory Byrnes of this world have got all these things on the table to deal with. You've got to cool the car, cool the brakes, you've got to make the suspension stiff and make it light, you've got to clean up the flow to the rear wing, to the radiators. All these things are contradictory. Deciding where to pitch that midline is what makes the difference between a really good car and an average car.'

According to Clear, with the exception of NASA or aerospace, there are very few fields of engineering where performance gains far outweigh cost in terms of importance.

This was particularly prevalent, of course, in the pre-cost-cap environment. As a design engineer, he feels that he developed his skills in the golden era.

'The fact that you could go down any area you liked, was so motivating. We were only just starting to get into computer simulations in those days. You felt like you were treading new ground every single day. Designers' wings have been clipped a little bit because the regulations are now much more restrictive. But there are little things that make me think, *If I'd thought of that, I'd be a god by now.* Things like the F-duct that McLaren invented.* It's so simple, how could I not have thought about that years ago? But, of course, these things pass you by, because you are just looking too deeply into specific things.'

It was this basis in the design and development of racing cars that gave Clear a fundamental understanding of vehicle dynamics and the engineering principles critical to success in motorsport, but then that's true of almost every engineer up and down the pit lane. When Clear moved to Lotus he decided that race engineering was an area that suited his traits more. It goes back to that basic desire to get into the thick of the sporting action, as he had been when playing rugby.

'What you hear a lot of on Sunday is that there is a fundamental trust between the driver and his race engineer, and over the years with Jacques, developing that trust was incredible. I've often said it was like the relationship between a golfer and his caddy. As a driver, the race engineer is the one guy that has just got your back. You don't even know if that is the case with your team principal. So it's a unique relationship within the sport. You are a team within a team. As a pair, you are out to do everything you can to beat the pair on the other side of the garage. I would play mind games and try to get under the skin of the opposition, and your team-mate is fair game for that. When I was Rubens Barrichello's race engineer in 2009, I would enjoy locking horns with Jenson and his race engineer Andrew Shovlin, and really try to piss them off a bit. Same

---

* The F-duct was a system used in Formula One around 2010 that allowed drivers to reduce aerodynamic drag on straights. By covering a vent inside the cockpit (often with a knee or hand), the driver redirected airflow to 'stall' the rear wing, decreasing downforce and increasing top speed. It was later banned for safety and regulation reasons.

in 1997 with Jacques. We were often on the front row alongside Michael Schumacher, and I would go and stand next to Ross Brawn in front of their car so that Michael could see me. I'd stay there for a few seconds until the pair of them were staring at me. I would never say anything, but I knew it might just get under their skin. It was that sporting dynamic, like sledging in cricket, that attracted me to being a race engineer.'

But as Clear's career progressed, so his job titles morphed. As the sport grew, the delineation of the different engineering roles in Formula One became more pronounced. Clear moved from Williams to BAR [British American Racing] with Villeneuve in 1999 and remained with the team through its various iterations for the next 15 years. As BAR became Honda and then Brawn, when Mercedes took over, Ross Brawn was one of the first team principals to realise that sometimes it was the personalities of his engineers that defined their specific roles, rather than fitting square pegs into round holes.

Traditionally a performance engineer's role is more focused on the technical aspects of the car's performance, and involves a broader scope of responsibilities beyond the race weekend. It is a position that requires a deep understanding of vehicle dynamics with a massive emphasis on data analysis.

'The race engineer was the more experienced and outgoing personality. The performance engineers tended to be a bit geeky. They're in the background just number crunching, telling you about floor pressures, tyre pressures, plank wear etc., and basically supporting the race engineer with all the data. As I mentioned, Ciaron Pilbeam was my performance engineer when I was with Rubens and Jacques early on. He was outstanding, a complete planet-brain and one of the cleverest people in the paddock.'

Clear had a moment of clarity about where his future lay in the sport when the Mercedes Formula One project got underway in 2010.

'I was race-engineering Nico Rosberg opposite Michael Schumacher. Nico would be constantly looking at the data and questioning why Michael was quicker in turn two and what he was doing on the brakes or the steering. Although it is quite natural for team-mates to look at each other's telemetry, I was thinking, *Nico, the difference is not in the bloody data!*

'Eventually I slammed the lid of the laptop down and said to him, "Nico, just look at how Michael engages with people."

'At the time Nico wasn't popular. He was quite brusque, dismissive and blunt with everybody, so people didn't warm to him very easily. Michael wasn't the fastest racing driver in the world. He fully admitted that Mika [Häkkinen] was quicker than him. But he made the most of what he had, because he was so emotionally intelligent. He won people over and got them on his side, because he would motivate them so well. And that's the bit Nico missed, the *only* bit he missed. Nico and I didn't get on in a working relationship. We do now and I would say he's a good friend, but back then, we didn't.'

It was because of this incompatibility that, towards the end of the 2010 season, Brawn took the decision to bring in Tony Ross from Williams. He and Rosberg had worked together for three years there and Brawn felt Rosberg would be more comfortable with him as his race engineer.

'When Ross told me, I said, "OK, no problem," and the interesting thing was that as soon as he told Michael about the change, he had said, well, if Nico doesn't want him, I'll have him.'

At that time Schumacher was being race-engineered by Mark Slade, who'd had great success winning two championships with Mika Häkkinen at McLaren, but he and Schumacher weren't clicking. Brawn made the decision to change the team on that side of the garage too, replacing Slade with Andrew Shovlin, with Clear stepping in as Schumacher's performance engineer.

'Ross had seen that the role of the race engineer was becoming more procedural. There were lots of things you had to do with legality and documentation. Teams were getting bigger very quickly. Race engineers were no longer doing strategy, strategy teams were doing that. They were no longer doing tyres, tyre engineers were doing that, so the role was becoming narrower. Ross saw that there was now a lot more support, with a lot more geeky people in all the other areas, and whole banks of remote support from back at base, so actually the performance and race engineers could now get on with looking after the needs of the driver.'

Brawn then brought in a young Pete Bonnington at the start of 2011 as race engineer for Schumacher. 'Bono', as he is known, went on to great things, winning six driver titles alongside Lewis Hamilton. Clear was tasked with mentoring him, while at the same time getting on with what he really enjoyed, talking to the other GOAT about how he was driving, in a newly created role as head of trackside engineering.

'With Ross realising that the roles were shifting, there was now the opportunity for somebody to be looking at what the drivers were doing more specifically, coupled with the more widespread availability of GPS and onboard videos. It made it much easier to analyse what the drivers were doing at any specific corner on the track. We could easily compare exactly where drivers were turning in, whether they were taking slightly more kerb, if they were picking up the throttle earlier. It began to open up more conversations about this aspect of driver preparation. Michael really enjoyed the discussion and quickly came on board, which carried through to when Lewis joined the team in 2013.'

At this point, Clear was already getting deep into the psychological aspect of driver preparation, but also recognised that most of the drivers that he came across weren't preparing themselves physically in the way that elite athletes in other sports were.

'If you took an Olympic rower, the level of discipline was just unbelievable. These guys were training every day of the year without fail. Christmas Day they were on the water at 6am because they knew that's how they were going to win a world championship. Most drivers didn't do that because they didn't think it was important. Fine if you were a rower, but if you're a Formula One driver you could do a bit of gym work once a week and then turn up. It wasn't until the late 2000s, after they saw Schumacher winning multiple world championships, that the penny dropped. He was so physically fit.'

With Clear's rugby-playing background, he began to look outside of Formula One for ideas that he could bring into the paddock to help the drivers. Marginal gains were nothing new in sport. Sir Clive Woodward always talked about finding the one-percenters, things that mounted up to give his side an edge on England's way to winning the Rugby World Cup in 2003. Clear spoke to the coaches at Saracens Rugby Club and Chelsea FC. He also took the team up to the FA's centre of excellence.

'We did some pit-stop practice and they did some football training with us and you got this realisation that there was an obvious cross-pollination. The fundamentals are that mental strength comes from preparation, believing that you are in the right place by putting yourself in the right place. So I said to my wife in 2012, when Lewis arrives it's going to be great because McLaren took this kid from 12 years of age and he's going to have had the best Formula One education anybody could have had. I presumed he was going to be a finely tuned, streamlined, really well-structured athlete and that he was going to know exactly what the workload would entail. But he arrived and he was a mess, a complete mess to the extent that I almost felt like ringing up McLaren and saying, "What the fucking hell have you done with this bloke?" I don't know what they told him between him being 12 years old and arriving at the Mercedes works team, but he didn't have any discipline or structure. And that's what we delivered very quickly. Ross instilled it into him and so did Toto Wolff when he arrived at the team.'

Clear's role was becoming more holistic and he was beginning to carve out a niche that moved him away from pure engineering and back to the sporting side that he'd enjoyed when race engineers were as close to the action as you could get. It comes back to the fact that he is an excellent communicator and had the ability to be the connective tissue between the burgeoning groups of more specialised engineers and the drivers.

'It was about putting support structures around Lewis, improving his fitness and mental preparation, but also giving him engineering guidance so that he knew enough about the car for his feedback to be relevant. Lewis never enjoyed simulator work, and it was always a bit of a challenge with him. But because we weren't allowed to go testing anymore, we had to get across to him that this is how we developed the car. He used to tell us that the sim wasn't realistic, but we needed his help to make it more realistic. I think he found a lot of it frustrating, because we were just cutting our teeth in getting the simulator up and running. He persevered and it quickly paid off. You can say what you want about Lewis, you can love him or hate him, but he's a very, very bright guy and he knows what works. So, whilst he might not understand the background in aero or the chassis, when he stops and says, this is the thing you need to fix, we listened. He has an innate ability to know which part of the car is the biggest issue and in the end it was why we developed the car so quickly. His natural talent was huge, so we put a complete structure around him and we started to fly.'

Clear was lucky enough during his last two years at Mercedes to be able to compare the two greatest drivers of all time. Michael Schumacher had, of course, won all seven of his titles already but when Lewis joined in 2013 he only had one to his name. Observing them up close was a privilege that very few got to experience. Two different personalities, whose achievements are unparalleled, but with very different approaches to winning.

'There's an obvious cliché you hear when you are at school. Don't worry about what you can't control, focus on what you can. Well, Michael obviously heard this when he was young and thought, *Yeah, but what if I can control everything?* When you look at his time at Ferrari, he made sure that the team principal, the technical director and everybody around him were the people HE wanted. He didn't control Jean Todt (then CEO of Ferrari) or Ross Brawn, but he made sure he had their ear and that they were HIS people.

'Lewis took the opposite view. He was more selective. He also only focused on what he could control. He would just review the situation and, if he thought he could only control this, this and this, he would decide to do those particular things perfectly. That was Lewis's skill. And he was mentally super, super strong. He got people to believe in him in a different way from Michael. Michael had an aura, because he had all the titles by then, whereas Lewis didn't. I think Michael was more humble when he arrived at Mercedes and put more effort into the emotional side of the team, whereas Lewis would focus on being clinical. You might think it would be the other way round. Michael used his emotions to manipulate the team around him from outside the cockpit. Lewis just focused on driving and managed it from within, so when it didn't go well he would be down. If it went well he would be elated. But it was incredible to watch two masters at work.'

In 2015, on the recommendation of Ross Brawn to James Allison, who was by then technical director at Maranello, Clear left Mercedes to become head of racing at Ferrari. His new role was to run everything trackside, overseeing the race engineering but also ensuring effective communication between drivers, engineers and management, which at that stage was no easy task.

Ferrari is the most political of all the teams. They last won a constructors' title in 2008 and their last drivers' title was Kimi Räikkönen's back in 2007. After team principal Stefano Domenicali, now the CEO of Formula One, left in 2014, the Scuderia found themselves in a turbulent phase. Marco Mattiacci lasted only seven months in the job before Maurizio Arrivabene took over in November of the same year. So when Clear arrived, it was a complicated environment to operate within, and then tragedy struck when Allison's wife passed away in March 2016.

'Whilst, ironically, it's all one team, it was at that stage a bit disjointed between the chassis and engine side. So you needed someone to umbrella the whole thing. I saw Ferrari probably at its worst in the first few months after I arrived. The behaviour of some of the people was just disgraceful. James needed to be back with his family in the UK and, in the end, rejoined Mercedes, but it was a difficult time for the whole team and even Sebastian Vettel wasn't enjoying it. I think Seb was suffering from the same sort of lack of trust, faith and support that the rest of us were. It wasn't really until 2019 that we sort of stabilised and things got back on track.'

So what was it that stabilised it?

'I think Laurent Mekies coming in as sporting director. A top guy and a good human being. That's what we needed. Mattia Binotto replacing Arrivabene also helped because his was an internal promotion and he knew how to deal with all the different factions. There was a lot of infighting within Maranello back then.'

When Charles Leclerc arrived in 2019, Clear became his senior performance engineer but, with over 30 years' experience in the sport, in 2020 he also took on the responsibility of becoming head of driver coaching for the Ferrari Driver Academy (FDA), while maintaining his position as head of racing. It was a lot to take on but another natural progression for someone who had seen it all. On every Formula One weekend he is fully focused on getting the best out of Charles but during the week he works with the next generation. These days, the best talent is spotted earlier and earlier. All the teams will keep an eye on what is going on in karting but the youngest drivers tend to get picked up by the FDA at the age of about 14 or 15.

'I'm not going to teach the young drivers to drive but I am going to teach them how to get the best out of themselves. That is what will make the difference in the end. Karting is not like football. Every kid in the world plays football and therefore the standard is extremely high. Karting is not like that. You can get to national or international level before you meet someone who has the chance to make it to the very top, someone who's won everything up to the point they enter Formula Four or Formula Three. Suddenly they are up against the likes of Kimi Antonelli, Ollie Bearman or Lando Norris and winning becomes a lot harder. That is when the demons creep in and they think there must be a problem with the team or the car. No, no, no, this is life from now on at the upper reaches of motorsport. Lewis, Lando and Max are up against people every race who are as good as them. But these kids take a while to realise that what makes the difference, at that stage, is not how quick you are, because on any given day they are all as quick as each other – it becomes a mental thing and about discipline. From nine years old any decent footballer has had to deal with the fact that there are other kids as good as them. Racing drivers haven't had that.'

Clear is of the opinion that once young drivers accept the fact that there is nothing between them at the very highest levels, only then can they look at what the differentiators can be. One of those differentiators is whether they can communicate to the engineers what the limiting factor of the car is.

'Telling an engineer that there are six different things wrong with the car is no use to us at all. We need to identify what the main priority is to fix and then establish the secondary factors. And that is my role. Some young drivers still think that all they need to do is just turn up and be fast, but the smarter ones increasingly don't do that. They need to put in the simulator work. No, it's not the same as a race track, but a sprinter doesn't go up against the best in the world on any given Tuesday at Crystal Palace. They are running up a piece of track with a tyre tied behind them because they know it's going to improve the muscles they are going to need when they do it for real. You train in the simulator to improve your precision and the muscle control you are going to need on Sunday. That's what being an athlete is about and you need to drill that into them as early as possible.'

Clear's experience has also taught him that the top drivers build the best support structures around them. In the early years many young drivers are reliant on the advice of their parents, particularly their dads. Most have been guided by and financially supported by their fathers and it creates a natural, unshakeable bond that has propelled them to the higher echelons of motorsport. But that doesn't necessarily mean, as they reach for the summit, that they are the best choice to continue with their children, on a professional basis.

'When Lewis arrived at Mercedes it coincided with his father not being ever-present. His dad was undoubtedly the most important and influential person in Lewis's career. Toto wasn't ever trying to alienate his dad, he was just trying to show him the most productive way to operate. Lewis understood for himself that perhaps his dad wasn't the best person to have around him between sessions, because he wasn't going to be the most objective. Nico Rosberg had realised that years before, because his dad was too emotional about it. We were suggesting, use your parents when you need to use them, but we wouldn't allow them to undermine their kids or disrupt race weekends. So, managing all that sort of thing is the kind of thing we work on at the FDA, so that they can operate independently.'

Jock Clear is a man who has carved his own unique path in Formula One. Having occupied most of the trackside engineering roles he understood early on where his strengths lay and what he enjoyed most, and he has endured in the most highly pressurised of arenas. By learning from the best behind the wheel and on the pit wall he has used that knowledge to help make drivers faster and created a template for success for future generations of racers. Now reunited with Hamilton at Ferrari, it would be hugely rewarding to see if he can help him come to terms with, and get on top of, a car that the seven-time world champion struggled with early on in 2025, and perhaps lead him back to glory when the new regulations begin in 2026.

CHAPTER 14

THE RACE ENGINEER

While the role of race engineer has changed since Clear first entered the pit lane, their relationship with their drivers remains critical to a team's success. Gianpiero Lambiase, known to the paddock as GP, has been Max Verstappen's race engineer since he made the step up to the senior Red Bull team four races into the 2016 season. Now a multiple world champion, Verstappen made his debut the year before, at the Australian Grand Prix, at the age of 17 years and 166 days. He is the youngest driver ever to compete in Formula One and arrived with an expectation befitting a generational talent. That wasn't lost on Lambiase right from the start.

'I had a phone call from Helmut Marko [Red Bull advisor] after the Chinese Grand Prix and he said we've got to make some changes. We are going to put Daniil Kvyat back in the Toro Rosso and you'll have Max from the next race onwards. He'd already created a bit of a buzz in his early years and so there was a reputation about him. And so to say I wasn't a little bit intimidated by him, even though he was still a kid, would be lying.'

The following Wednesday, Verstappen arrived at the Red Bull factory where they had arranged for three days on the simulator to go through a whole host of familiarisation exercises. They guided him through the basics of the steering wheel and the car. Expectations for procedures on track during a race weekend gave him a broad brush of set-up options to gauge his initial feel for the car and assess how his technical feedback was. They then put him through some more pressurised scenarios such as qualifying simulations and a few blind and placebo tests to see how he performed.

'What stood out immediately was the capacity that this kid had. He took on absolutely everything. And I'm not just blowing smoke up his arse. It was like playing a PlayStation for him. Some of the instructions we were giving him for if a particular system goes down were pretty complex, especially whilst you are still trying to drive the car at 99 or 100 per cent on track, and he didn't miss a beat. After those three days on the simulator, you kind of knew what you had under you. The fact that I was quite an experienced engineer at that time is what stood me in good stead to build a relationship with him, because I think if I had been in my first or second year of race engineering, he would have eaten me alive.'

Verstappen's first race weekend for Red Bull was in Barcelona, a track that all the teams know so well from the amount of testing they have done there over the years, and the young Dutchman hit the ground running. He was on top of his new team-mate Daniel Ricciardo in the other Red Bull pretty much immediately, and quicker than him in both the first two qualifying sessions. During qualifying in Formula One there are a few little things you can adjust as you progress to help with the balance and therefore performance of the car. This includes changing the front wing angle, tyre pressures, control systems, the differential (i.e. the mechanism that allows the wheels on the same axle to rotate at different speeds) and brake bias (the adjustable distribution of braking force between the front and rear wheels).

'You would normally refine and hone your limitations through qualifying, but Max was adamant that the time was within him, and he just wanted to retain the car that he knew and try and keep it where it was. In the last part of qualifying, Daniel was four tenths quicker than Max but it was hard work for Daniel to put this young boy in his place. We could have helped with the balance and limited the time difference, but Max was happy enough and it was already an incredible weekend up until that point.'

Verstappen qualified in fourth and was alongside his team-mate on the second row of the grid with Lewis Hamilton on pole and Nico Rosberg in second. This was the race where the two Mercedes drivers famously collided at turn four of the opening lap, ending both their races and setting the narky tone between the pair for the rest of the German's championship-winning season. However, with the two of them out, it presented a massive opportunity.

'Once the Mercedes had gone off we were in a battle with the Ferraris of Sebastian Vettel and Kimi Räikkönen, who had started just behind us. Daniel was ahead, but Max was on his tail the whole time. To be able to follow a car around Barcelona with the tyre degradation that you get round there was incredible. He was all over his rear wing and proved that he was the quicker car. Ultimately, Daniel felt hard done by, because we put him on a three-stop strategy and Max on a two, but I think what hurt Daniel is that deep down, he knew Max was quicker and he hid behind the strategy. Max won the race, and it was the perfect ice-breaker, the perfect start to our relationship together.'

It meant that another record had been broken: he became the youngest driver to win a Formula One race, at the age of 18 years and 228 days. A bar had been set immediately and it had a huge effect on the team.

'He just wasn't fazed by anything that we put in front of him that weekend. He would tick it off like it was a routine job that he'd been doing for five or ten years and, of course, he was quick. But he expected to be quick. He brought an expectation to the team that we would be winning races and championships imminently. "Don't worry, Max Verstappen's here everybody, we're going to be OK!" It was that kind of arrival. And that's the kind of impact he had on the team. The only target from then on was that we had to provide Max with a championship-winning car.'

As Red Bull's head of race engineering, GP has remained as Verstappen's race engineer since 2016, but these days he also manages a team that includes the second-car crew on the performance and race-engineering side. GP began his career in Formula One at Jordan in 2005 and worked with the team at Silverstone as it morphed to Midland, then Spyker and then Force India. From 2008 he worked with Giancarlo Fisichella, as a performance engineer, before becoming race engineer for Vitantonio Liuzzi in 2010. He took the same position when Paul di Resta joined the team, and stayed with him for three years, until Sergio Pérez replaced him in 2014. The following year, GP was poached by Red Bull. He hasn't looked back and has been absolutely integral to the team's success. You can tell by the frank and honest conversations that you hear over team radio between GP and Verstappen that the pair have an implicit trust.

'We are at very different stages in our lives, even though he's in a serious and steady relationship with a child on the way. I mean I could almost be his dad. He is a very straightforward, honest guy. What you see is what you get and he definitely doesn't have two faces. Ultimately, I'd like to think I'm a genuine and sincere person and so I think that's the mutual bond that we've got together. The trust that we have is based on doing the absolute best for each other and the team. I will tell him when he's wrong and I will tell the team when he's right. We just know where we stand with each other.'

The most successful and trusted race engineers have something more than just an innate understanding of the data. They are the primary point of communication between the driver and the pit wall, but nowadays their job is a hybrid of strategist, problem-solver and driver coach. Many go on to senior management roles and it is a position that is often a rite of passage. There is something of a standard career path at Red Bull as an aspiring engineer, as there is at all of the teams.

'You would begin in the vehicle dynamics group back at the factory, then the suspension group and the performance-simulation groups, so that you learn the dynamics of the race car. You would also have an interaction with the aerodynamics department, where you learn the principles. If that is your interest, and an opportunity arises, you would traditionally move into performance engineering.

That's where you bring in the skills of vehicle dynamics, before you start learning data analysis and ultimately optimising the performance of the car based on data. (Suspension, aero, powertrain, control systems, brake balance, differential etc.) It is also where you learn your trade trackside. It's not too often that an inexperienced race engineer jumps into Formula One, especially nowadays. The natural route, like I took, is through performance engineering, which is a 100 per cent technical role. A race engineer is more 50/50 and very different. A large part is related to human performance, and you have to have an emotional intelligence to you, not just be a brainbox.'

But how does that work in practice?

'From a technical perspective, as a race engineer your main role is car set-up for each track you go to and every condition that you are facing, be that differing tyre compounds, differing tyre behaviour because of track roughness or environmental conditions. All the sensitivities around the car in terms of the mechanical and aerodynamic grip. How do you trade power, downforce and drag? So that is one area. The other is dealing with the driver, and this is such a complex problem. I've had a different challenge with every driver, but that is the fun of the role as well. Knowing how to get the most out of the driver is an art and a fundamental skill for a race engineer to be successful. Building that relationship, the rapport, the trust between you is absolutely paramount in your potential to be successful as a pairing.'

Anyone who has watched a race in the last decade can see that Verstappen can be extremely demanding over the team radio during the stresses and strains of any given weekend. GP is on the front line dealing with this.

'I don't know whether he detests this or not, but he knows that I've got the power over him on a Sunday! Whilst he will sometimes not be shy in telling us what he thinks of some of our decisions, he has to be able to trust us to make those decisions for the right reasons, and then we can have it out in the office if we need to.

When he disagrees, usually, it's an emotional rant based on instructions from the pit wall. I used to get a lot more upset about it than I do now. It is water off a duck's back these days. Obviously it's still a bit frustrating when he's fighting back because he hasn't understood you. I then feel that I've failed at either communicating our intentions for the race, or in providing him with what he wanted or needed. Sometimes I bite my lip, but that goes back to the fundamental skill of a race engineer. You need to know how to manage someone in very different environments. He's the one in the pressure cooker. We are all making split-second decisions that could affect the outcome of the race but, ultimately, he's the one operating at elevated core temperatures at 350km/h, fighting with 19 other cars, and me trying to keep calm, rationalise the whole situation, keep him in line and on side, is the essence of the job.'

During a race, Red Bull are one of the teams who are universally admired. It is very rare that they make a strategic mistake on track or during a pit stop, and they pride themselves on this. Verstappen, as we've explained, is an extremely intelligent driver who doesn't mask his frustration at all well if he perceives that the team has made an incorrect decision. So how do Red Bull operate on the pit wall in the heat of battle, to avoid incurring the wrath of their star driver? In 2024, as well as GP on the perch there was Hugh Bird (Sergio Pérez's race engineer), Jonathan Wheatley (sporting director), Hannah Schmitz (strategist), Pierre Wache (technical director) and Christian Horner (team principal).

'For a team principal, Christian has a pretty high involvement in the calls made from the pit wall. He has a very good sense of how the race is unfolding and is a good backstop at picking up the external factors that we might have missed by being too involved in the detail. He's very much a big-picture person in race terms and for a TP, who's not into the day-to-day detail of running the cars, he's excellent and ultimately will sign off every pit-stop call. As race engineers we feed into that by liaising with the whole back bench of engineers in the garage and remotely. We are simply trying to optimise our own car's race result by communicating with the driver and relying on his feedback as well as the car's data. That data then feeds into what the strategists are looking at. They will have some very basic numbers that they input based on past races and free practice to start the event, but during the weekend they are basing all of their simulations on what is actually happening across the field and, primarily, on both our cars. So again we are constantly in contact with Hannah and you've got the driver as the middle man giving you the feeling, on top of the lines and numbers. We are looking ahead and thinking about the stop and therefore keeping Jonathan abreast of when that might be as he must talk to his pit crew in the garage to ensure they are ready with the correct sets of tyres.'

GP is the conduit between the driver and the rest of the team – the lightning rod for Verstappen's invective – and although it's his ears that may get burnt every once in a while, there is no doubt that the message is received loud and clear by everyone else in the team, especially if GP is on his driver's side.

'The pit wall may be saying, "What's up with him now, GP?" And I'll give them, "Well that's because he wants to stop and we didn't stop, for God's sake! I can see it as well: his tyres are falling off a cliff!" And whilst you might see me being calm to Max, the conversations we have on the pit wall, that thankfully aren't broadcast, are a lot more heated. Nobody will say anything with any malice but you are at the coalface and decisions need to be made and whilst it's helpful if all these decisions are based on fact and you've tried to stay away from subjective opinion, there needs to be a freedom of speech on the pit wall and that is something that, thankfully, Red Bull has encouraged. If you are treading on eggshells it doesn't work.'

That freedom of speech has helped lead them to four back-to-back world championships for Verstappen. It is clearly a process that works and has been tried and tested over the years. They have dominated this current era of ground-effect rules but if we go back to 2021 they were attempting to hunt down a Mercedes team that had dominated the turbo-hybrid era, and who had won seven titles on the spin. In fact, when you count Vettel's four titles in a row between 2010 and 2013, these two teams have split the last 15 years between them and that's not counting Jenson Button's win for Brawn in 2009, in the team that was to become Mercedes. It's unsurprising then that 2021 was a highly charged year for everyone involved, particularly for GP and Verstappen.

'Once we realised we were in a championship fight, so the last six months of that season, it was incredibly intense and also really exciting for the team. But the one thing that I will say about 2021 that I really disliked was that I felt that it went beyond sport. It became so personal at every level – drivers, teams, team bosses, engineers – it felt like every time you went out on track it was a battle and it got to the point where it went beyond a sporting battle. I think the crunch point came at Silverstone, after the accident [when Verstappen hit the wall after contact caused by Hamilton attempting a high-speed overtake at Copse], when the season took on a different light. It actually wasn't that fun at times. I'd come home beaten up after a race weekend because it was so mentally draining. Not only are you trying to do your normal roles, you are constantly coming up against this adversary who is just trying to have you over. And they will say the same about us, no doubt. It was just war.'

As a member of the British media, I can say from a personal perspective, in my role as a presenter, that I try to remain neutral. We are, however, a British broadcaster whose main audience is British, so stories featuring British drivers are always of interest to those watching. In recent years and with the growth of the sport, Sky's coverage is now broadcast to over 80 countries, including the States. We try to bear that in mind, but that is not the feeling within Red Bull.

'I mean, I won't lie. There is a general feeling that the British media is naturally going to stick up for the British driver and it just so happens that the two closest championships that we have had have been against British drivers. Max, whilst he's very good at compartmentalising it when he steps into the car, outside of the car he is a very honest guy, quite a reserved character with a very small circle of friends. He will only let people in once they've really gained his trust and he's quite sensitive too. It does affect him in more ways than perhaps you can imagine. It's not only the media. He's also been subjected to, in my opinion, unfair scrutiny from the FIA at times with some of the decisions. I'll be the first to admit that he can make a rod for his own back by airing what he does on the radio but that's just him. He doesn't have two faces. If that's his only weakness, then so be it; he can't play those games that the likes of Lewis can.'

Having worked in sports broadcasting for over 25 years I have been lucky enough to witness, first hand, some of the world's best sportsmen and women competing at the highest level for the biggest prizes and to reach the top in any chosen field clearly requires a mental armour that most mere mortals don't possess. The level of scrutiny in Formula One is unique in that there are only 20 seats on the grid.. So when there is a title on the line, that scrutiny intensifies exponentially and I've seen it change drivers and break some. Seb Vettel never really recovered after his crash from the lead in the German Grand Prix in 2018, Nico Rosberg felt he had achieved his life's ambition by beating Hamilton to the crown in 2016 and promptly retired, and we will have to wait and see how it will affect younger drivers like Lando Norris who, by his own admission, made too many mistakes trying to chase down Verstappen's big lead in his first title contention and struggled in the first few races of 2025. So when the pressure ramped up from all angles in 2021, GP and Verstappen had to circle the wagons and focus on developing the car together.

'You can only control what's within your remit. And, of course, between races as a trackside engineer, part of your job is to decode the drivers' feedback into an engineering problem and try to ensure that the factory is on board. There are inherent ways to efficiently produce a competitive car, but the driver will have a significant impact on the final path that development goes down. Max has so much spare capacity when he drives that he is able to really tune in to the finer things that the car is talking to him about. It's this that you definitely notice between the great drivers and the standard drivers. It's those extra bits that he can focus in on, that help develop the set-up during a race weekend. He's not a man of a thousand words and he will keep it very succinct during a debrief after every session. He's very good at breaking down what the main limitation is to going faster, but then can also identify trends that are becoming a problem between races and will ask us to go and have a look at something in particular, where he feels there is lap time.'

As well as deciphering information and turning it into workable engineering problems, they also had to cope with the external pressures and noise by tuning it out. They focused on not getting too high or too low as the season reached a crescendo in Abu Dhabi. We will return to this race a number of times, but GP was at the very heart of it and living and breathing every second of that season with Max. It was a weekend he will never forget, as none of us will.

Lewis Hamilton and Max Verstappen were tied on points coming into the final race and it was a winner-takes-all finale.

'We had already had a bit of a setback on the Saturday because that year those that made it into the third part of qualifying had to start on the tyres that they used in Q2. In attempting to get through on the preferred starting tyre, the medium, we flat-spotted it, which meant we couldn't risk the time we set on them, getting us through to the shootout for pole. We had to go back out on the soft tyre to set a time, and therefore had to start on those softs, which was far from ideal as Lewis got through Q2 on the mediums and so would begin on them.'

In fact the flat-spotted lap on the mediums would've been good enough to progress to Q3, so they had shot themselves in the foot on that front. Verstappen managed to put it on pole, three tenths quicker than Hamilton, who would start alongside him on the front row of the grid but on the preferred starting tyre. It meant that they had to recalculate their strategic plans for the following day.

'We had to get away well off the line, as we knew that we were going to have a little bit more tyre degradation on the softs. I think we had set ourselves up to be a bit faster in a straight line as a defensive measure against the Mercedes, but unfortunately we didn't get off the line very well and Lewis immediately took the lead. That was a bit of a heart-sinking moment – *shit*, I thought – first requirement, failure. And then Max tried to overtake at the turn six to seven chicane up the inside of Lewis. I think, although maybe I'm biased, he pulled off a perfectly acceptable manoeuvre within the regulations. He stayed with it on track and Lewis took to the outside to stay in front of him. The FIA didn't do anything about it. So we knew that we were facing an uphill battle. We were now second, we were on the wrong tyre and that decision didn't go our way. We were up against it.'

In that first stint Hamilton began to extend his lead by three or four tenths a lap but GP and Verstappen tried to stay pragmatic and deal with the reality of the situation that they now found themselves in, but it was difficult.

'A race is a long time. And you are just dealing with it lap by lap as you normally would, but nothing really changed; even when we both pitted for the hards, the Mercedes was just a quicker car, as it had been for the last three or four races. And then your mind starts to wonder. You start to think about the points lost during the year – *We've got so close, how can this be happening?* Ultimately we threw everything at it but it didn't work and I think we had accepted defeat. It was just emptiness. I imagine if we go back to the race recordings there wouldn't have been much communication between us because, of course, Max knew as well.'

And then, on lap 53, the safety car came out. And that changed everything. There were six laps remaining.

'It was all too much to take in but, as the car behind, it was a much easier decision. They stayed out on their very used hard tyres, so of course we pitted. But the only thing I will say is that you do plan for these situations and you know if you are going to be a sitting duck. These are conversations we have within 10 or 15 laps of the finish, when all the regular stops have been completed.

More often than not, you don't want to be that sitting duck. Not only were they on a used set of tyres but also the temperature had bled away from them and so on a restart they were in a much worse state than a new tyre would be purely because they are much more difficult to get up to temperature. I go back to thinking about what we would've done in their situation. If you disregard that Michael Masi only let through the lapped cars between Lewis and Max, I don't know how, at the time the safety car was being deployed, Mercedes could've been 100 per cent sure that the race wouldn't have been restarted.'

But Mercedes hedged their bets that the race wouldn't restart and refused to give up track position. So what was GP communicating to Max as the last few laps counted down and while Jonathan Wheatley and Christian Horner were lobbying the FIA and Masi for a restart?

'On the one hand I was pushing as well, trying to work out what could be done to clear Latifi's car [which was the crash that brought out the safety car] as quickly as possible, but on the other hand, after we'd decided to pit, I was making sure that the car and Max were primed, armed and ready for if it did get going again. So I was trying to contain my excitement whilst thinking, *My God, if this restarts, we are on the soft tyre, Lewis has stayed out on a used hard, we are going to be world champions.* I was making sure the battery was topped up, that Max was following the safety car deltas, we'd got sufficient temperature in the tyres, sufficient temperatures in the brakes, we'd made the right flap adjustments at the stop for this one-lap shootout or whatever it was going to be. So the excitement levels were ramping up but we still didn't know if it was going to restart.'

And the rest is history. Masi pulled in the safety car a lap sooner than he should, Max made the move past a helpless Hamilton at turn five and the title was his. Controversy aside, as his race engineer, in Formula One terms, GP had reached Valhalla.

'My wife and daughter were there that weekend and it absolutely made it for me. I remember when the chequered flag came down, I turned around to look back at the garage and they were right there on the pit-wall railing. It was amazing to be able to hug them both. It's a photo on a shelf and a memory that I've got that will stick in my head for ever.'

Andrew Shovlin, known to all as Shov, is Mercedes's head of trackside engineering and was on the other side of it that night.

'It was a bit surreal because Lewis had to be faultless for the last three races to even put him in position to win but as the races went by, that long shot started to look more and more possible.'

Hamilton won the three races prior to Abu Dhabi in Sao Paulo, Qatar and Saudi Arabia to set up the grand finale.

'And a handful of laps from the end in Abu Dhabi, it looked like it was going to come true. It was months of pressure at work, just trying to make sure we did what it took to help give him the chance. So it was difficult. And no one felt it more than Lewis. You could not believe quite what was happening and how it slipped away from us. I don't blame Red Bull or GP or Max. Not for that. I think if they [the FIA] had followed the rules, Lewis would have won the championship but the rules weren't followed.'

And that is how it will remain, for those who were part of it, that night. It was utterly brutal for Mercedes but for GP and Max, who had worked together for so long to achieve their dream in the face of the Mercedes dominance of the turbo-hybrid era, it was *simply lovely*.

GP – 'I have to say though, the next morning we were immediately back at work for the young driver test. I had a bit of a headache from the night before and we were sat around discussing it all. I will never forget Shov coming over and congratulating us despite what had happened and how raw and fresh it must've been for them all. I can't imagine what they must've been going through, but he had the heart to walk over and be the first to say well done. Full respect and kudos to Shov for doing that.'

If the shoe had been on the other foot though, you just know that GP would have been the first person to do exactly the same.

CHAPTER 15

THE PERFORMANCE COACH

While on track, the race engineer is a driver's right-hand man. Off it, that role falls to the performance coach. When you look back at footage of the early days of Formula One from the 1950s you might have noticed a couple of heavy-set Argentinian fellas clambering into their vehicles. One of them was Juan Manuel Fangio, five-time world champion and one of the greatest ever to step into a racing car. The other was José Froilán González, who delivered Ferrari their first ever win in 1951 at the British Grand Prix. González weighed in at 90kg and was nicknamed 'The Pampas Bull' by some of his contemporaries and 'El Cabazon' or 'Fat-Head' by others, depending on whether or not he'd cut them up on the race track. Either way, his robust and powerful frame belonged to an era long gone in Formula One as he would have been almost 15kg heavier than today's average driver.

In those days the drivers smoked, drank, partied and generally had a lot more fun than those on the grid today. Their lifestyles were so far removed from modern-day elite athletes, and more redolent of those in the media! In that first decade of Formula One the cars were heavy and needed wrestling around circuits that were significantly longer, during races that lasted a lot longer. So a few extra pounds didn't hurt.

In the 1960s, Colin Chapman was the first to strip his cars down to size-zero levels with mid-engines and monocoque chassis making them as light and nimble as possible. As the cars shed weight,

Chapman demanded the same from the men driving them. This led to a decade of leaner drivers like Jim Clark and Bruce McLaren.

The arrival of wings and downforce in the 1970s increased the G-forces on the drivers' bodies, making the cars more physically demanding once again. Battling against these forces required greater upper body strength and endurance. It led to some taking a more professional approach to fitness. Niki Lauda was one of the pioneers in this field and started experimenting properly with training when he returned to racing after his near-fatal crash at the Nürburgring in 1976. He had worked with a physiotherapist and masseur by the name of Willi Dungl, who was then known for his work with the Austrian ski jumping team. Dungl helped nurse Lauda back into shape and was the first to apply dietary ideas and psychology on top of physical fitness regimes to help Lauda gain an edge.

The turbo cars of the 1980s were beasts. With engines reaching over 1,000bhp, they were brutal and required drivers to bulk up further to cope with the demands. When Ayrton Senna arrived in 1984, he took the concept of driver fitness to another level. Working with Josef Leberer out of the Dungl clinic, he ensured that he worked harder than any other driver had ever done and left no stone unturned.

As the 1980s became the 1990s, competitors like Michael Schumacher understood that to be able to compete with Senna's talent, they needed to implement their own 'professional' training methods and, from then on, as the science of training began to improve dramatically, it became the norm for every driver to work as hard as athletes in any other physical sport.

With every regulation change in Formula One, there is a change in the optimum body shape for the drivers. When energy recovery systems came in in 2009 they added 30kg to the car but the minimum weight limit for the car and the driver remained at 605kg. The engineers felt that the easiest way to save weight was for the drivers to lose it themselves. It produced an era when drivers had to stay as light as possible, while maintaining the strength to cope with the demands of the cars. They just couldn't consume the things that they wanted. There were virtually no treat days and carbohydrates were scarce because they had to stay fit, without bulking up. It wasn't fun and it can't have been that healthy. I seem to remember there was almost a revolt over the work-life balance being forced upon them by the dietary and physical requirements of the job.

But with the cars getting much heavier again in the turbo-hybrid era from 2014, it meant that the drivers could again begin to eat a more balanced diet. In 2024 the minimum car weight was 798kg, with the driver's minimum weight requirement (measured post-race) including helmet, suit and shoes being 80kg. This increased to 800kg and 82kg in 2025. It still poses massive challenges and great commitment to stay at the perfect weight, so these days the attention to detail for the drivers and their performance coaches is at a level never before seen in the sport.

Martin Poole had looked after Nico Hülkenberg since 2016. He began in motorsport with the Ricky Flynn Karting team and, specifically, former Formula E driver Sam Bird, back in 2002. Even then, you required a sizeable annual budget to race in the Karting European Championship. It would cost the drivers (or their parents) about £100k per year to take part and, with that level of investment at stake, many of them deemed it necessary to begin thinking about proper training regimes to help with their progress, and therefore hired help. Poole started training many of the up-and-coming talents, including Nyck de Vries, George Russell and Lando Norris, at around the age of 13, but as their career trajectories steepened, they needed full-time coaching. With so many young drivers on their books at the time, Poole and his business partner Dan Williams, whose company Elevate Human Performance have looked after more than 350 drivers in total, weren't in a position back then to commit to just one driver. A path to the top is never guaranteed in single seaters, so it was simply too risky to take a chance on one. But as their stock rose, they realised it was time to focus on fewer clients, but at a more elite level.

'These youngsters had spent so much time at kart tracks that their general athleticism, the way that they moved and lifted weights and played other sports, was very basic. I remember trying to play squash with a young karter and he couldn't hit the ball. Most kids spend the weekends playing a variety of sports. They didn't. And whereas ball sports are transferrable, motor racing is unique and uses specific muscle groups. You don't move side to side or run and jump, yet it is still athletic. So a lot of the time with junior drivers, we were just trying to make them better athletes, because this would help them eventually improve strength, endurance and tolerance against injuries.'

Poole is one of today's breed of performance coaches who take a holistic approach to all their top-level clients. It is not just about ensuring they are in peak physical condition. They need to understand basic nutrition as well and that also starts when they are young.

'Back then, it was more theory based and we were teaching drivers about their macro needs, complex carbohydrates, protein balance, that kind of thing. But now, it's a lot more practical where we try to get them to look at what they are eating, how it affects them, and we work with the chefs to give them recipes and practical advice on how to prepare it, so that they can actually understand what they are eating.'

With the amount of data and biometrics now available to every individual with a smart watch, anyone can become more aware of themselves. Whereas the advice 15 years ago was more standardised, now there is increased demand for Poole and trainers like him to go into much greater depth with their roster of clients, adapting training plans that are much more bespoke.

The Formula One season is incessant. A relentless grind for the athletes who change time zones, travel approximately 200,000km in a season and must stay at the top of their game to be able to compete. There really is no other sport like it, and therefore the attention to detail required to keep the drivers in peak condition falls on both the athlete's shoulders and his training team, because keeping them there is a year-round process.

'Nico will take a week's holiday over Christmas but even then we are constantly chatting about programmes for the following season. Literally the first of January, he will phone me up and say, can you come tomorrow? He's done the holidays and the family thing and is itching to get back to work. We tend to work in blocks, so I will come over and do an intensive training stint with him at his home in and around Monaco, and then disappear for a week and leave him to train by himself. This continues all the way through January and February. Although we are very close, he doesn't want me there all the time and I don't want to be there all the time. We used to travel further afield to places like Punta Cana, in the Dominican Republic, where Nico had some friends. but nowadays we are always thinking about travelling and energy expenditure, so we just do training camps as close to home as possible.'

In the first couple of the months of the year during these training blocks, Poole is solely focusing on building up Hülkenberg's VO_2 max, i.e. his aerobic fitness. Without that backbone, he cannot begin to work on the strength and endurance training. So, in the first couple of weeks of the new year, the pair will focus on running and swimming at a relatively low intensity, just to get his base level ticking over, before moving into the gym to ramp it up with HIIT training and exercising with a purpose, at a more elevated level. The cycling fraternity within Formula One is an extremely tight group of individuals who take to the hills around Monaco to stay fit. Drivers like Valtteri Bottas will spend two or three hours a day building their aerobic capacity on the bike, but Poole and Hülkenberg simply don't have the patience for cycling and focus on getting what needs to be done in as short a time period as possible. They pride themselves on efficiency, but that still means running 10km in 40 minutes, which is no mean feat. Quite simply, they know what works for them.

'Compared to other athletes, Formula One drivers are more in tune with their bodies than most. A lot of athletes would push like hell, beast themselves and then do their recovery process, sleep and be ready to go and hurt themselves again in the evening. With racing drivers, it is all about quality. So yes, we will do two sessions in a day, harder in the morning, but it's counterproductive to go to bed with lactic acid build-up in their legs knowing they've got to do it all again at seven in the morning. They need to feel that they've worked hard, recovered and balanced down again, because they are extremely sensitive to how their bodies feel.'

One of the areas that the performance coaches really need to focus on from a strength perspective is the drivers' necks. This is the area of the body that is under the most repetitive strain over the course of a 300km race. The human head plus a standard Formula One helmet weighs 5–6kg. If you multiply that by the G-force of any particular corner then you can quickly get an indication of how hard the muscles in a racing driver's neck have to work. For example, in a 4G corner you will have roughly 20–24kg of force acting on the neck at multiple different angles that are constantly changing – backwards, forwards, torsionally – and it means they have to work extremely hard in the gym. In fact, if you ever see a Formula One driver up close, have a look at their neck. They all look like Buzz Lightyear.

'The way we do it is manually. I provide the resistance on Nico's head. At some angles we find I can push as hard as I can against his neck and he can resist, that is how strong those muscles have become. In your neck you have the trapezius, the major muscle group that goes up into the base of the skull, which we build up. But the main one that they rely on is the sternocleidomastoid, which for most of us is quite small. However, in drivers it's a big chunky muscle you can easily grasp. And you have scalene on the front, which are really small jaw muscles that they use a lot to stabilise against the vibrations and also under braking.'

While he is working on resistance exercises with Hülkenberg, Poole can provide vibrations and impulses, using devices to help simulate the violence that the drivers are exposed to within the cockpit of the cars.

'Nico once told me how it felt. Imagine you are sitting here now, and someone is asking you really hard questions against the clock and you are under immense physical strain anyway. You are doing a cognitive test, whilst someone shakes you constantly for an hour and a half. That is what it feels like to be in the cockpit of a Formula One car. The viewers can't see this from the outside. The drivers are getting thrown around the whole time and, whilst we try to replicate it in training, when we get to the first day of testing, it is always a shock to his system.'

This is why Poole aims to get Hülkenberg at peak fitness before the start of the season. As soon as the lights go out in the first race, you are then into a pattern that those of us who follow the calendar know well. If you are to retain a healthy work–life balance, you have to have time to focus on family and friends when you do get home. For the drivers, fitness then becomes about maintenance and ensuring that they spend enough time resting and in recovery from the travel between countries.

'When a driver has been in the sport for about five years, they undergo a mentality shift. I've spoken to a number of trainers about this. When they come in as rookies, they need to be the best prepared they can be, because they have a deficit in experience. And I'm not just talking about physically. These new guys now coming in from Formula Two like Jack Doohan, Franco Colapinto and Ollie Bearman have done a lot of simulator work and are physically and mentally extremely prepared. That's how they are able to get up to speed so quickly. Nico, having been in the sport for as long as he has, has had a change in philosophy and values a work–life balance that ensures he's a happy human being and therefore a top-performing athlete. One does follow the other and you see it a lot in the older drivers.'

So, what does a typical race weekend look like from the performance-coaching point of view, when a driver gets into the bread and butter of his day job? Thursday is media day and, for every driver, having to answer the same question a thousand times over makes it their least favourite part of the week.

'It's important for us as a team within a team to hit the ground running and with a really positive outlook. Raoul [Spanger,

Hülkenberg's media manager] will navigate Nico through his media commitments, some of which might be a bit painful, and I will just be ensuring everything is set up for the weekend, preparing for every eventuality with regards to his kit, speaking to the catering team about our requirements, doing treatments with Nico, potentially a track walk and talking to him about his last race and beginning to think about all his concerns for the coming weekend. But overall, simply trying to create a really good vibe ahead of Friday.

'Friday is homework day unless it is a sprint weekend. It is about knuckling down and learning about the track and the car. Again, it's not his favourite day because there is no competitive action. We have to try to keep him motivated, making sure he's spending enough time with his engineers, giving him headspace to process everything, making sure everything is perfect and that his meals are on time, keeping him hydrated, just doing things without overcomplicating them or overloading him with information.'

'On Saturday it lifts a level, and we get into the serious business of the weekend. If it is not looking good in practice, then we try and put him in a positive mindset for qualifying. But if it is looking good, we might just try and bring him down a little bit, so expectations aren't too high. The ten drivers in the second half of the field have the hardest job of everyone in qualifying. For the top drivers and teams, the qualifying format works really well, because it provides them with a gradual way to ease into the session.

'So, in Q1 Max or Lando don't need to put in their best lap. In Q2 they are getting a feel for how the track is evolving and getting into their sweet spot, before they can really start hammering their best laps in Q3. For us, we need to hit top form with our first lap in Q1. Then we have to reset and do it again, all the way through. That's why qualifying is the most fun for us, but also the most tense. We have three sessions and five runs, if we get through to Q3, and we are under pressure for every single one, whereas the top teams can build into it.'

After qualifying, Hülkenberg heads to the massage table. Usually, Poole will treat him twice a day but sometimes more on race weekends if something doesn't feel quite right. He is constantly assessing Hülkenberg's mental state, which also requires management.

'He's allowed to be completely fucked off with qualifying if it's gone badly on Saturday afternoon but he has to be back in the room for Sunday. Sunday is a totally different prospect. What is done is done in qualifying, but on race day we are trying to stay relaxed. You can't go into the race with the same intensity as qualifying, because it is a much longer session. Starts for Haas in 2024 weren't easy and if we started overthinking it, it got worse. We go through our routines, but we've done all our talking by this stage. What he really wants to focus on is different strategy decisions for the race. He's heavily involved in that and leads those discussions in the engineering meetings. Before the race we will do our warm-ups, talk about what he's going to drink in the car and just make sure everything is as chilled as possible.'

The most physically demanding of all the events on the current calendar is the Singapore Grand Prix. The heat and humidity, despite it being a night race, can mean that drivers lose up to four kilos in liquid over the course of the race. With Formula One following the sun, though, there are a number of races on the calendar where it is essential for the drivers to stay hydrated and keep their core temperatures as low as possible, so that they can perform at their best. It is why before most races you will see them wearing ice vests, but Poole and Hülkenberg went one step further.

'In 2023 it was great because the grid procedure was different. From the moment the car arrived on the grid, we had an extra ten minutes before we had to head back. The idea was that there would be more time for the drivers to talk to people like Martin Brundle on his grid walk, and that it would make for a better show. But, of course, all that happened was that they disappeared off the grid. So we had time to come back to the hospitality, jump in an ice bath, get into a fresh race suit and then head back for the anthem. Physiologically, the benefits are incredible. You get a dopamine hit and your cardio-vascular system switches on because you've just had this shock to the system and your brain says, "I need to be alert." At the anthem in Qatar, everyone else was sweating buckets, but Nico was asking for his jacket because he was freezing!'

The demands, though, on racers' bodies are more than just short-term exhaustion. With a return to ground-effect cars in 2022, to optimise performance, it was necessary to run extremely low ride heights. It meant that we started to hear complaints from drivers about the toll it was taking on their joints.

'The vibrations and bouncing caused by this current generation of cars is having a long-term effect on drivers' bodies. There is simply no cushioning for them and it's not good for their spines and necks. I know that some younger drivers are suffering from back issues that are only going to get worse, and I think in the future we could see more of that, as well as disc issues, nerve impingement and other problems that are often more associated with high-impact sports. On a muscular level, I can see there being hamstring and glute issues in later life, because of the jarring in the lower half of the body. They are occupational hazards, though, and these guys do put their bodies on the line.'

• • •

Ultimately, of anyone in the team, performance coaches spend the most time with the drivers over the course of a season. Good ones, like Poole, cater for their every whim and are massively in tune with their emotional and physical needs at any particular time. Poole prides himself on pre-empting anything that might cause Hülkenberg any undue stress.

'I have a holistic approach to managing everything that I can over the weekend. I get a lot of satisfaction from making sure that all the details are correct. Not because Nico is high maintenance, but because I believe it does make a difference to performance. So I make sure the hotel room is right, the pillows are right. If he likes a particular room, I will make a note of it and ensure he gets the same one the following year. Nico is a highly sensitive character, and I mean that in a good way. He's always saying, "Can you hear that?" or "Can you feel that?" And that transfers into the car. This is why Formula One drivers are so special because most of them have this. Anything that is slightly off can have a negative impact on their performance. I'm there to ensure that I give him this platform and sit underneath it, putting out all these fires to ensure that the platform stays rock solid so that he can do his job to the best of his ability.'

After several years working together, Poole and Hülkenberg amicably parted ways at the end of 2024. Initially it was a shock to Hülkenberg. Poole told him he was moving on after Singapore and the pair didn't speak for a short period but subsequently the German driver came to understand that he required a fresh challenge with a driver at the very start of his career, Ollie Bearman.

'I want to apply my model to a young lad who doesn't have that kind of structure in place yet. Hopefully he will benefit massively. I want to be right at the centre of his decision-making, and we are going to try new things and experiment to find out what works for him. That's really exciting, because he's under some pressure to get off to a good start in his Formula One career, and because he has an opportunity perhaps to move to an even bigger team. I could have worked with Nico for another three years, and I love him like a brother, but this is a chance to work with a young British driver coming into a sport where I'm at the peak of my understanding of it. I didn't take the opportunity to go with Lando or George on their journeys early in my career. This one has come at just the right time for me to hopefully escalate Ollie's development.'

CHAPTER 16

THE CHEFS

The performance coaches work closely with the team chefs to make sure the team's nutritional requirements are met throughout the Formula One weekend, and these days some of the best chefs in the world are working in the paddock from race to race.

There are now more than eight billion people on earth spread throughout 195 countries and it is estimated that there are approximately 15 million restaurants in the world. The ultimate guide to a restaurant's quality is still the Michelin guide. As of 2024, there were 2,290 with one coveted Michelin star, 414 with two and just 113 with three. In 2002, Karlheinz Hauser, a German chef, took over the Seven Seas restaurant within the historic Hotel Süllberg in Hamburg, perched above the River Elbe. It gained its first star in 2003 under his direction and a second in 2012. A lifelong motorsport fan, in 2021 he left the Süllberg having built his immaculate reputation there to work in his dream job, as chef for the McLaren Formula One team.

Each weekend Hauser must provide for approximately 250–350 guests, plus the team itself. He produces four different menus that cater across the paddock, from those in the garage to billionaire sponsors expecting haute cuisine and everything in between, including the very specific dietary requirements of the drivers.

An army marches on its stomach, and so the most important thing to get right is the team itself. If you ever cross a hungry mechanic or get in the way of a rigger's dinner, they'll let you know about it. Most teams these days travel with 60 to 70 people in the garage, but these numbers will swell when the marketeers arrive at the bigger races for the sponsors. The first thing for Hauser to get right is the garage and the mechanics. They work long hours and are on their feet or underneath a car all day long doing the hard yards, so they have to be fed and watered accordingly.

'Our performance coach looks over the menus, along with the team doctor, Justin Hughes. I typically work six races ahead in preparation. Those in the garage need healthy food, but also something that they can eat quickly because quite often they are time limited. We won't just do them a piece of meat. There is always something they can grab and go, or eat in a hurry, for instance stir-fries, a stew, tacos or pasta when they come in for lunch. But my service team will also be ferrying sandwiches and wraps into the garage throughout the day for when they are especially up against it.'

There is always a buffet lunch set up in the motorhome for the marketeers, management and engineering staff to help themselves to and then there are the drivers, who have to follow much stricter diets.

'They have a special menu plan which they follow from the moment they arrive at a Grand Prix weekend. Everything is calorie counted and consumed at set times to ensure they get exactly what their bodies need, depending on the specific demands of the race. But I have to be careful. Lando doesn't like fish. He loves chicken, wraps and poke bowls, whereas on the other side you have Oscar who loves all sorts of fish and sushi and everything. But whatever I get, I source it myself and have to ensure I get the best possible ingredients.'

That is what Hauser changed when he first arrived at McLaren. There used to be certain local distributors that the team chefs could order from, who would bring the products to the paddock directly, but the quality and variety of the produce was not good enough for Hauser.

'The first year was difficult, because it was really hard to find the local markets. But now we are organised, and have identified where we can go in every country to view the produce ourselves and we know who we can trust to deliver the quality we desire. So that's why I'm OK with Oscar eating a lot of fish, because I know where the fish is sourced.'

Hauser's VIP menus are always built around the local cuisine, but it is harder to source the right produce in countries such as Azerbaijan, Japan and China, partly because of the language barrier.

'We will always have a soup and two appetisers, as well as a chicken Caesar salad. One fish dish, one ravioli and one meat dish, as well as dessert and a cheese plate. I had a supplier at the Süllberg who provided me with caviar, and he had some links in China, so I have been able to get produce that I can trust, as it is so difficult there. The last thing we need is anyone coming down with food poisoning. We have to be extremely careful.'

Hauser's company has a contract with McLaren, and within that he must absorb all the food and beverage costs, as well as travel and accommodation. Food and beverage sit outside the cost cap that was set up in 2021 to limit spending on performance-related areas and so Hauser's company budgets for the year and they run and staff their operations themselves. He will tender with others to win the contract going forward, as there are now plenty of chefs who will want to be associated with the 2024 constructors' champions. It is high pressure and it takes its toll, but Hauser has the added benefit of travelling the world with his son Tom, who runs front of house in the motorhome. Together they make a great team.

Hauser isn't the first high-end chef to work with a Formula One team. In fact, as the sport has grown in recent years so too has the demand for the top-level experiences at every Grand Prix. In 2024, the most expensive package cost $40,000 for the five-day VIP experience in the Las Vegas paddock club. To most, that is an absurd number but Formula One has become the hottest ticket in town since Covid and the guests that are paying these prices expect the best, which has provided opportunities for the world's top chefs to get involved.

At the Singapore Grand Prix in 2019, Heston Blumenthal brought his gourmet cuisine to the paddock club in the form of his Michelin-starred gastropub, the Hind's Head. Guests could experience the dishes that he serves up at one of his two restaurants in the village of Bray in Berkshire. Unlike his more famous three-Michelin star restaurant the Fat Duck, which features his high-end molecular gastronomy, in Singapore, if you had the cash and a ticket, you could expect to be served up a menu of Lapsang Souchong tea-smoked salmon with sour cream butter, caviar and soda bread, followed by a veal chop with celeriac puree, as well as roasted scallops with scallop tartare, white chocolate foam and more caviar. If you are prepared to pay top dollar it will veritably rain caviar.

He wasn't the only one either. The Singapore Grand Prix also featured a NOBU restaurant experience, by another award-winning chef, Nobu Matsuhisa. His restaurants have become perhaps the most well-known high-end chain in the world. He now possesses 59 establishments of the same name, spanning five continents, and he also had a presence in the paddock club for guests wanting to sample his Japanese–Peruvian fusion dishes.

Phil Eagle has been the head chef with Aston Martin for the past four years. He started helping out in the kitchen of a local hotel when he was 16 and now runs his part of the team with the same military precision as everything else in Formula One. He has a consistent group in his kitchen, and they all work exceptionally hard 80-hour race weeks.

'For a European race we travel with the team on a Monday and, as soon as we get there, we will split. Some of us will go and source the produce, but the rest will then build the kitchen and restaurant for the motorhome. We have people that will plumb in and set up all the equipment, but my team lay the restaurant and make sure everything is washed prior to service. On Monday and Tuesday there are normally only 20 people in the set-up team that we have to cater for. The numbers start to swell from there.'

Since Brexit, regulations have changed, with rules that dictate that they have to shop in the city that they go to. But they also have to be wary of varying food regulations, which change from place to place.

'You've just got to be aware that in places like the Americas they have such different additives and sugar contents in their food that aren't allowed in the UK. For example, in Mexico, a couple of years ago, one of my chefs, who has a peanut allergy, was stuck in the notorious Mexico City traffic on the way back from a shop and opened a pot of Pringles. He's been eating Pringles for years, but he phoned me and said he thought he was having an allergic reaction. He's got an EpiPen and is very rigorous, so he obviously knew that he wasn't feeling right. It turns out that in Mexico, at the time at least, Pringles weren't safe for those with a peanut allergy. He was very lucky because those reactions can be deadly. Thankfully, he got to the hospital on time, despite the traffic.'

Like Hauser, Eagle found sourcing ingredients in China and Japan tough at the start, because of the language barrier.

'All the chefs talk to each other and give advice on the best places to shop, and we started sourcing the best local suppliers. But we also will use the bigger chains like Costco and Metro. We start planning way in advance of the events and I have a team that will look at menus for every race of the season. The race team runs at about 90 people at Aston Martin and, on top of that, we will have about 50 guests per day on Friday, Saturday and Sunday, depending on the race. Most of the meals are planned to the race team's agenda that is set by Formula One or the FIA. We do breakfast, lunch and dinner all three days, and fit in the guests around that with a VIP menu, which is normally a three-course meal, although we are moving towards sharing platters.'

On top of all that, Eagle and his team do sponsors' dinners, which usually take place on Friday or Saturday. They are the first to arrive and the last to leave, starting at seven in the morning on a Friday and often not finishing until 11 at night: long, tiring days that require an enormous amount of food. They are always on hand, though, for those that need to be fed.

'When we go to the big cash and carrys at the start of the week, we will fill 12 of those flatpack trolleys and then, at the end of the week, our kitchen logistics guy will go out to get the fresh meat and fish that we need. We set a budget at the start of the year and it works out at about £20,000 per race on food and beverage, although every team's budget varies.'

At Aston Martin, Eagle has a close relationship with the performance coaches of each of the drivers and stays in constant communication with them.

'I wouldn't say that the diets for our drivers are that strict, compared to others. I know that some other teams can be extremely regimented. Fernando Alonso went vegan for a bit because he wanted to see what it did for him. But our guys are really easy. When we were cooking for Sebastian Vettel, we would just do him chicken stir-fries but with no flavourings in it, low on salt and plain. It's normally berries, yoghurts, granola or eggs for breakfast. Lunch can be ham and cheese toasties or something with chicken and rice. Lance [Stroll] likes to have chicken Caesar salads. They will eat early on race day and then use protein shakes in the build-up and just keep the fluids going.'

Aston Martin have a relationship with another world-renowned chef in Wolfgang Puck, who is friends with owner Lawrence Stroll.

Eagle continues, 'I used to work with an executive chef from one of his restaurants, 45 Park Lane. So I went down there for a few days and had a bit of training, stole a few recipes and rustled up a few ideas and that's kind of how we started the project. It just means, from the guest side, we could offer his steaks, which he is famous for, and tell them a little bit about his story. We activate this association when we race in cities where he has a restaurant, because it is easier to get the support from them. A lot of these celebrity chefs have certain suppliers or produce that they like to use. He has restaurants in Bahrain and Budapest, where it's easier to get meat and his specific seasonings from his guys.'

The range of cooking that Eagle and indeed every chef in the paddock must do each weekend requires a huge level of skill, but also versatility.

'One minute we are cooking a shepherd's pie, handing out a bacon sandwich or making a salad for a team member and the next we need to flip it and make some fine-dining food for the VIPs or sponsors. Our cooking style fluctuates, but I'd say for the team now we are moving towards giving them comfort food. We are a British team and when you are on the road for two or three weeks, most of them are craving British dishes like roast dinners, gammon, egg and chips, pies, mash, toad-in-the-hole. We try and give them a big selection and keep it exciting.'

They might sit outside the cost cap but the chefs on the road are clearly providing an advantage if they can keep the drivers, team members and guests happy. If the food isn't right, the troops won't perform at their best. Formula One is a pressure cooker and they are the pressure cookers of the paddock.

CHAPTER 17

THE STRATEGISTS

As one of the most disorganised people on planet earth, I don't often have a plan for the day, let alone further ahead. Getting the kids (and myself) fed and dressed is about as detailed as it gets. Therefore, writing a chapter on strategy wasn't one I was particularly looking forward to tackling, as my brain simply isn't wired in the same way as an engineer. That's why, in life, everybody should have a Bernie Collins to turn to. Strategy to her and those like her is effortless. I imagine she breezes through each week, knowing exactly what she's going to do next and always with a failsafe plan B and C, should her well-thought-through plan A go wrong. In her day job, on a pit wall, as a Formula One strategist, these decisions often have to be made in a split second, but she's equipped to make them because of the thorough preparation she goes through before every race.

'The best thing about being a strategist is the influence you can have on a race. That's going to sound very bigheaded, but there are very few roles where you are definitely making a direct difference to how the race finishes.'

A Formula One strategist has a unique position within the sport. It is an engineering role yet it's different from the others. A strategist is solely focused on optimising the number of points that the team can get on any given Sunday. They can't change the pace of the car or the inherent pace of a driver, but they work and develop models to plot the best possible finish for both of their cars. A high percentage of the current strategists in Formula One are female, and they are becoming clear role models for other women who are considering entering the sport. Many of them studied maths rather than engineering, and while that mathematical knowledge is key to the role, they also need to be effective communicators who can make informed decisions quickly and relay that to the rest of the team, while reacting to various situations in the highly charged, testosterone-fuelled dynamic of the race itself.

Bernie grew up in Northern Ireland and we now have the pleasure of her company on Sky for several race weekends over the season, during which she imparts her incredible knowledge to us all. She has added so much to our coverage, bringing a depth of understanding built up over 15 years on the inside of the engineering offices of both McLaren and the team that is now Aston Martin. Bernie studied mechanical engineering in Belfast and enjoyed subjects like maths and physics, where there was always a right and a wrong answer. That's why, I imagine, making the transition into television was probably harder than any for her. In my experience, people in TV are more often than not 'creatives', with concentration spans akin to goldfish and a propensity to waffle on for hours. Engineers are quite the opposite. Over the years at Sky Sports F1 we have tried to make our production meetings on race weekends more like engineering meetings. We now have headsets to try to keep focused. It has helped, because in the early days our meetings were more like a coffee morning with conversation often veering off on wild tangents or disappearing down rabbit holes of nonsense. I won't mention names but, David Croft, you know who you are. I remember when Pat Symonds, the former technical director of Benetton, Williams and Formula One, joined the team for a season or two. Having witnessed one of our meetings for the first time, he simply shook his head and admitted that he couldn't believe how we got anything done as it was so completely at odds with any meeting he had ever been involved in. For some of our team, this was a rude awakening – to others, a badge of honour!

Bernie's Formula One journey started in the graduate scheme at McLaren. Over the course of a year, she spent three months in the design office, three months in systems engineering where she got to understand car systems and the wind tunnel, three months in vehicle dynamics gaining experience in the simulator, before a final three months covering each of the other departments. It gave her a solid grounding in every aspect of Formula One engineering from the gestation of the car to its fully functional operation.

At the end of that year, she moved into the design department full time, starting with suspension systems and then moving on to gearboxes for the next three years. It was during this period that she decided that she wanted to end up trackside with the race team. It's not a natural route from the design office, so she started to volunteer on the race weekends at mission control in Woking, before moving on to work with the now boss Zak Brown as his race engineer in British GT. Eventually, in 2013, she got the opportunity to replace Jenson Button's performance engineer Tom Stallard when he was on paternity leave.

As we have seen, the performance engineer works closely with the race engineer of any given driver. The race engineer is the one that communicates with the driver during the race and is effectively his right-hand man/woman. They are responsible for the physical set-up of the car, wing adjustments or suspension set-ups. The performance engineer is concerned with getting the best out of the driver, by focusing on the data. They will spend time looking at the telemetry and the overlays and working out where the driver can gain time, be it through adjusting braking points or throttle application. They will look at the brake bias or the differential, and help with any of the switches on the steering wheel that can help make the driver faster that particular weekend.

At the end of 2014, Collins was told she wouldn't be racing with McLaren the following season and so she had a decision to make. Having had a taste of the adrenaline of a race weekend, the desire to return to a factory-based job wasn't there, so she started looking for opportunities elsewhere. It came almost immediately from Force India, where she had the chance to take a role that was split down the middle: half performance and half strategic. She grasped it with both hands.

'Upon arriving at my new team, I immediately noticed the difference. Force India has never been as well funded as McLaren, who are the second most successful team in the history of Formula One, and for that reason I was afforded an opportunity that I would never have got at a bigger team. But in my hybrid role, I had a very short space of time to learn something that was completely unknown to me, the dark arts of strategy. To be precise, I had two races before being thrown in at the deep end.'

The job of the strategist begins well ahead of time. Planning can begin a couple of months in advance, but the intensity of the work steps up early in race week. On the Monday or a Tuesday before a race, they will begin prepping in the factory. They start with some of the wider questions garnered from historical data. What do they think the basic overall strategy will be? How many pit stops will there be? What is the risk of a safety car? What tyres are they going to run? What are the predicted levels of degradation? The interaction with the other engineers, particularly the tyre engineer, at this stage is critical in determining what the most important factors are for them to learn in practice on Friday. On Wednesday, they will travel to the track with the rest of the team and on Thursday they get to work with the drivers for the first time. They will talk about the plan that they've formulated and do the track walk with them, go through what happened the week before, discuss any decisions that were controversial and what might have been done differently with hindsight. They consider what the other teams did and might do this weekend, and discuss the run plan for the Friday sessions.

In Formula One, other than on sprint weekends, the teams have three hour-long practice sessions to prepare themselves for qualifying and the race. The first hour of practice isn't of particular interest to the strategist. This session is for the aerodynamicists to work out the best wing levels and for the teams to optimise the mechanical set-up of the cars. The second hour is when the strategists begin to come alive! It is during this hour that they start to work out their run profile for qualifying, and where they get information from the long runs on what their consistency looks like for the race ahead. They start the weekend with lots of ideas on how the race will go and from there it is about trying to reduce the unknowns.

The strategy team is largely made up of a central strategist, who sits on the pit wall and is in overall charge of decision-making during the race, supported by two strategists at mission control back in the factory, who look after the needs of each driver. Some of the larger teams will have two further strategists analysing the opposition.

On Friday night, the strategists do a detailed analysis of what they have seen in the practice sessions and adjust their thinking accordingly. Can they prove, from the models that they have built and adapted with the data acquired from those sessions, that they have the right thinking for Sunday's race strategy and for qualifying? By Saturday, unless there is a dramatic change in the weather, attention moves towards the race. With qualifying done and the grid position set, Collins and her team further refine their plans, assessing what is achievable relative to the pace of the other teams and where they line up.

By Sunday morning, the ideas are set, but the strategy team spend a fair amount of time with the drivers, going through the specifics of the plan and balancing it with the drivers' preferences. It's also important to take into account the relative strengths of individual drivers. Some may be better off the line, others at managing their tyres. They try to ensure that they are all on the same page when it comes to the scenarios that are most likely.

'You know the starting tyre, but the bit you can't plan for is what will happen at the start. Say, for example, you've done the plan for starting P7 or P8, what you can't predict is what will happen on that first lap. By turn one, you could be anywhere. But if you do start to plan, the next thing that you are trying to assess is whether your next pit stop is correctly timed. Ideally, your tyres perform exactly as you expected, and everyone else's pace is just as you thought, and therefore you run the number of laps that you want, and you are not being pushed from behind or having to react to someone else's pit stop. So you remain on plan and do your pit stop as predicted. However that is very rare.'

Even if this happens, the job of the strategist is to keep thinking a step ahead by constantly asking themselves what would change the plan if the safety car came out at any point. This information will be relayed to the driver so that they know whether to pit if the safety car is deployed. Usually, towards the end of a tyre's life, the driver will be instructed to pit. However, if it is deployed just after a scheduled pit stop, then the driver will be left out because the tyres are still fresh enough.

'In places such as Austria or Bahrain, where it is relatively easy to overtake, the race tends to finish in pace order. However, in places like Jeddah, Monaco or Singapore, where the opposite is true, stopping one lap early or one lap too late can have a really detrimental effect on the result, because it is easy to lose position during the pit stops.'

Everything in Formula One is measured in a constant quest for marginal gains. Sporting performance these days is never left to chance. As an elite athlete in your chosen sport, paying attention to the one-percenters, the tiny things that all add up, is now a given, a bare minimum; no stone is left unturned. Strategy teams are no exception, and they measure their success by adding up the positions gained or lost every weekend, versus the predicted result, given the pace of the car.

'For strategy to work consistently, you need a couple of things. You need the driver to buy into it. Sometimes strategy will be heavily based on which tyre you start on. You might not start on the tyre that everyone else thinks is the best starting tyre. You might want to run a little longer in that first stint, and some drivers are more comfortable managing their tyre wear than others. That's why the meeting on Sunday morning with them is crucial in order for them to understand your thinking and get on board with it. And secondly, you need to react correctly to what happens in the race. You need to have the structure in place to trust your pre-planning and empower the strategist to make their decision based on the data that their team has modelled, so that decisions don't go to committee as there simply isn't enough time. But the answers aren't always in the data and that's very hard to teach people. This happens particularly in changeable conditions. There is an element of leaning on the experience you have gained from the past and using common sense.'

James Vowles is now the team principal of Williams and, along the line of his ascent within the sport, he has taken on many roles. Until he got the top job at Williams, he was best known for being chief strategist at Mercedes. He started at the team based in Brackley, in its initial iteration as British American Racing, and stayed for 22 years as it morphed into Honda, Brawn and eventually the Mercedes team that we know today. Like Collins, Vowles came from a mathematical background, having studied the subject alongside computer science at the University of East Anglia. Upon realising he wanted to pursue a future in motorsport, he decided to apply to all 11 Formula One teams that existed at the time he was graduating. He was rejected by every single one, but two teams replied with a singular reason, that he didn't have an engineering qualification. Vowles is not one to give up lightly. Undeterred, he applied for and then undertook an engineering conversion master's at Cranfield University, which ultimately led to that first job at BAR.

'I interviewed as a test engineer. but wasn't successful. However, there was also no one else in the business that had the mixture that I had of computer science, mathematics and engineering, so they created a job for me. It was basically sitting between race engineering, vehicle dynamics and the electronics department, acting as a conduit of information. They had all these supremely clever engineers that didn't understand what was possible with software to help improve these areas.'

Vowles had been training as a race engineer with a Formula Three team alongside his studies and having that as another string to his bow allowed him to quickly forge a unique skillset.

'I'm someone that is able to bridge a number of areas and understand how to automate them to move things forward, and that is what I did. It was the perfect job. I wanted something where I could learn everything about the business that I possibly could.'

Like Collins, Vowles spent time in R&D, in electronics, in vehicle dynamics, in performance meetings and with the race engineers. It was the perfect grounding for stepping into the world of strategy when it was in its infancy.

'Back in the early days, we would sit down on Saturday evening with the drivers and an Excel spreadsheet and say, "Do you want a one stop? Good, tick. Do you want a two stop? Good, tick." And again with my mixture of maths, computer science and engineering, I thought, *This doesn't feel right*. We had a hundred channels of data at the time, we had simulations, so why were we doing it this way? I put together a proposal to fundamentally modernise strategy by applying scientific techniques.'

Vowles set about some pioneering work in the field of strategy using techniques that had previously been applied in the stock market to assess volatility. The aptly named 'Monte Carlo Method' is a broad class of computer algorithms that rely on repeated random sampling to obtain numerical results. They are primarily used to model phenomena with significant uncertainty of inputs and provide approximate solutions to problems that are otherwise too complex to model mathematically. In other words, things such as tyre degradation.

'So alongside my other jobs at BAR, in the evenings I was developing software that allowed us to just take in timing data and then calculate what the tyre degradation was, what the pit-stop time loss was and, from there, determine what everyone would do within those parameters. We ran about 1,000 simulations through this software and, by the end of 2002, we were beginning to make headway.

It wasn't heuristics anymore, there was a level of science to it. It was very basic and you weren't always going to get it spot on, but it was far better than what we were doing prior to that.'

From there, Vowles began to build out the strategy team at BAR. As it grew, they started to develop increasingly complex systems that you could no longer run on a laptop. They needed more and more computing power.

'We started at 1,000 simulations and you'd be sat back and could go and get a cup of tea before you got the results. Nowadays you run millions, and they come back within a few seconds. And you do that in real time during a race. Originally the inputs started off with a single value. So a lap time was a lap time, the pit stop would take this long and you can simulate it. But there's not much variability in that, so armed with the same data there's little as a strategist that you can do differently.'

Vowles and his team started to bring in variance, probability and standard deviations to their modelling to give them an edge. They were weaponising their data in order to gain an advantage.

'Instead of the individual values we turned the timing data into distributions. You could take a lap time of a certain driver, whether your own or a competitors', and say, for example, they were doing a 1 minute 30. You could apply a probability of 5 per cent that they would do a 1 minute 29.2 second lap and then start getting spreads on how the drivers actually perform. And as it turns out, and this is very boring, that driver performance isn't actually a standard distribution, it's more like a Weibull distribution [a high peak with a long tail]. So basically, a driver is very good at getting close to their peak lap time but they make mistakes, hence the long tail. That is actually how you describe a driver in mathematical terms and how you can more accurately model them to make better strategic decisions!'

Vowles continued to build out his strategic software while continuing as a race engineer at BAR, but in 2007 he decided to make the full-time switch to strategy, because he felt race engineering had become a little too one-dimensional.

'As a race engineer you are working with one driver in one control condition with the set-up of the car dictated by systems and tools. As a strategist I saw it as having strings and puppets and you could basically move things around a big chessboard and try and get people to do things in reaction to you. You're not just changing what's happening within the team, you can control what other teams do.'

To Vowles, strategy is not just pulling numbers out and judging when the perfect time to stop will be. In his opinion, there is not a strategist out there that knows what the race is going to look like when the lights go green.

'Strategy is fundamentally creating a set of plans beforehand, so that when something happens in the race, the first human reaction isn't one of surprise and shock, and so that we aren't caught off guard because it's not something we didn't anticipate. Whatever words come out of your mouth as a strategist on the pit wall will set into motion actions conducted by around 40 people. In seconds, you know whether you've made a good or bad decision. And that's empowerment in the best way that you can have in Formula One.'

Vowles was known as a guru of strategy during the period of Mercedes's sustained dominance in the turbo-hybrid era. He made countless good decisions and, by that, he means converting a car that the data says wasn't the fastest that weekend, into a winning one. He cites Monaco 2016, when he took the decision to stay out on the extreme wet tyre (while others pitted for intermediates) and wait for conditions to dry enough for slicks, as one of them. Budapest 2021, the race you may remember where Hamilton was the lone car starting from the grid on intermediates at the restart, with the others on slicks in the pits, was another. This conversion to a two stop when Verstappen stuck to the one stop led to Hamilton finishing third, and later promoted to second, and Mercedes overtaking Red Bull in the constructors' championship. But he also made mistakes.

'Monaco 2015 was the obvious one. I'm normally incredibly calm under pressure. It was the one time where Lewis's commentary was the only thing resonating in my head. I wasn't looking at the data anymore. I was listening to his words, which were, "My tyres have gone." I boxed him and I immediately knew we were in trouble at the restart. When we went back over the race and we listened to the audio from Lewis, I had approximately 2.5 seconds to make that decision, before he got to pit entry, and that's what creates the mistake. When you try and rush the decision without thinking it through. That's when the pre-planning goes out the window.'

Inevitably, in a Formula One race, there isn't always enough time to make the right decision, and Vowles is the first to admit that. His strategic genius helped lead Mercedes to eight consecutive constructors' championships and of course he was there for 'the one that got away' for Lewis Hamilton at the last race of the season in Abu Dhabi in 2021. But did he feel helpless in that bizarre set of circumstances that led to Verstappen winning the championship? Surely it was a strategist's worst nightmare?

For those who don't remember the sequence of events that led to the most controversial end to a championship in a generation, and possibly the history of the sport, allow me to try to refresh your memory. I know I've already mentioned this in a previous chapter, but it is easy to forget the specifics!

On lap 53 of a 58-lap race, Nicolas Latifi crashed at the Yas Marina circuit. It brought out the safety car. Now, normally when the safety car comes out, because the cars are going slower around the track, you lose less time taking a pit stop, so when it comes out earlier in the race most of the field will take advantage and pit. However this close to the end of the race and with Hamilton leading, had he pitted, Verstappen would have stayed out and the Mercedes driver would've lost track position. This is a massive risk should the safety-car period not end before the chequered flag, so Vowles and his strategy team had only one option and that was to keep Hamilton out. Verstappen therefore pitted for fresh tyres and retained second but, at that late stage, there were five lapped cars between himself and Hamilton. Ordinarily, lapped cars can only unlap themselves when it is safe to do so and when the obstruction

[Latifi] is cleared. But because this hadn't happened, Michael Masi, the race director, instructed the lapped cars not to unlap themselves. With laps fast running out, Christian Horner and Red Bull lobbied that it was the wrong decision and that those cars should be allowed to unlap themselves. On lap 57, Masi acquiesced to Red Bull protestations and, not wanting the championship to finish behind the safety car, he gave the instruction for the five cars to unlap themselves, while at the same time ordering the safety car to come in immediately, to allow one racing lap. This was the mistake that has been discussed ever since, because under the specific rules, the safety car is only supposed to come in at the end of the lap *after* the lapped cars have unlapped themselves. The rules weren't followed to the letter of the law and the race should have finished behind the safety car. With fresh tyres Verstappen overtook Hamilton relatively easily on the last lap and the rest is history.

'I didn't feel helpless until the message came on the screen that said some of the lapped cars could overtake and the safety car was coming in a lap early. I was in shock and disbelief. Normally this doesn't happen to me, but I went silent. It's a message that no one had ever seen before. I thought, *This isn't right.* I'm incredibly transparent, incredibly honest, I play fair and by the rules in every respect. It was just a smack in the face. I just couldn't understand what was going on anymore. What I felt like is that we had started on the right tyre, we had pulled a gap, we did everything right. We got to the safety car and it shouldn't have restarted, we did everything right so I felt robbed, I felt sick to my core. And even today if you speak to everyone who was with Mercedes that day, no one has let go of it, they really haven't. You can see that with Toto, you can see that with Lewis. They struggle with it, and rightly so.'

But did he think it was simply a refereeing error?

'I do not blame Michael Masi. He is a human being, who was under immense pressure from both Mercedes and Red Bull. There was pressure from the teams to make sure that races finished under green-flag conditions. That's what he thought his role was. As a human being, I don't know many that wouldn't have crumbled and got it wrong under those circumstances. I've been there, in Monaco in 2015. And so it's why I don't apportion any blame to him, particularly. But it allowed me to move on to the next chapter of my life as a team principal. It made me want to move on from life as a strategist.'

But as with everything in life these days, you wonder about the future of humans making decisions based on past data. Are the days of the strategist numbered? Will the Bernie Collinses of this world be taken over by robots and artificial intelligence or should the use of it be vetoed?

'I don't think they'll veto it,' she says. 'Teams are using AI already for lots of things. They will use machine learning for car set-up as you can do lots of experiments very quickly. In strategy it can be used to calculate what the others are going to do. Where it could be really useful is potentially in the race situation. On lap ten, say I decide to do a pit stop. If I make that pit stop it would be good if AI modelled what would happen if I make that move and it can challenge that decision by representing all the other cars like pieces on the board in a chess game. So, if I make the stop, what is the best case for everybody else? For AI to fight me back. At the moment we have quite good models, but AI can help improve those in terms of how teams would fight you.

'The second thing is understanding how we can model other teams' natural reactions to certain situations, and how particular individuals, be it drivers or other teams' strategists, will behave, using historical data. We should be able to know where and in what situations the drivers will drive defensively or aggressively. AI will be able to more accurately model team interaction and predict patterns of team behaviour during a race. The possibilities are endless, but it throws up so many other intangibles. What happens if the strategist moves to a different team? Will the AI be able to model what that change means for future team behaviour?'

For now though, the Formula One strategist remains one of the key team members that can affect the outcome of a race. Aside from the drivers, they have the power to get the best out of both cars for the good of the team. A good strategist can plan better and react smarter. In doing so they can help their teams maximise their points return on any weekend. It's as close as an engineer can get to driving the cars themselves and that, in itself, is quite a responsibility.

CHAPTER 18

THE SPORTING DIRECTOR

While James Vowles and the rest of the Mercedes team were coming to terms with the cruellest defeat of their lives, one of the men at the centre of the drama in Abu Dhabi was the Red Bull sporting director at the time, Jonathan Wheatley, who is now the team principal at Sauber (which will be the Audi works team in 2026).

'I've spent a long time thinking about this. It's not like I'm sat there with a pen and paper ticking off each lap as it goes. A tremendous amount can happen in a race, in a short period of time. You're not stood back from it, like you are the moment the race is over, when you get time to think about it. And, as the years go by, you get even more time to mull it over. It would be foolish to underestimate how competitive people on the pit wall are, and for me, more than anything, the race isn't over until the chequered flag.

'We were dealing with a lot because we were retiring Checo's car at the time, which took some managing, and then we had the situation on the track with the safety car. So we had to bring Max's car into the pits to change tyres. I was concerned that the race director, Michael Masi, wanted all of the lapped cars to catch up with the main pack before starting the race again and my feeling was that it wasn't necessary and that he had, within his control, the power to not let that happen. And yeah, so I tried, from a competitive point of view for the team, to convey that. I wasn't being Machiavellian. I was just pushing for a race to the flag and, looking back on it now, I wasn't aware that I was a lap out at the time.'

In the wake of the 2021 Abu Dhabi Grand Prix, his role in the finale became the subject of intense discussion. While some praised his shrewd handling of the situation and his ability to capitalise on a unique set of circumstances, others criticised a perceived manipulation of the rules.

During the safety-car period, Wheatley engaged in a direct conversation with Masi, suggesting that only the lapped cars between Hamilton and Verstappen should be allowed to unlap themselves, rather than the entire field, allowing Verstappen to close up directly behind Hamilton for a one-lap shootout to decide the championship. The decision by Masi, and the role of Wheatley's communication in influencing it, sparked widespread debate and led to months of scrutiny and investigation by the FIA. Mercedes protested the result, arguing that the regulations had not been applied correctly, but the protest was ultimately dismissed, and Verstappen's title was confirmed.

The FIA's investigation into the Abu Dhabi Grand Prix revealed that team communications, including those from Jonathan Wheatley and team boss Christian Horner, did play a role in the decision-making process, but it did not conclude that either had acted inappropriately. It found that Masi had contravened Formula One regulations, but had acted in good faith and cited human error. It also set out the need for clearer communication protocols between teams and the race director.

As a result of the investigation, the FIA made several changes, including removing Michael Masi as race director for 2022 and revising the rules regarding team communications with the race director during races. The inquiry did not find any direct wrongdoing by Jonathan Wheatley, or suggest that he had unfairly influenced the race outcome.

Whatever happened that day, you cannot deny that Wheatley's calm communication and encyclopaedic understanding of the rules was key to the outcome of the title. I, for one, do believe that he was ticking off the laps with a pen and paper though as he never misses a trick and that, in essence, is one of the fundamentals of being a good sporting director.

In Formula One, the sporting director is absolutely integral to the success of the team. You could also call them team managers. Their responsibilities span everything from strategic planning and race management to team co-ordination and regulatory compliance. They are also the voice of the team when representing themselves to the FIA. That means having a thorough understanding of every single sporting and technical regulation, as they are the ones that will fight their teams' corner when called to the stewards.

Andy Stevenson is a former colleague of Jonathan Wheatley's from their time at Jordan. They remain good friends, even now as competitors. The pair of them started as mechanics and have worked their way up through the ranks. They are both racers in the purest sense of the form and Stevenson was still in his teens when he got his chance in motorsport.

'So I'd been doing some weekend warrior stuff for a friend's Formula Three team when I met a guy called Bosco Quinn, who was Eddie Jordan's old mechanic from the time he used to race in Ireland. He liked my attitude, so when he moved back to Jordan racing, he invited me in for an interview. My mother Julie drove me to it, which Eddie never forgot, and I'm being interviewed by Bosco when Eddie walks in, takes one look at me and says, "Bosco, Who's this c**t? Don't like the look of him. Don't employ him."'

Stevenson was one of EJ's closest friends and was devastated when he passed away in March 2025 but he still smiles and laughs when he thinks about the times they had together.

'I mean I was 17 years old, and Eddie's team had just become the British Formula Three champions and I was thinking that this was my big break. I'd never been spoken to like that. But Bosco said, don't worry about him, you're hired. So I turned up for my first day at work, and I was the first to arrive. I'm in the car park sitting in my car and Eddie arrives to unlock the factory. I go up to introduce myself and he says, "What the fuck are you doing here? I told Bosco not to hire you, I don't want you." *Not again*, I thought, so I had to go back and sit in my car until Bosco turned up.'

It didn't end there. He now knows it was Eddie's way of working out who really wanted to work for him.

'So I carried on working and a couple of weeks later, after EJ's already had me doing some really dodgy things to three Vauxhall Carltons, I'm in the factory and we had some electronic control units from some old cars. We'd worked out a way of updating these to use for new engines. I was converting these boxes, saving Eddie an absolute fortune. I'm upstairs on a mezzanine floor soldering away and putting all these bits into the ECUs and Eddie comes along and barks, "Don't you dare fuck 'em up."

"'No, I'm all right, I've got 'em sussed," I replied.

"'And why are you still here? It's ten o'clock at night."

"'I'm doing my job," I said.

"'I'll give you two weeks." He laughed.

'And I'm still here, 37 years later!'

While Wheatley has recently moved on to become team principal of what will become Audi, Stevenson has remained at the team that was formally Jordan, from its inception all the way through its various iterations, and is still in position as sporting director at Aston Martin. He is their longest-serving team member, so he must be doing something right.

The only item on Stevenson's desk, apart from his computer, is the latest copy of the sporting regulations.

'I'm never without a copy close to hand. When you first get this book, which for me was 2005, you have to know it like the back of your hand. But people like myself, Jonathan Wheatley, Ron Meadows [Mercedes] and Dave Redding [manager of Williams] know it inside out. To the man in the street, it doesn't make a great deal of sense, but we understand it as sporting directors because we've all been involved in its evolution. Much of it was written by former race director the late Charlie Whiting but what we are finding is that a lot of the new regulations are more foolproof, where Charlie used to like to leave things quite open to interpretation.'

Jonathan Wheatley had been in his role at Red Bull for 19 years and had way more responsibilities than is probably healthy for one individual to have and so when he left to become team principal of Audi, his job got divvied up between a number of people. Both he and Stevenson are almost irreplaceable.

'When Christian [Horner] first installed me as team manager, the most daunting aspect was to learn all those rules and regulations and really understand them. If I'm out of my comfort zone, I roll my sleeves up until I get to the point where I am comfortable. And that meant reading and re-reading, and driving Charlie mad with questions and trying to understand what I would do in certain situations. I haven't had a look, but I wouldn't be surprised if the sporting regulations were a quarter of the size back then. Nowadays, there's not just the sporting regulations, there's the International Sporting Code, the financial regulations, you have to learn the technical regulations and then there's all the technical directives as well.'

Like Stevenson, Wheatley always carries a copy of the sporting regulations around with him and buffs up on certain aspects on long-haul flights, looking for nuances within them that he might not have seen before. It's being armed with this knowledge and knowing when to go into bat for your team that can be worth points and affect championships. Stevenson is one of the most modest people in the paddock and a master of the understatement, but he thrives under pressure. They both innately know when they can put all their experience into practice.

In 2023 Stevenson was able to apply his knowledge to help his team at both the Austrian and Saudi Arabian Grands Prix.

'Prior to Austria, whether working in our simulator or in our briefings before the race, we discussed the importance of track limits. We know how key they are at the infamous turn 11, coming down the hill into the final corner. We told ourselves that we could not exceed them, we must observe the regulation at all times. So, in the simulator we were doing that, and in the race we were doing it. The drivers were incredibly disciplined. But, after the race we saw all these track-limit violations that hadn't been penalised. So we had a quick tot-up, and I went and protested the result to Steve Nielsen [the then FIA sporting director]. I asked if they were going to apply them all as they were supposed to. The response was there were too many, the FIA couldn't keep up. Steve pleaded with me not to protest, but it's my job. When you have Fernando Alonso sticking to the rules behind Esteban Ocon, who is exceeding the limits each lap, and it's us that's being penalised for sticking to the rules and not them, then what was I supposed to do? I couldn't go back to team owner Lawrence Stroll and say, "Yeah, I know they should have had a penalty, but I didn't want to upset anyone!" Anyway, the long and short was that the FIA had to go through the video of every lap of every car and total up the violations, which no doubt would have been a massive pain in the arse, but when the penalties were correctly applied it changed the result. We actually helped McLaren out; they went further up than us!'

Stevenson's protest led to the review of more than 1,200 track-limit breaches and meant that Fernando Alonso moved up from sixth to fifth and Lance Stroll from tenth to ninth. Stevenson's actions resulted in three extra points for the team. How did that feel?

'It felt fucking brilliant.'

In Saudi Arabia in 2023, a five-second penalty was given to Fernando Alonso for positioning his car incorrectly on the start line. The team decided to serve the five-second penalty during the pit stop, as per the rules. However, after the race the FIA penalised him again, claiming that the rear jack had touched the car while the penalty was being served, which is a breach of the rule prohibiting mechanics from working on the car during the five-second penalty. There is, however, a lack of clarity on this subject. The jack man didn't jack up the car, he merely touched the rear crash structure. Led by Stevenson, Aston Martin contested the penalty, arguing that there were inconsistencies in how such penalties were applied. They provided video evidence of seven occasions from the previous year where exactly the same situation had arisen, and further penalties had not been applied. He even brought up the minutes from the last Sporting Advisory Committee meeting where everyone had agreed that merely touching the car with the rear jack was not deemed to be 'working on the car', and thereby proved by precedent that the stewards had incorrectly applied the penalty.

While discussing the minutiae of individual rules could get very boring indeed, it is at the very heart of a sporting director's remit. If the ten-second penalty had not been overturned by the stewards, Alonso would have been relegated to fourth place. Stevenson's intervention meant he kept his third place and the Spaniard thereby secured his 100th podium in Formula One.

'Whenever you go into the stewards' room, you have to be fairly confident with your argument against whatever they have levelled against you. As big a buzz as it is when it goes your way, it's a massive kick in the teeth when it goes against you, especially when you absolutely know that they've got it wrong. And that really hurts because you've run out of options. You've given them everything you can to sway their decision, or allow them to make the right decision, and then it goes against you. I really struggle with that. I'm down for days when that happens.'

Again, for the teams and the sporting directors, it's knowing what you can and can't appeal against. You cannot appeal against 'in race' time penalties, for example. So going back to Jeddah, Stevenson couldn't appeal against the five-second 'in race' penalty, but what he could do was ask for the stewards to review why they gave it to them.

Stevenson is one of seven people on the pit wall, but he has a team of 20 to 30 people that are his eyes and ears during the race, helping to spot infringements.

'You have to have your pragmatic head on, as well. So I don't scream at the race director every time someone pulls out of the pits and might be slightly too close to us. There's a certain element of just playing on. You don't want to be crying foul every two minutes or the stewards will think, *Here we go again with this fucking idiot. The next time they do that, we'll show them.* I have to act as a filter and assess whether incidents are actually worth the argument. If I look at it and I think, *Well, it hasn't affected our race*, then even if it's a bit dodgy I'm not going to try and get someone else a penalty, whereas others would. Some of the younger ones, the younger bucks, are onto the stewards for everything. And it doesn't pay to do that, it will come back to bite you on the arse.'

Wheatley is also not the kind of person to jump around and get overexcited. Both he and Stevenson are from the school of thought that effing and blinding at the stewards is going to get you nowhere in the long run.

'Everything in this business is about relationships. I've tried hard for a really long time to understand how the stewards arrive at decisions, helping guide the regulations along with other members of the Sporting Advisory Committee. You know how to prepare for each battle. Sometimes I'm armed with evidence for them to take into consideration, and sometimes I say very little. If it's a driver-related matter, obviously the most important information comes from the driver. Precedence helps allow the stewards to make the correct decision but I would say that post-Covid there was a bit of a reset in the sporting guidelines, where the teams agreed on principles moving forward, and forgot about certain ones from the past. So, suddenly, a huge body of work by those that sit on the SAC goes in the bin. But the tidying up of the clarity of the regulations has allowed stewarding to get so much better in the last four or five years. The quality has gained by an order of magnitude, and there is a huge amount of respect for the people who do the job now, across the board.'

One of the jobs that Wheatley took the most pride in during his tenure as the sporting director at Red Bull was getting the pit crew as sharp as possible. They won the Fastest Pit Stop Award seven years in a row. In the post-refuelling era, they have dominated in this department more than others. It is, frankly, a remarkable achievement to do it as often as they do, and Wheatley had overseen a group of people who had worked extremely hard to make them the best of the best at it.

'We decided to put together an instrumented/intelligent wheel gun and launch system and looked at the entire pit stop holistically. We'd worked out what was the best failure mechanism for every single thing that we could think of that could happen in the pit stop. It had levels of security and safety built in that we never had before. So, from that point you could let the guys off the hook a bit. There's 22 people in the pit stop, plus the driver. Everyone is wired and thinks differently. So you had to find a way to communicate with these people in the same way. They might be mechanics, IT guys, engineers or the truck drivers and you've got to pull them together into this elite performance crew. Most of the teams now have similar equipment, but [at Red Bull] we had this incredible ethos in this team where we'd go out and nail pit stops. And it was probably the single most rewarding aspect of my managerial role. We didn't just have a good "A" team, we had a pretty good "B" team as well.'

Ensuring that nothing was left to chance meant Wheatley could sleep better at night and when you look at how the Red Bull pit stop times deteriorated in the early part of 2025 after he left, you wonder if it was a coincidence. He, like Stevenson, has always believed in working as hard as possible so that in all areas of their responsibility, mistakes are minimised. But what is the best part of being a sporting director?

'Not screwing up,' says Wheatley. 'When you are responsible for so many things that can go wrong that can directly affect a race, a good job is when you can breathe and get to the end of it and go, *Oh, I can enjoy myself now.* It's hard to do that whilst it's happening.'

'Everything,' says Stevenson. 'It's a competitive sport where every weekend you've got another chance. We can't always win. Every team wants to win, but we can go out each weekend and get a better result than we did the weekend before. And then every year you get a clean sheet of paper and away you go again. I just love everything about it.'

Both men are paddock lifers who have witnessed the sport change dramatically. At Aston Martin, Stevenson is seeing the team that he has worked at for more than 600 races morph in front of his very eyes. As of 2024, it is estimated that owner Lawrence Stroll has invested upwards of $600 million across the Aston Martin automotive and Formula One team. He has turned Eddie Jordan's vision for a team with a small budget but grand ambitions into something enormous, and with the ultimate ambition to win championships. They have rebranded, built a state-of-the-art factory and wind tunnel on the original site next to Silverstone, and Stroll is putting together his dream team ahead of the 2026 regulation change. He has brought in Andy Cowell as the CEO, the man who was responsible for designing the dominant V6 turbo-hybrid engines that powered Mercedes to their most dominant era and Enrico Cardille from Ferrari, who will become their chief technical officer. Then of course, there is the biggest signing of them all, Adrian Newey, who brings his creative genius and a combined total of 25 constructor's and driver's titles as a designer and chief engineer to his name. Stevenson can rightly feel proud that he remains part of something so significant. For him and the team, perhaps the best is yet to come.

Wheatley has been granted the opportunity to step up another rung on the Formula One ladder. When Audi decided to enter the sport from 2026, they initially appointed Andreas Seidl as their team principal. But a couple of years before an Audi-branded car had turned a wheel in Formula One, he had left his position. Audi have brought in the former team principal of Ferrari, Mattia Binotto, as managing director of Audi Sport, and Wheatley will report into him as the team principal.

'I'm incredibly loyal; I worked for 16 years with Benetton/ Renault and 19 with Red Bull, and when you've been with a team for that long you build up a strength in depth. And whilst I'm busy every day, there are days when I'm here that I don't feel like I'm actively doing something, because everyone's doing such a good job around me. I'm at my happiest when I'm completely rolling my sleeves up, trying to make it better.'

After four back-to-back drivers' championships, starting with that night in Abu Dhabi in 2021, cracks were appearing in the Red Bull armour early in 2024. All empires crumble, as is true in all dominant eras in sport. With Newey having left for Aston Martin, chief designer Rob Marshall a few months previously for McLaren and all the early season off-track controversy surrounding Christian Horner, had Wheatley seen the writing on the wall?

'I couldn't see the trees out the window when I moved into this office at Red Bull because they were still saplings. Now they are all that I can see in the summer here. Do I spend another five, six, seven, eight or nine years here watching the leaves fall and grow again or do I start a fresh challenge? I left Renault in 2006, when Fernando was in a championship-winning year, to come to Red Bull and build something from the roots again. And I'm doing the same now. I'm prepared to go because of the opportunity that I've been offered.'

A good sporting director knows their team better than anyone. From running the day-to-day operations to helping write the rules, fighting their team's corner, motivating and managing both sides of the garage and looking after the needs of the team from race to race, they oversee it all. They are the epicentre of a Formula One team, and the really good ones are extremely hard to come by. Wheatley and Stevenson are two very fine examples.

CHAPTER 19

THE STEWARD

Facing the prospect of going up against sporting directors like Wheatley and Stevenson every weekend, who would want to be a referee? All of the aggro and none of the glory. On the plus side, you get the best view in the house, but you never get to enjoy the show because you're too busy working!

In Formula One, the job of refereeing falls upon the stewards. At each race there are typically four of them appointed to oversee the event, comprising a chairman, who is a senior steward, plus two others, nominated by the FIA, who hold the necessary FIA super-licence. One of these is normally a driver. The fourth steward is nominated by the race's own national sporting authority, because they have more experience of the intricacies of the track where the Grand Prix is taking place.

While the race director controls the sessions and the timetable and is responsible for the deployment of flags and the safety car, the stewards are responsible for monitoring on-track behaviour, investigating incidents, applying penalties, and ensuring that all the teams and drivers adhere to the regulations and standards set out by the FIA.

Garry Connelly's family is steeped in motorsport. His grandfather was Australia's first motorcycle champion back in the early 1900s. He then moved to England and designed the Douglas racing bike, finished second in the Isle of Man TT and won the French Grand Prix. Not a bad haul! Connelly himself got involved in rallying while at university and, in 1985, was asked by the Confederation of Australian Motor Sport to try to bring the world rally championship down under. The bid he put together was successful, and Connelly ran the race out of Western Australia for 20 years. At the same time, he became involved in the FIA rally commission, as well as stewarding in the world rally and touring car championships. In 2006, he was appointed Australia's representative on the World Motor Sport Council before Max Mosley, then president of the FIA, asked him to become a Formula One steward. In 2009, when Jean Todt replaced Mosley, he put in place the position of rotating chairman of the stewards, and Connelly has remained in place as one of them ever since. The 2025 season is to be his last performing the role: a role that he has never been paid for.

'After getting my degree, I taught high-school mathematics in a rough part of Sydney. I think it gave me the skills required to help me in stewarding. I find that stewarding is an educational process. It's all about explanation and communication. It requires a lot of soft skills. When I started teaching I was 21, and the students were 16 and 17. The kids were excellent, but the parents left a lot to be desired. I learnt how to present difficult news, how to listen and how to judge when people are not telling you the truth.'

Connelly commutes from Australia to all the events that he covers. Like most of us, he lands on a Wednesday to be able to get to the track first thing on a Thursday morning.

'The first thing that we do upon arrival is walk the track and do an inspection. We will take note of all the areas that have changed, new kerbs, run-off areas and places where track limits could be an issue. We will look at the pit entry and exit, the two safety-car lines and all the DRS points, and just familiarise ourselves with the layout. That usually takes a couple of hours, and then we go and sit down in the stewards' room and review the most recent race. We will go through other things that have happened in the season that are noteworthy, and then look at the same event from the previous year.'

The stewards are responsible for overseeing all the racing categories taking place at the event, so Formula Two and Formula Three are part of the same governance framework under the FIA, but will have separate race directors. It means that they are kept busy over the weekend.

'On Friday morning, we'll have the team managers/sporting directors meeting, take on board what they have to say, come back and discuss any issues with the race director. After the two practice sessions, you have the drivers' briefing, which usually finishes about 8.30 or 9pm and then, the next day, we are into the sessions like everybody else.'

Once the action starts on the track, the stewards don't stop. As chairman of the stewarding team, Connelly will be in constant dialogue with the race director and his second-in-command, Tim Malyon. Typically, when an incident arises, the race director will communicate directly over the intercom and then a link will be sent to the stewards for review. That is the only communication between them until they have taken a decision. When the incident is noted by the stewards, a message will pop up on the screen to tell the TV audience that it has been noted, and will update to 'No further action' or 'Stewards investigating the incident between car x and car y'. They usually allow a minute between noting an incident and deciding whether it warrants further investigation. If they decide to investigate, it is usually the chairman and the driver steward who will have the initial look at the incident, while the number two and the local steward keep their eyes on the live feed.

'We generally only see about two or three minutes of live action. The rest of the time we are heads down, looking at replays. They come thick and fast and it's pretty intense. Once we've got all the relevant information, what we typically do is ask the driver steward what their first impressions are and, interestingly, these impressions are usually right. We will then get consensus from the other stewards. If we all agree it's a breach, we will say, OK, what's the penalty, and look at our guidelines. These were brought in about seven or eight years ago, to try and get more consistency. We then decide whether we are going to mitigate or stick with those guidelines.

Upon unanimous agreement, I will get back onto the intercom to race control, inform them of our decision, it will pop up on page three of the timing screen and be put up to air.'

These days the stewards have all the equipment necessary to help them make the most informed decisions. As well as all the camera angles that are available and cut up on the world feed, they can view every onboard, as well as the FIA-installed closed-circuit TV cameras that amount to about 30 at every track, positioned on every corner, designed to pick up track-limit violations and driving incidents.

'The best angle for incidents is usually from the helicopter. On most of the other cameras, the cars are either coming towards you or, on the onboards, going away from you and they distort distance. When you are looking from the helicopter, it gives you the most accurate positioning of the cars on the track.'

On top of that, over each pit box there is a fish-eye camera, which is used to help with decisions about unsafe releases, or whether someone has served their penalty correctly.

The telemetry (real-time data) can also tell the stewards a great deal about what happened. This includes acceleration, speed, braking and steering angles on the individual cars. The data can be overlaid while flags are deployed on the track enabling them to see what a car was doing when it entered, for example, a yellow-flag zone. Also at their disposal is GPS, plus the ability to replay all the radio communications, which are now instantaneously transcribed to text.

'When the race is over, we still have to type up all the decisions. You need to set out all the reasons because these days we don't believe it's appropriate to simply say, "That's the decision and you are all stuck with it." We need to explain how and why we took it. If the decision we reach is different to a previous incident that looked similar, we need to explain why a different penalty has been applied. This is particularly relevant when applying driving-standard guidelines, as they are constantly updated. If there is a protest it can go on late into the night. If there is a decision that someone is not happy with, that can lead to a right to review, which can take place the following week. If there is an appeal to the International Court of Appeal then that can go on for three or four months!'

Of course, it is very rare that decisions go to the International Court of Appeal, but it shows how things can mushroom if decisions are disagreed with, and there's therefore huge pressure on the stewarding team to get it right in the first instance. That's why they have so many tools at their disposal.

If the stewards can't reach a unanimous decision about who is to blame and it is unclear from all the information that they have, then they are obliged to have a hearing after the race. This is where the drivers involved and their sporting directors go to see the stewards together.

'They can tell us so much about what was going on in the car, and I can honestly say there has never been a situation where I've felt disrespected or been abused. Sometimes it can get heated between the drivers, and we always shut that down quickly by getting them to talk to us, not each other. We will also revert to the sporting directors, just to diffuse things and calm things down a little bit. When it gets to the stage that we feel it's 70 or 80 per cent someone's fault then we will apportion blame, but if it's at 60/40 or 50/50 we will let it slide.'

It doesn't stop the criticism, though.

'It is incredibly difficult. As Derek Warwick [a regular driver steward] says, "You give me a consistent incident and I'll give you a consistent decision," because everything has nuance. Every decision these days gets vilified by probably 50 per cent of the fans, even if it's for a technical infringement that is black and white. I mean what's the expression, "You can't please all the people all the time"? Well, we can't please all the people, any of the time!'

The only answer for Connelly and all the FIA-accredited stewards is to keep working hard, as everyone does in Formula One, to constantly improve. In 2010, Connelly designed a three-day course for this very reason, but the FIA couldn't find the budget for it. That was until Laurent Mekies, now team principal of the Racing

Bulls, who was the head of safety at the FIA at the time, managed to change that and, since 2016, all 100 FIA stewards have received formal training. Their first big conference was in Geneva of that year, and since then they have met regularly.

'On top of the conference with stewards from all the different forms of motorsport, the Formula One stewards will always meet pre-season and then regularly throughout the year, and the Formula One chairs get together after every four events. After each event, we write up a very detailed report featuring all the major incidents and our explanations of why we took the decisions that we did. We have a section on recommendations to our fellow stewards for the future, and we recommend changes to the regulations and equipment or resources that we need to help us do our job. That gets circulated to all the Formula One stewards and the FIA all the way up to the president.'

One of the recent major topics for discussion has been driver standards, particularly in light of the incidents on track between Lando Norris and Max Verstappen in Austin and Mexico, at the business end of the 2024 season.

'The drivers are constantly asking for more guidance on what they can and can't do. I don't like grey areas because it puts us in an impossible position. The rules for racing are based on a set of rules that were designed in 1954 as an appendix to the International Sporting Code. If you look in the Formula One regulations, there is hardly anything on driver conduct.'

As far as the decision-making process goes, where driver behaviour is concerned, the first document that the stewards will look at is the code of driving conduct from the International Sporting Code, because it includes more than the sporting regulations do on the subject. Then they have the driving standard guidelines, but this is not an official document like the other two and therefore is not something that the stewards can hang decisions off by themselves.

'Our role is not adversarial. All we are here to do is to provide a level playing field between one driver and another, or one team and another. So actually it's not a battle between us and them, it is a battle between them and them.'

Connelly is an advocate of having an open-door policy with regards to transparency and extends regular invites to journalists to sit in the back of the stewards' room and watch how they operate.

'I wouldn't want people in the way whilst we are deliberating a protest, but I think it's important for the media to understand the processes that we go through to try to arrive at the right decision. Do we always get it right? It is hard with our rules to always know what is right. If you talk about tennis, it's easy, the ball is in or out. I liken Formula One to synchronised swimming or gymnastics, where you can give a four or five. It is not an exact science. It is with the technical regulations, but not always on track. Take that incident between Max and Lando at turn 12 in Austin in 2024.'

To refresh your memory, during the United States Grand Prix, an incident occurred between Lando Norris and Max Verstappen on lap 52 at turn 12. Norris, after several attempts, overtook Verstappen by running off the track and rejoining ahead of him after Max had braked exceptionally late on the inside. The stewards, including Connelly, reviewed the move and determined that Norris had gained an advantage by leaving the track, resulting in a five-second time penalty. This penalty demoted Norris from third to fourth and elevated Verstappen to the final podium position.

The decision sparked debate among drivers and teams regarding the consistency of track-limits enforcement. Some questioned why Verstappen was not penalised for his role in the incident. McLaren's team principal, Andrea Stella, described the penalty as 'inappropriate', expressing frustration over the stewards' interference in what he considered a 'beautiful piece of motorsport'.

'We agonised over that, and we still do. Could we have come up with a different set of circumstances? Yes. Could we have penalised both drivers? Yes, but we went with a mitigated penalty for Lando. Perhaps in hindsight, we should have given Max a five-second and

Lando a ten-second as they both left the track, but that would have put them both behind Oscar Piastri.'

So it goes back to the question of whether the current regulations and guidelines have been at odds with fair competition.

'I do believe that the driving standard guidelines need to be adjusted [they were at the end of 2024] because there were a couple of manoeuvres in Texas which we felt shouldn't have had to have been penalised but, if we wanted to be consistent with the driving standards, we had to give a penalty. Instead of giving a ten-second penalty, we only gave a five-second penalty, because we felt a really good overtaking move had been done.'

Either way, this question of consistency reared its head again towards the end of that year, and with it the discussion about having a permanent team of paid stewards, rather than the revolving door of unpaid volunteers.

'If you go back to the time when we had a permanent chairman of the stewards at every race, the teams hated that. There were constant accusations of favouritism. That would also happen if you had the same panel of stewards. They don't have the same referees at every match at the football World Cup. So to me it is all about getting the training right. As far as getting paid is concerned, it happens in other sports so I'm all for it!'

Connelly was the steward in direct communication with race director Michael Masi in Abu Dhabi 2021, and understands better than most people what happened that day as he was right at the heart of the decision-making processes during those eventful final laps.

'I'm happy to talk about it, even more so, because there was a recent case that had great relevance to what happened that night.'

Following a similar disputed use of the safety car in an International GT open event in 2023 that went to the FIA International Court of Appeal, it was declared wrong to nullify the final result because of a mistake by the race director.

'In sport, there is what you call a field of play decision, where once the eggs are broken, you can't unscramble them. In general play in football, outside of VAR and a goal decision, if there is an infringement and the referee says play on, you can't go back ten minutes later and redo it. So Michael Masi was under enormous pressure. He was, I believe, acting in good faith. It was not a conspiracy. We could hear what he was doing. Clearly, as the report said, he erred. On the day, as stewards, we got two protests from Mercedes.

'The first was that Max had overtaken Lewis under the safety car. That was relatively straightforward because our view of overtaking is that it is when you start behind and you end up and stay in front. Our penalty guidelines say that if you overtake under the safety car and give the place back, there is no penalty. So that protest was dismissed.

'The second was that the race director had made a mistake on the restart.'

Mercedes claimed that there were a couple of breaches of the sporting regulations. Article 48.12 states that 'any cars that have been lapped by the leader will be required to pass the cars on the lead lap and the safety car' and 'once the last lapped car has passed the leader the safety car will return to the pits at the end of the following lap'. Mercedes argued that if this had been adhered to, the race would have finished under the safety car and Lewis Hamilton would have won the race.

In response to this, Red Bull argued that 'any' did not mean 'all' and that article 48.13 stated that once the message 'safety car in this lap' had been given it was the signal that it would enter the pit lane at the end of that lap. They argued that 48.13 overrode 48.12 and that another article, 15.3, gave the race director 'over-riding authority over the use of the safety car'.

Michael Masi stated that the purpose of 48.12 was to get rid of the cars that would interfere with the racing between the leaders, and that's why he applied article 48.13 to the restart. He also made the point that he had the clear impression from the team principals and sporting directors that they wanted the race to finish under green not yellow flags.

It was a massive decision, and Connelly was right at the centre of it. The stewards considered all the arguments from both sides and determined that while 48.12 might not have been applied fully, 48.13 did indeed over-ride it as it was mandatory to withdraw the safety car at the end of that lap, and that Masi did have the authority to remove the safety car when he did. Therefore, that protest was also dismissed.

Mercedes had the right to appeal but chose not to because they felt there was no mechanism with which to overturn the result.

The FIA's report into Abu Dhabi 2021 cited Masi's human error and was an admission that a mistake had been made. He paid the price with his job. It was a night that will be talked about and debated forever, but Hamilton fans will never forgive those at the FIA who reached the decisions that they did, including the stewards who supported the race director's actions in light of the Mercedes protest.

Connelly and others like him know that they have to wear the criticism when things go wrong and at times it must seem like a thankless task, but he's insistent that, like the teams, the stewards and the new race director Rui Marques are constantly working as hard as they can to be the best that they can be. It can't change what happened in 2021 but perhaps it might stop it from happening again.

CHAPTER 20

THE TEAM PRINCIPALS

The sight of Toto Wolff throwing his earphones down in disgust that night at the back of the Mercedes garage and shouting 'No, Michael, no. This is not right!' after the restart, is etched into the memory of Formula One fans forever. It showed that acute pressure affects not only the FIA decision-makers but also the drivers, all the way up to the top of the organisation and everyone in between. There is so much at stake in the most watched motorsport series on the planet, and the role of the team principal is to absorb as much of that pressure as possible and take some of it away from team members themselves. That's leadership.

OTMAR SZAFNAUER

Otmar Szafnauer was born in Communist Romania in the 1960s to a Romanian mother and American father, living behind the Iron Curtain under the dictatorship of Nicolae Ceaușescu. After repeated applications to leave the country were denied, Szafnauer's father inexplicably won a car in a lottery that was linked to his bank account. It meant that his family became the proud owners of only the second car in their village, the other belonging to the local doctor. While young Otmar loved it, his father believed it to be a government bribe designed to keep him in the country and when he tried to escape in 1971, he was thrown into prison.

'He was lucky they didn't kill him. Thankfully whilst he was incarcerated President Nixon did a deal with Ceaușescu to allow all remaining US citizens in Romania to leave. We were one of 40 families and my dad asked me where we should go, anywhere in the world. I was seven, I loved cars, so I said, Detroit. We could have gone to Germany, but our story would have been a whole lot different.'

When Szafnauer arrived in the States, he didn't speak a word of English and the only German speaker he knew was a dinner lady with whom he would converse for ten minutes a day while waiting in the lunch queue! It forced him to learn the new language very quickly, and within six months he was fluent. During this time, Szafnauer longed for a go-kart and every birthday and Christmas he would beg his mother and father for one. Alas, to no avail. Over the years, unwanted soccer balls and basketballs piled up in the back yard, until he took matters into his own hands after leaving home. He went to study electrical engineering at university, before beginning work at the Ford Motor Company in 1986 and saving all the money he could in order to buy his first racing car.

He enrolled in the Jim Russell Racing School in Laguna Seca, completed their entire racing pyramid, got his racing licence and rewarded himself with a brand-new Reynard Formula 2000. He began racing locally, then regionally, and then the National Pro Series came to a circuit nearby, Elkhart Lake in Wisconsin. 'Nearby' in the States means anything less than an eight-hour drive, and so Szafnauer drove all night and arrived at the circuit at six in the morning. Three hours later and with no sleep, he was taking the treacherous long right-hand corner 'The Kink' flat-out in his F2000 at 140mph. You have to be able to drive to do that. Of the 55 open-wheel races that he competed in, Szafnauer won five. A modest return, but one that opened up a whole new world. At Ford, because he drove that Reynard, he met the man who built them, Adrian Reynard. They began to work together on a programme called the Indigo in 1995. After that project finished he, Jacques Villeneuve, Craig Pollock and British American Tobacco bought the old Tyrrell team and started their own Formula One outfit called British American Racing. Szafnauer was appointed operations director. He was just 34. It was the genesis of the team that is now Mercedes. Their first race was Australia 1999.

'In Australia I remember Villeneuve's rear wing fell off! The car was unreliable, but we would qualify really well. [Villeneuve didn't finish any of the first 11 races.] In those days you scored points down to sixth and we had a few seventh-place finishes, but we didn't score any points in our first year, largely because of reliability. But we got on top of the issues and, come the second year, we managed to finish fifth in the championship.'

Szafnauer left BAR to go to Jaguar in 2001 as chief operating officer. He stayed for 12 months and then moved to Honda, where he remained for eight years as part of the management team on the engine side. He left in 2009, the year it turned into Brawn.

'This is a little-known fact. When Ross Brawn [technical director of Ferrari] became available, there were three people at Honda that wanted to hire him: myself, Ron Meadows [team manager] and Robert Weatherstone [communications director]. We convinced the Japanese to go after Ross. The team principal at the time was Nick Fry, and Nick didn't want Ross, but the minute that he knew that he was coming, regardless of what he wanted, he claimed it was his idea! So, when Ross first came, Nick kind of convinced him that he should sideline me to Super Aguri. Nick saw me as some kind of threat. Then Honda decided to leave, and I was working with Richard Branson and Bernie Ecclestone to buy the team. On the other side was Ross and Nick. I mean, they weren't buying the team, they were being given the team, plus money to run it for a year. And Richard wanted a little bit more, about 30 million more, than Ross and Nick, and so Honda gave it to them and that's when I left.'

That year, Szafnauer created the Formula One timing app that many people subscribe to on their mobile devices, before joining Force India as chief operating officer as 2009 drew to a close. The team, run by Indian tycoon Vijay Mallya, were in their second year in Formula One and were the latest iteration of the constructor that had started life as Jordan, would later become Midland and then Spyker. When he joined, they were dead last. Szafnauer was there for 12 years and by the time he left they had finished fourth for three years on the trot, and were constantly at the head of the middle of the pack. While Mallya was the team principal on paper, he was only at the factory for four or five days a year. It was Szafnauer who was his right-hand man and who drove the team forward on a day-to-day basis.

'I said to Vijay, when he hired me, "You need to build your commercial department so that you don't have to put all the money in yourself. You should be getting between $30 and $50 million in sponsorship and, even if you get the lower end of that, it means you put in $25 million instead of $55 million. It's more palatable for you!" He said to me, "You worry about the performance, let me worry about the money. If, after a while, we are still not getting out of Q1, then I'm not going to need you." So it was pretty clear to me that I needed to worry about the performance. But not only did I worry about the performance, I also started the commercial department because I knew that, even if you are a billionaire, if you are putting in $50 million a year, in ten years, that is half a billion, and no one likes to do that!'

Within a month and a half of arriving at Force India, the then technical director James Key had handed in his resignation and moved to Sauber. Szafnauer replaced him with Andy Green, who he had worked with at BAR. Between them they started growing the spine of the team that began to take them in the right direction. There were 280 people working at their Silverstone HQ when he arrived, and 408 by the time it became Racing Point in 2018. Szafnauer knew he had to take some key strategic decisions and prioritise at this point.

'First and foremost, we knew that we could never stop the learning, and by that I mean always keep the wind tunnel going. And when I arrived, we simply didn't have the money to buy the resin to create the wind-tunnel models. So we righted that, and then we moved from our 50 per cent tunnel [using a car model 50 per cent of actual size] at Brackley to our 60 per cent model at Toyota in Cologne, which made our Reynolds numbers better.'

In Formula One wind-tunnel testing, achieving the correct Reynolds number is crucial to simulate real world conditions. It's the critical parameter in fluid dynamics and represents the ratio of the inertial forces to the viscous forces in fluid flow. It works better with a larger model because it is closer to the real-world conditions experienced by the full-sized car.

'Then I started hiring people in areas where we were lacking in skills. When Bridgestone stopped supplying Formula One in 2010, I hired all their best engineers so that we weren't guessing on tyres. We bolstered the vehicle science department and also started hiring more aerodynamicists and formed our Aero Performance Group. We hired Tom McCullough from Sauber and one of the top guys from Red Bull and, to be fair to Vijay, he always wanted the best drivers he could afford and attract. Guys like Sergio Pérez, Nico Hülkenberg, Adrian Sutil. I hired Esteban Ocon, when Toto Wolff was pushing me really hard to sign Pascal Wehrlein. It's just simple stuff. Understand the racing car, understand the areas of performance that can be improved, hire the best drivers, and we also had a massive debate about which powertrain to use. So, when the regulations changed in 2014, Andy Green and I wanted to stay with Mercedes and some of the others wanted Ferrari. We won.'

Again, when you are a midfield team, it is about being nimble in order to keep up with the big boys, and Szafnauer and Force India quite quickly forged a reputation for being a team of racers that punched above their weight.

'We were always fast followers. So if we saw a bit of technology that looked like it made the car go faster, we were always the next team to get it. The double diffuser. Yeah, we didn't think of it, but we were the second team to have it. The F-duct, when McLaren came up with that in 2010, we were probably the second team to deploy it. That was our way, and lo and behold it got results.'

So what does Szafnauer think makes a good team principal?

'You have to have a deep understanding of the sport and you have to sometimes be the arbiter of decisions at a senior level where, internally, some say go left and others say go right. But most importantly there are two things that a team principal needs to do. One is to motivate the staff that you have, to work together and do the best that you can do for on-track performance, and two, attract the right people. The way you attract the right people is to make the team the best place to work in Formula One, and you do that through creating an atmosphere of psychological safety where everybody loves their job, they like contributing and they get patted on the back when they do well and don't get their heads torn off when they make a mistake.'

I've witnessed, first hand, Szafnauer, the person. We've spent a fair amount of time away from the circuit together and he is equally at home sharing a bucket of his beloved Kentucky Fried Chicken with a cleaner as he would be with the president of the FIA, because he sees the person rather than the job title. In the dog-eat-dog world of the paddock that's a rare skill in senior management. From what I've witnessed, it's rare in any sort of business among the ambitious, most of whom spend their time managing up rather than down.

It was clear to see that the culture that Szafnauer created at Force India made it a good place to work and the results got better and better. In the time he was there, the trajectory was upwards and that was reflected in their finishing positions in the constructors' championship: tenth, ninth, seventh, sixth, seventh, sixth, sixth, fifth, fourth, fourth, fourth. But during this time Vijay Mallya, their owner, was facing increasing pressure back in India over allegations of financial fraud and, by July 2018, with debts reportedly exceeding £200 million, the team was forced into administration.

It was then that Szafnauer did an extraordinary thing: he personally paid the salaries of all the employees while working with the eventual buyer, Lawrence Stroll, an act of incredible generosity that he didn't mention at the time.

While we could get into his departure from Aston Martin and brief time at struggling Alpine, that would be to miss the point on the bulk of his Formula One career and his leadership. Szafnauer was someone who led a team of real racers and excelled in the motivational style of his job, but that isn't all a team principal has to do on a day-to-day basis.

'You had to be on top of all the political wranglings. There was always something afoot. Mercedes or Red Bull are always winning, how do we change the regulations to stop them? You had to be in on all that stuff to affect it. It was funny, in the team principal meetings, those teams that had a common interest or goal, three or four of you, would get together and say, well, that Haas is just a replica of the Ferrari, for example. That's wrong. And all those that were affected by it would get together and say, we've got to go to the FIA. So, you'd find yourself having different friendship groups amongst the other team principals, depending on the subject matter! And you could force an outcome by lobbying for enough votes at the Formula One commission. You just had to get the will of the collective.'

There is no hard and fast rule about what makes a good team principal, but certainly the new crop coming through like James Vowles (Williams), Ayao Komatsu (Haas) and Laurent Mekies (RBs) are all from engineering backgrounds. It remains to be seen whether they have the full set of skills to remain in place for a long period of time, but they have all had impressive starts. They are all blooding themselves in the midfield, where they have the space to earn their stripes. Szafnauer, though, with his experience at Force India and then Alpine, has witnessed the difference between managing a works team and an independent.

'The independents are much more nimble, because they are smaller. But that means you can't do everything a big team does, and people often have to do more than one job. A large works team obviously has more resource at its disposal. If it has no interference from the parent company, like Mercedes, then it can do well and win. If the parent company thinks it knows better than the people that have been racing their whole lives, then they will never, ever win. And that's what happened at Enstone and my time with Alpine.'

Don't be surprised to see Szafnauer back in Formula One in the future. He has the experience and, during his time at Force India, took the fight to the big guns and landed some heavy blows. For the moment he's watching from the outside and looking for a way back in. Potentially by starting his own team.

GUENTHER STEINER

Guenther Steiner grew up in South Tyrol, in the northern mountains of Italy, an area famed for its skiing and ice hockey. The son of a butcher, as a child he worked in the family shop. His introduction to motorsport was a hill climb that took place about 40 minutes from his home. His family weren't into racing, but this was the era of Niki Lauda, whose success served as an inspiration to young Steiner, who lived so close to Austria. Despite being academic and already a card-carrying chatterbox, from a young age he only had one desire, and that was to work in motorsport. So he took an apprenticeship as a mechanic, prior to doing his national service and, upon returning, saw an advert in a magazine looking for rally mechanics in Belgium. That's where it all started. He spent the following decade working his way up to director of engineering with the Ford World Rally Team with Colin McRae and Carlos Sainz. He helped them secure consecutive runners–up finishes in 2000 and 2001, before an opportunity presented itself in Formula One with Ford's official Formula One works team, Jaguar Racing. It was Niki Lauda who headhunted him.

'His secretary called me up and said, "Can you come to dinner in Vienna? Mr Lauda would like to speak to you. You can go for dinner, get a schnitzel, Mr Lauda will be there for 20 minutes and then you can say goodbye!" So I went and got my schnitzel and we were talking for two hours. I called my wife afterwards and she asked how the dinner was. I had a good time. I mean it was nice for me to meet Niki, as I had never met him before. Anyway, the next morning, he calls me up at eight and says, "Thank you for coming last night, you are going to come and work for me!" And I said, "Yeah, Mr Lauda, but what am I going to do?" He said, "I will tell you later," and put the phone down.'

Steiner worked as managing director at Jaguar until Lauda left in 2003. Steiner was asked to stay, but his allegiance was to Niki and so he too departed. He took a year's gardening leave and went to DTM (the German touring car championship) in 2004. In 2005, the Austrian billionaire Dietrich Mateschitz purchased Jaguar and Red Bull was born. Having known Steiner for a few years, Mateschitz asked him to come and guide the team and their young team principal, Christian Horner. As technical operations director, together they helped the team to seventh place in the championship in their first year but when Mateschitz poached Adrian Newey from McLaren, he offered Steiner the opportunity to establish a NASCAR team in the United States, and Steiner accepted. He stayed with the team for a couple of years until a disagreement with Red Bull advisor Helmut Marko precipitated his exit. Steiner and his wife decided to remain in the States, where he set up a composites company and, despite offers from Europe, waited for his next opportunity.

Stewart-Haas racing is an American professional stock car racing team, based near Charlotte, North Carolina, that started life in 2002. In 2009, there was a failed attempt by their former technical director Ken Anderson and journalist and former team manager of Williams Peter Windsor, to start the US Formula One team. Despite being granted an entry into the 2010 world championship, they never made it to the grid, but Steiner's interest had been piqued by the attempt.

'I thought the idea of opening a US Formula One team was a pretty good one. I wrote up a business plan and went around to shop for investors. One of my first ports of call was Gene Haas. It took me two years to convince him, but eventually he said, let's do this. Starting a Formula One team from scratch, though, when a lot of people have failed, was not easy but back then, the sport was so much simpler. These days there is so much more money involved. We bought in for $350,000. I did not even use a lawyer to get the licence, I did it all myself. I mean try and fookin' do that now.'

It shows you how fast things have moved on. It is estimated that General Motors and TWG Global will pay $450 million to enter Formula One as Cadillac in 2026. This fee is to compensate the existing teams for their loss of prize money, effectively an anti-dilution fee.

'In the beginning nobody knew you and no one was interested in your team, because so many others were failing. The biggest challenge was to get the team together, focus on building it up, fighting off the naysayers and establishing ourselves. It took a couple of years, but finishing fifth in our third year was quite an achievement. But then we had eyeballs on us asking how we had done it. The critics and the people that said we were cheating and doing something with Ferrari [their engine supplier], meant we had to come out and defend ourselves. Everything was starting to get bigger, and then Covid struck and we had two years of survival. Gene wanted to close the team down. I just had to find money to survive. And then came the post-Netflix years. All of a sudden everything was going crazy and everyone now recognises me. It was like a whirlwind. It is utterly amazing how it has changed.'

Ten years ago, as Steiner recalls, the disparity between the budgets of the teams was astronomical. It was the days before the cost cap, and the only way for Haas to be competitive was to get creative.

They took an unprecedented approach to cost efficiency and outsourcing, entering a technical partnership with Ferrari that allowed them to buy their non-listed parts (i.e. parts that teams were allowed to buy from third parties under the regulations at the time). This included the power unit, gearbox and suspension. Also, rather than building their own chassis in-house, they outsourced to Dallara, a well-known racing car manufacturer. It reduced the need for extensive infrastructure and engineering staff, thereby embracing the 'customer' team model like never before. They still designed the bits of the car that were listed, and therefore required to be designed independently, but by not investing heavily in facilities or a large workforce, they were able to field a competitive car with a fraction of the budget of the top teams.

There were many, including the purists, who argued that Haas had blurred the boundaries between a customer and a constructor, with some calling them a Ferrari 'B' team.

'In the beginning our business model worked pretty well. Because it was new, we had the advantage of surprising the others. We didn't do anything illegal, we just used the regulations. But after we finished fifth in 2018, the rules began to be bent against our model. The loopholes got closed down more and more. For example, in the beginning we could buy the brake ducts, which have a big effect on the aerodynamic capabilities of the cars, but then they outlawed that and so we had to design more and more of the car and ramp up our engineering capabilities. Also, when the budget cap came in, in 2021, if you bought parts from another team it would be an unfair advantage, because you hadn't spent money on tooling and engineering. So, it made it very difficult and Gene never wanted to manufacture our own parts. He wanted to stick to our original business model.'

And therein lies the challenge for a team principal of a smaller team scrapping for minor points. You are still the leader, but you must wear many hats.

'You need to be a good negotiator. You need to have a good understanding of the technology, or have someone that you really trust that does. You also need to be a salesman. Sponsorship in the end is down to you. You need to be a politician, in order to work things in your favour when you are in discussion with the other nine team principals or with Formula One and the FIA. You have to be a leader that is believed in, and give your team confidence that you do what you say and that you are not just a mouthpiece.'

So how did Guenther Steiner get the best out of his people?

Jock Clear (left) celebrates with Hamilton and members of the Mercedes team after the driver's 2014 victory in Austin, Texas.

Gianpiero Lambiase poses with Verstappen, marking his 2024 driver's championship win. It was his fourth consecutive title.

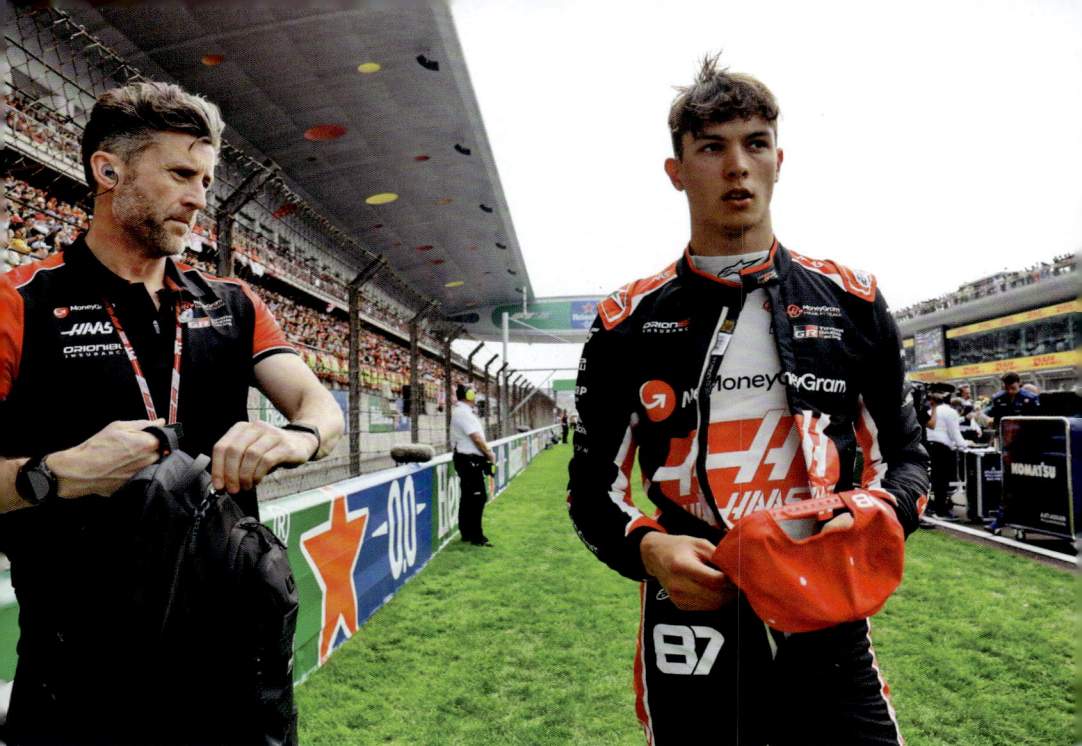

Martin Poole with HAAS driver Oliver Bearman on race day at the Chinese Grand Prix.

Head of race strategy, Bernie Collins, on the Aston Martin pit wall in 2022.

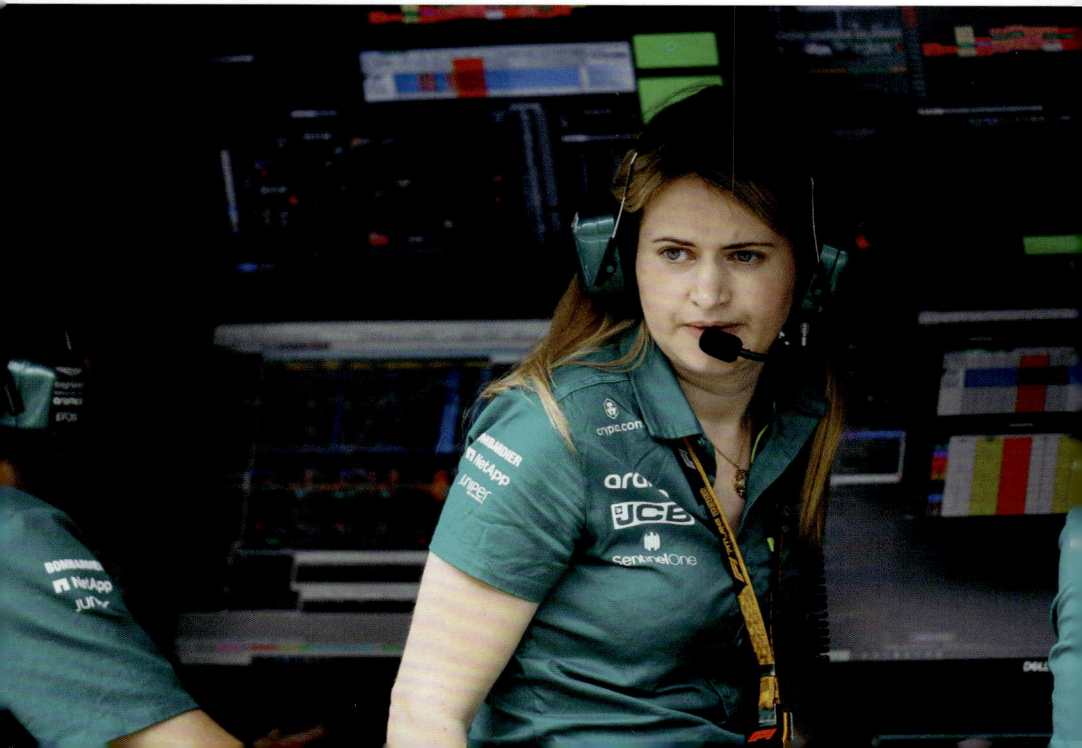

A moment between Hamilton and Verstappen in the aftermath of the 2021 race in Abu Dhabi. It was a cruel defeat for Mercedes, but Hamilton went straight over to congratulate the new world champion.

Steward Gary Connelly and Bernie Ecclestone on the grid at the Belgian Grand Prix in 2012.

James Vowles on the Mercedes pit wall ahead of the Saudi Arabia Grand Prix.

Gwen Lagrue with Kimi Antonelli, one of the many talents he has recruited to Mercedes's young driver development programme.

George Russell on the track at Monaco. Having learned a thing or two from Hamilton during their time together at Mercedes, in 2025 he is the team's lead driver.

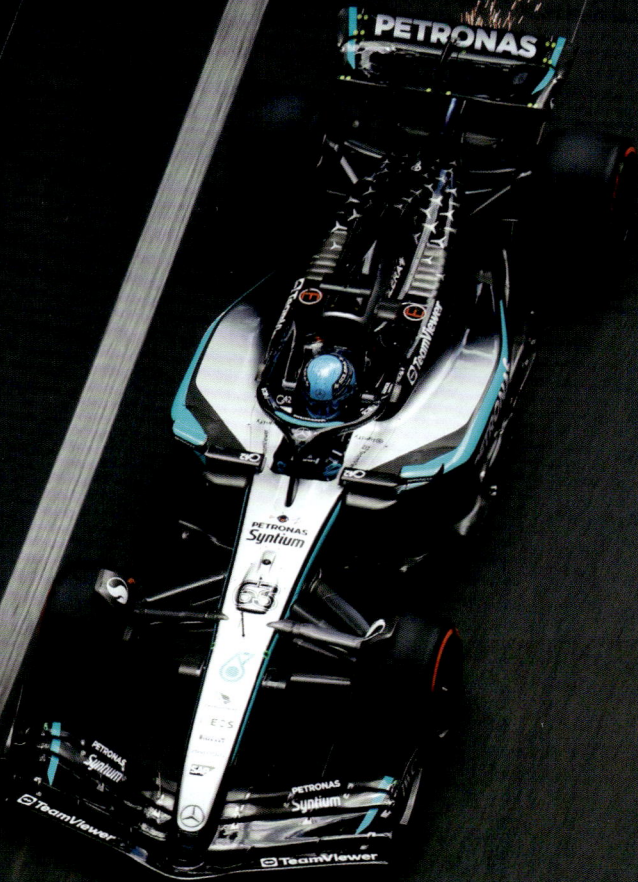

F1's head of broadcast and media, Dean Locke, stands inside the event technical centre at the Las Vegas Grand Prix.

In the commentary box, Martin Brundle and David Croft have a built up a huge amount of trust and an innate understanding after many years of working together.

Paddy Lowe and Damon Hill pose in front of Zero Petroleum's innovative fossil-free fuels. The fuels are manufactured using just carbon dioxide taken from the air and renewable hydrogen made from water.

Andy Cowell on stage during the F1 75 launch event at the O2, with Aston Martin drivers Lance Stroll and Fernando Alonso.

Spraying champagne on the podium at the Abu Dhabi Grand Prix, Zac Brown celebrates winning the 2024 constructors' championship.

'By always telling them what is achievable. For example, if I told them that we wanted to win the world championship in two years' time, then everybody would have laughed at me. You need to give realistic goals, and explain to them how you are going to do it. And that is the most challenging part of the job, keeping the people behind you. So, some years, like 2020 in Covid, it was just a survival year. When we finished fifth in 2018, it was, *How do we replicate that?* and so you get more into the technological side of the job, and then, in 2021, it was going out and again finding money to keep the company going, by selling the sponsorship and building the team back up. And that's the thing with being a team principal, the challenges change and you need to adapt whilst still being seen to be improving ever year. It's really hard.'

Steiner left Haas at the start of 2024. He was undoubtedly a great fit for a start-up team a decade ago and steered the team well but, as I mentioned earlier, in that time the sport has moved on and is swaying towards ever more technical leaders. He paid the price for finishing last in the standings the previous year but he was, undoubtedly, the star of *Drive to Survive*. He's always possessed a great sense of humour, and I've always found him a pleasure to interview because he doesn't take himself too seriously. That's a rare trait in a team principal and one that has allowed him to move seamlessly into television. He might well stay there, as it's a lot less stressful.

JAMES VOWLES

James Vowles has quickly become something of a cult figure in Formula One. When Jack Whitehall gave most of the paddock a roasting at the F1 75 launch event at the O2 at the start of the 2025 season, it was Vowles, among others, who was singled out by Whitehall, but the Williams team principal took it in good faith. He was also more than comfortable introducing his team in front of the 20,000 fans who had packed out the arena. He is not a man short of confidence and is revelling in his leadership role at the historic marque.

When he moved from his job as chief strategist at Mercedes, it was a massive step up but, in the quarter of a century that he has been involved in the sport, he has been able to learn from some of the best. He started life at British American Racing before it morphed into Honda, Brawn and then the Mercedes team with which he became a senior figure.

'I wouldn't just put it down to Toto, it was also Ross Brawn and David Richards. They are all different. When Dave did a speech I wanted to follow him. He was a brilliant public speaker. Dave was not me, though. Dave's way was telling you what you wanted to hear, so that you followed. I'm different. I will be transparent, which is more of a Toto trait. That doesn't mean he always tells you everything. He tells you what he believes at the time, but that might change a week later. And then Ross was different. Ross was about how do you get the right people in the right room talking. That was his forte. In terms of how do you create a structure that over time is successful, in not just one angle but all angles, and how to use honesty and transparency in order to gain respect from your peers? Again, that's Toto.'

It is clear, as one of the newest team principals on the grid, that Vowles has drawn inspiration from all three men and assimilated some of their leadership characteristics. He has witnessed what it takes to win multiple championships up close. That is something that not many in the paddock have had a chance to do, and it is obvious that most of his learnings will therefore be taken from his time at Mercedes and their sustained period of success.

'Even today I talk weekly to Toto. I was fortunate, because as Toto had more and more responsibilities applied to him, I had more and more responsibilities afforded to me. Initially young drivers, then young drivers and sim drivers, and then race drivers as well. Then I was responsible for more series like Formula E and GT3, and other elements within the company. I appreciated the fact that he trusted me with these and used me as a sparring partner. We had sensible discussions as two human beings rather than a leader with a subordinate. We would talk things through. I'd have my opinion and he his and we would walk out the room agreed on whatever the direction ended up being. And that is one of Toto's strongest traits and why I learnt the most from him.'

The challenge for Vowles is that he needs to prove himself as quickly as possible, and taking a struggling team forward is no easy task.

'Williams isn't Mercedes. We don't have the facilities or the depth that we need in our organisation, just yet. In this first year [2024], it is not time to empower people. I've got to be in the depths of everything, trying to figure out what is going on and helping individuals perform at their best, because that is the background to what Williams was. That is not what I want it to be in the future, but that is what it needs today. At Mercedes, you had a thousand leaders and you would point them roughly in the right way and you would have to slow them down and hold them back a little bit. At Williams that is not the case. Yet.'

So how would he summarise the job that he now finds himself doing?

'It's very simple. Firstly, you've got to have the right drivers, and we have that now with Alex Albon and Carlos Sainz. You have to have the right power unit, and I'm confident with Mercedes that we have that, and then you have to have the right people in your organisation leading the team. We are starting to get there with that as well.'

As far as Vowles is concerned, they are the three very simple basics of being a team principal. The difference now, he says, is that he has to fulfil several roles, as he takes the learnings from his time working in a winning team and applies them to dragging Williams in the right direction. That involves being a bit of a technical director, and understanding the finance and the cost cap, on top of his role as leader. His first year was spent gaining as much knowledge as he could about the workings of the team and, now in his third full year, it's about applying the structural changes that he wants to implement.

'I need to understand the strengths and weaknesses and where we needed to prioritise investment. I mean investment in both financial terms and time. What you see on TV isn't really Formula One. The build of the car is what really stretches an organisation, and what you can't do is change that organisation when you are doing the build. If you do you will catastrophically fail. So, after the first year of my time here, we made a lot of changes in March and April. That is not the end of the journey, it is just creating the foundations for what we need in the future.'

Under Vowles's leadership the team has recruited nearly 250 new staff members, including Pat Fry as chief technical officer, Matt Harman as joint design director and Angelos Tsiaparas as chief engineer. Signings of this calibre are beginning to make a difference to the team, and they started the 2025 season strongly.

Some of the first structural changes that Vowles made were to the operations department (i.e. how they fundamentally produced the car) and the design office. Vowles changed how both of these departments were led and how things were communicated. He then set about identifying the individuals he needed to work within that new framework.

'In the design office, it is a multi-year journey to get the right individuals into the right positions. I could fill it in six months, but that is not the solution. The solution is to build the right long-term structure, which is what I am constantly talking about externally and also to our investors. We don't want to rush it.'

They don't call Formula One the Piranha Club for nothing. Vowles is now dining at the top table and up against nine other extremely determined individuals, all trying to pull their teams towards the same goal. So how does a young team principal deal with the politics?

'I'm OK with it, as it was one of the things I was exposed to with Toto. I know Zak and Fred [Vasseur, team principal of Ferrari] extremely well from before. In fact, I have bonds with most of them, stemming from my time looking after the Mercedes young driver programme, where we had many good young drivers and not all of them could stay with Mercedes, which meant going out and forging relationships with the other team principals. My way of working is to be open and honest and that helps build strong relationships with people up and down the pit lane. And that includes Christian Horner, by the way. Christian and I can have a sensible conversation. There is no politics, it is just business. Zak and Fred are kind of the same people. They are both about getting to the point and not playing games around it. And then there are some trickier characters, and with them you just have to play a slightly different game.'

He doesn't mention names.

As we've seen earlier, one of the key drivers of growth within a Formula One team is being able to attract sponsors. At the start of 2025, Williams announced the biggest sponsorship deal in their 48-year history. The multi-year agreement with Atlassian marked them as the official title partner, official technology partner and software partner to the team. The numbers haven't been disclosed, but it was a big moment for Vowles and a sign that the commercial flywheel was beginning to spin faster at Williams.

'Our USP is quite straightforward. It has never been about 2024 or 2025 for us. I will keep saying this until I am blue in the face. There has been so much to do here, and it will not be fixed in a day. I can produce more performance in the short term, but that is not of interest to us. Last year the repair bill was enormous, but the letters that I got from sponsors all said they were here for the journey. They know it is not about today, but the future projects. We have laid out to them where we are investing and why. You can join other teams and have exposure on the grid, but you will be small fish in a big pond. We have an incredible heritage, beyond most of the others, and we are on an amazing journey that excites them. We are not where we want to be, but we are building out and can see the pathway forward. When I joined, commercially, we were very, very poor, but that is not the case now.'

As you can imagine for a young engineer who has now found his way into his dream job, Vowles lives and breathes it every day. It is the only way to be in one of the most highly pressurised jobs in the paddock.

'What I love the most is that every day is different, and you can understand why it links to strategy now. Everything I do, every decision I make has a tangible effect on this workforce. It's not that you are fine-tuning small elements, you are making huge structural changes and we are beginning to see the outcomes.'

But how long will it take to get this storied team back to the front of the grid?

'Five years, or maybe more than that, and that is simply because there is infrastructure there that is still 24–36 months away. There are people missing, which also takes between 12–24 months because they are locked into contracts. And beyond that, we need time to learn. We will catch up with similar facilities to Red Bull and Mercedes, eventually, but they have already been winning for years. We have to challenge ourselves to do things differently, and that carries an enormous amount of risk. It may fail, but it may produce a better result in the end. And that is why it will take more time than many would like.'

Time is not something that is often afforded to struggling team leaders, so what makes Vowles think the board of Dorilton Capital (Williams's owners) will grant him that luxury?

'Will I be afforded the time? Yes, because when I first joined I laid out the plan and I have a very good board. I sit in the office with them and show them where we are today. You can literally walk them to a specific department, and show them what is going on and tell them why it is going to take 36 months to fix. They have been here long enough to see where the problems are themselves. Even 2026 will only be the start of the turnaround. There is not a person here that is not on board and on the journey. If I wasn't comfortable that I had the time, I would go for a short-term fix with people who are average. It would look OK for a period of time, and then it wouldn't move forward. That's what you do when you are risk averse, you take decisions that are easy. I am doing things that I hope are the opposite of that.'

CHAPTER 21

THE DRIVER DEVELOPMENT ADVISOR

Taking the time to get things right is essential in all sports. When Neymar was six, he was hauled off the streets of Sao Vicente in Brazil by coaches who saw his preternatural footballing ability and enrolled him in Santos FC's youth academy by the age of 11.

Lionel Messi was also first spotted at the age of six, when he joined his local club, Newell's Old Boys, in Rosario, Argentina. There he became the standout player, scoring hundreds of goals before he got picked up by Barcelona when he was 13.

In football, they have always started them young, and kicking a ball is one of the first things every kid does. Dutch club Ajax's pioneering football academy, where they revolutionised youth development and produced players such as Johann Cruyff, dates back to the early twentieth century. In the UK, the Lilleshall Hall Elite Training Centre was officially opened in 1950 by the FA in order to develop young players and subsequently, all of the current 92 clubs in the English Football League have some form of youth academy.

It's different in motorsport. Proper organised mini karting starts at the age of eight, and Red Bull were the first to establish a young driver programme back in 2001. They did so four years before purchasing the Jaguar Formula One team, and entered the sport believing in the importance of building from the grass roots up. It provided a constant pipeline of talent that understood the culture of their team. The programme has been hugely successful, and has produced drivers such as Daniel Ricciardo, Carlos Sainz, Sebastian Vettel and Max Verstappen. Helmut Marko is still in charge, and has been from the start, but it is known to be an unforgiving environment where you are either up to the task or you are not, and, in recent times, they have hit a snag in that those coming through aren't matching up to the phenomenal talent of Verstappen.

Mercedes set up their equivalent young driver programme back in 2009, the year before they re-entered the sport, and since 2015 it has been run by Frenchman Gwen Lagrue. He's responsible for scouting, developing and nurturing talent, much as Marko has been, and guiding them as far as they can up the motorsport pyramid, hopefully all the way to Formula One.

It was after 13 years in karts and rally that Lagrue realised his talent wasn't going to propel him any further. He went back to school and gained a master's in law, economics and sports management, then took a job in a car dealership. But in 2005, he gambled on a year's sabbatical managing a young French driver by the name of Guillaume Moreau, who was competing in the Formula Three Euro-series against Lewis Hamilton, Adrian Sutil, Paul di Resta and Sebastian Vettel.

'It was an important year for me because I met Fred Vasseur, Toto Wolff and Éric Boullier, who were themselves supporting a few young drivers and I began to build my network. But at that stage none of these guys were involved in Formula One.'

That was until 2009, when Genii Capital bought the Renault Formula One team and inserted Boullier as team principal. He quickly brought his friend Lagrue in to run their young driver programme.

'I told him we needed to rethink and restart the programme from karts, because that was the base, the root of our sport, and that's where I think we needed to start to create the relationships with the drivers.'

Lagrue spent most of his first couple of years with Renault at kart tracks around Europe on lookout trucks, trying to spot the next

Lewis Hamilton or Ayrton Senna. It didn't take him long, because around 2010 and 2011, the crop of karting talent he was watching every weekend was a golden generation.

'Max Verstappen, Charles Leclerc, Esteban Ocon, Pierre Gasly, George Russell and Alex Albon. They were all there racing each other. I think anyone who was able to sign one of those guys was going to have success, so I was lucky to have this generation come through WSK European and world championships together. Having five, six or seven guys all competing at the same time in karting, and all reaching Formula One, is unique in the sport's history.'

Lagrue picked up Ocon, and also decided to support Albon after Marko dropped him from the Red Bull junior programme when he started in single seaters. When he was eventually offered the Mercedes job by Wolff in 2015, his first move was to snap up Russell, who he had tried to sign way back in karting. Russell at that stage was looking at moving to DTM with BMW, and Lagrue snared him in the nick of time and kept young George's dream of a Formula One seat alive.

So what does Lagrue look for in his young drivers?

'I am most interested in the personalities and the human aspect of the driver. The way they interact with the team, with other people, the way they behave and the way that they approach a weekend and respond to difficult moments, like a technical issue or a crash. It takes months and months of investigation to get to know the driver, to get to know their family and to understand their back story. Only then will I decide whether I will sign them.'

When Lagrue looks at drivers, they will almost always be in the top 10 or 15 of the highest category in their age group, the best that are available at international level. He keeps an eye on the mini-series from the ages of between 8 and 11, and will monitor them over that time period, but prefers to sign youngsters after they have made the transition to the junior kart series, between the ages of 11 and 13. He signed Kimi Antonelli to his programme, just as he made this leap.

'When you jump into a junior go-kart, the power of the kart and the level of grip increases dramatically. Physically, it is therefore quite demanding for a mini when he moves up to this level.

'You will discover much more about them when they do this, than when they are winning everything in the minis. It's the same when they make the step up at 15 to single seaters. Again, they have to completely change their mindset and accept that they will have to learn all over again. It can take a few months to make them understand that they are not the champion that they were in go-karts, and that they need to work and learn and to explore new things again. That is where, most of the time, we get to see who they really are.'

Lagrue has a good network of scouts on his books, people like Mike Wilson, a karting legend who won six world championships in the 1980s and became the most successful driver in the history of karting; his nickname, 'Mike the Kart', says it all really. And Dino Chiesa, who was manager of the Mercedes-Benz McLaren karting team that included Hamilton and Rosberg, and also his Chiesa Corse team, which included Verstappen. A reasonable couple of names to help identify future world champions, you would think. He has a few other sets of eyes on the ground at any one time but will still attend the big races himself. It is a crucial part of his job.

'It's funny, all the other Formula One teams are involved in karting, but I have never seen anyone else at a race. Maybe we are not doing the same events, but I don't think they are as involved as we are. My team have developed our own approach, that is based on the human side. So we give the drivers time to learn, we accept that they may have a difficult season and we also understand that in your early teens life can be difficult and so the support that we provide is different and quite unique in our industry.'

In 2024 there were seven drivers in the Mercedes young driver programme: 13-year-olds James Anagnostiadis and Kenzo Craigie, who finished first and second in the OK Junior World Karting Championships; Luna Fluxa Cross, who made the transition to the senior karting category, the young Spaniard winning the title and becoming the first female winner of an FIA international championship since Susy Raganelli won the World Karting championship in 1966; Yuanpu Cui and Alex Powell, who were competing in their first season of single seaters in assorted Formula Four championships, with Powell taking the rookie championship in the Italian Formula Four and Euro Formula Four championship; Doriane Pin, who finished second in Formula One academy; and Andrea Kimi Antonelli, who made the step up to Formula Two and achieved his dream of reaching Formula One with the senior team for the 2025 season.

Five men and two women all striving to get to the promised land and follow in Antonelli's footsteps. Lagrue and Mercedes are providing a tailor-made package of support for each of them. If Lagrue believes they have the talent, then that support could mean full financial backing, as Mercedes have provided for George Russell, Alex Albon, Esteban Ocon and Antonelli.

'When we sign a driver, for the kid it is his life's dream, so I feel a massive responsibility to do my absolute best to help and support them every day. I wouldn't be able to look at myself if I hadn't done everything in our power to make it work, but we are working with humans and therefore sometimes it will work and sometimes it won't, but we will exhaust every possibility and all options with our young drivers. We don't just ditch them.'

Another of Lagrue's tasks is to match his drivers with the teams that he feels will best suit their personality traits and, once they are into the season and focused on maximising their potential, the support package includes doctors, performance coaches, nutritionists and sports psychologists.

'Once I know that they are with the right team, it allows me to focus on the individual. Sometimes, though, it can be an anomalous season, like we had with Kimi at Prema in 2024. It was an awful year, a new car and the team didn't adapt well to it. But it was a strange season in Formula Two, where all the top teams struggled to perform, and it had an impact on the seasons of Ollie Bearman and

Kimi [two drivers with Formula One contracts for 2025]. But that is very unusual. Maybe once every 10 or 15 years you can observe these difficulties where there is a new car, but most of the time we know that we are working with the best drivers and we will place the best drivers in the best teams in the junior categories.'

The 2025 season is the first since Lagrue's arrival that he has had two of his Mercedes young drivers in the top Formula One seats. Kimi Antonelli hadn't even passed his road driving test when he signed his first Formula One contract. Russell is now making the step up to team leader with the departure of Lewis Hamilton, and so, after three fallow years since the regulation change in 2022, how excited is Lagrue about the new line-up?

'The further you move up the racing pyramid, when you get close to the top, like Kimi is now, the more you begin to interact with the Formula One team. So when they arrive in Formula Three, they start to come to the factory and do some simulator sessions, they start to meet some engineers and marketeers and begin their Formula One education. It is only then that they start to understand how big a Formula One team is, and how many people are interacting every day to make it work. We also give them an understanding of the culture of the team.'

For Lagrue, they must be able to understand the ethos of what it means to be a Mercedes driver.

'It's very important to me, and to Toto and the entire team. We are defending some values that are important to us, and we want to make sure that they are aligned with them. I was supporting the decision to put Kimi into Lewis's seat straight away. We are not dominating the sport, as we were a few years ago. I hope I am completely wrong, but maybe in 2025 it will be a similar performance to 2024. For me, it was the right time to promote a rookie, when there is less risk than when you are fighting for a world championship every year. We are targeting to be very strong in 2026, and it's my focus to make sure the line-up is right to challenge for a title then.'

It is clear, though, that Toto Wolff trusts the man that he has put in charge of his young drivers. They aren't a team that will chop and change their line-up every year. Mercedes drivers by and large remain loyal and, from a personal perspective, that is one of the things that I most admire about the team. There is clearly a huge amount of respect for the boss, but Wolff is a man who is willing to put his faith in his lieutenants and likes to promote and give opportunities from within.

'Of course, ultimately driver line-up decisions lie with Toto and the board, but each time we have had to make a decision, I have been lucky to have been involved in the selection process for the top seats. It's funny, because when Nico Rosberg retired, I was in Dubai airport about to board a plane. Toto phoned and said, "Are you near a chair? You need to be sitting down, I have big news, Nico is leaving the team." And the next question was, "Who do we put in the car?"'

This was the end of 2016, though, and Lagrue was just starting his new job, and neither of the drivers in the programme were ready for the step up. Esteban Ocon and Pascal Wehrlein had respectively only half a season and a season's experience at backmarker teams under their belt.

'It wasn't the right time for them, and I was not as comfortable as I am now to discuss with Toto what I thought about who should fill Nico's seat. However, the second time he called, I knew something was up, because he never usually calls early in the morning. He said again, "Are you near a chair?" And I said, "Who has left this time?!" When he told me it was Lewis, this time I had the confidence to speak up for Kimi. We could have chosen someone else, but my role is not just to answer for the short term, but how are we going to be world champions again for the next ten years. That might not sound good for the spectators if it happened, but that is why we are here. We want to win again, and the driver is the guy that is finishing the job for the 2,000 people who are at Mercedes. I think Kimi can, in a short time, be a very strong answer to what we need, and now George is at the maturity to become world champion. So we are super well covered, but Kimi needs to be given time.'

Like Jock Clear at the Ferrari young driver programme, and others like him, Lagrue draws inspiration from other sports and has friends around the world from whom he tries to learn, particularly in individual sports like skiing, which have comparable programmes to motor racing. But if he was to give one piece of advice to any aspiring youngster, what would it be?

'Be honest, be yourself and believe in your dreams, because those like Esteban and George and Alex always believed they were capable and had the ability to make it into Formula One.'

Lagrue is an extremely humble and likeable man, who doesn't give many interviews and prefers to let his work do the talking. But in the ten years that he has headed up the Mercedes young driver programme, it has grown from an extremely small project into something that the team has fully embraced. He has now won every championship that he has placed drivers in, from junior karts all the way up to Formula Two. The only one missing is the big one, and he has two highly capable drivers in a position to make that happen. If and when it does, they might want to buy Lagrue a drink. But then what? Once he has the full house, what else is there left to achieve?

'My next challenge, I would love to be the first one capable of helping a girl get into Formula One. Of course, I think it is possible and I think we are leaders in that area. I signed Luna Fluxa Cross when she was 11 years old, and that was three years ago. That was before the Formula One Academy even started. So, the problem here is only numbers. There are not enough girls in go-karts. We need to change that. If there are as many girls starting as guys, then they have the same chances, because it is not a physical issue. I do not want to support and help a girl for marketing reasons, I want to do it for sporting reasons, because it will happen one day.'

Let's hope that day is soon.

CHAPTER 22

THE DRIVER

There is no doubt that they are the heroes. The chosen few. The ones who have dedicated their entire lives to making it into the highest level of motorsport. Some will appear fleetingly, others will become part of the midfield furniture, but a handful, and only a handful, will reach the summit. Since 1950 there have been just 34 world champions, but the question every year, which keeps us coming back for more, is who's next?

George Russell is striving as hard as any to become the 35th. He is famously one of the most determined drivers on the planet and extremely driven to achieve his ambition. He's not afraid to speak his mind and can sometimes rub people up the wrong way – ask Max! – but, I'm going to admit, I've always liked George. While some who reach the higher echelons of Formula One become affected and restricted by the fame that envelops them, George has remained grounded and open, and will always stop and talk even on the grid, when the national anthem has finished and we are moments away from lights out. There are some that I wouldn't dare stick a microphone in front of so close to the start of the race, but George, within reason, is usually prepared to give us an insight into what awaits him over the next 300km.

'It's been in my blood since I was a kid. My brother Benjy is 11 years older than me. He was a go-karter and I followed him around the race tracks when he was competing in Formula A which featured karts with air-cooled water radiators. I used to have a pedal tractor and a water tanker on the back of my tractor and would ride around so that the teams could fill up their radiators. I was two.'

At the age of three George received his first quad bike and would whizz around the fens and the farmland near his home in Wisbech on the Cambridgeshire–Norfolk border. It sounds like an idyllic, if adrenaline-fuelled lifestyle, even as a toddler.

'I always knew racing was my destiny, but it was only when I won my second British Championship in the Mini Max category when I was ten that I began to really comprehend how much I loved it, and that I might have a future in motorsport, so I started to watch Formula One a bit more regularly to get an understanding of what's what.'

George was one of the lucky ones, and had a family who just about had the means to support his burgeoning talent. His father, Steve, ran a successful wholesale agricultural business trading peas and beans, but still had to make sacrifices and be selective about his son's racing choices because of the enormous costs involved.

'Dad ended up selling the business in 2012, which allowed him to fund me for the coming three years until I got to Formula Three. At that stage Jost Capito, who was the head of Volkswagen motorsport, sponsored me £100k, which was about a fifth of the budget for that season. I had a couple of other sponsors, but it was the last year of my family's support, which amounted to about a quarter of a million pounds. I also had the money from the McLaren Autosport BRDC award for the best young British driver in 2014, which added £100k to the pot. But my father realised that this was our last shot so we put everything into that year.'

Being the youngest ever winner of the Autosport award, at the age of 16, made a lot of people sit up and take notice.

'I first got hold of Toto Wolff's email after I'd won the Formula Four championship and the Autosport award, on the Tuesday night after the Abu Dhabi Grand Prix. The season had just finished, and I was there testing GP3. I sent him a message hoping for a meeting and he responded within 20 minutes. We had the initial meeting at the beginning of 2015, to get to know each other, and so that he could understand what my intentions were and I could ask him his advice. This was the time that Prema were the team to beat in Formula Three, and the number-one Mercedes backed team, but it was owned by the Strolls and there was a bit of politics about me going there. Toto advised me to go with the Mercedes number-two team, Mücke Motorsport, but they were struggling, so I thanked him for his advice and wrote him an email saying that I had decided to go to Carlin and hoping that this would not close the door. I think I actually gained a lot of respect for ignoring his direction and going in mine.'

After a solid 2015 in the European Formula Three championship with Carlin, in which he finished sixth, he was picked up for the following year by Ollie Oakes, now the team principal of Alpine, who was then in charge of Hitech GP. They provided a seat and the much-needed financial backing. Having finished third in the championship in 2016, Mercedes showed a renewed interest and George was utterly determined not to let this opportunity pass him by. It was time for him to whip out his now mythical PowerPoint presentation, to show Toto.

'I wanted to lay out in writing why I felt I deserved a shot in Formula One. I created the PowerPoint to express more about me as a person and the traits that I thought were required to be a Formula One driver, as opposed to listing out my accomplishments. Because it was out of the ordinary, I think it stuck with Toto. I hoped that these little moments of doing something different meant that he would remember me and keep an eye out.'

Russell also highlighted to Wolff his consistency in the lower formulae, the fact that he always tended to move forward in the races and that he rarely crashed. When you look at his record, there were very few failures and he was a driver who finished most of the races that he started. This was something that was engrained in him by his father.

'I was scared of letting him down, so I never actually pushed myself to my fullest potential because I would prefer to finish one place lower rather than going for another position, failing and my father being upset with me. My mentality has shifted a bit in the last few years, and I'm hoping that recently I am striking a better balance, but these were some of the things I was expressing on my PowerPoint.'

He was also keen to stress his values, but he feels that Wolff understood those from the start.

'Loyalty has been with me from the beginning, but I'd also say that I am extremely ambitious. I always want more and I am willing to go above and beyond to achieve that because of my upbringing and having to fight for success. We didn't struggle when I was a kid, but my father worked incredibly hard to give me my dreams. I wasn't born with a silver spoon in my mouth. We were just from a very hard-working background and believed that the more you put in, the more you get out of life.'

Gwen Lagrue had been keeping an eye on Russell's progress through his time in karting and beyond, and it was he who eventually persuaded Wolff to take a punt on the young Englishman. So, from the start of 2017, Russell was absorbed into the Mercedes young driver programme and placed in the French team ART to compete in GP3. Here, he began his journey within the system that he hoped would take him to the promised land. It involved working hard with senior figures as part of his education. James Vowles was the head of strategy, but also mentored drivers like Russell, preparing them for a Formula One-level of racing intelligence, including tyre strategy, race-craft and data analysis, as well as introducing him to the way that the senior team operated.

'When I first arrived, Toto, Gwen and James were all, very much, aligned. They knew I had potential, and they were there to help get the most out of me. They told me that they believed in me and they were going to take me the whole way. I then felt a sense of duty that I had to give everything for these guys.

This was not a time when Mercedes had 10 or 15 drivers on the books. Red Bull did on theirs, but I was the sole junior driver for those two years. They were always very good at taking the pressure away from me by telling me to focus on today's performance and not get caught up in the dream of Formula One. When I was about 16, I was always stressing about what was next, because if I didn't perform, I wasn't going to get picked up and it put a lot of pressure on me.'

That wasn't the case in his formative years, when Russell believes he was quite naive.

'I would even call it arrogant, because I believed that I could beat anyone and fly to the moon. I took it to some extremes on the race track, to test my ability. I remember being 11 and I didn't think the driver who was leading one particular race was any good so I said to myself that I would overtake him at a particular point on the last lap and I did it.

'Pressure only crept into my life when I began to comprehend the responsibility that I had, and the financial support and time that my parents had invested in me. My dad worked seven to seven and I didn't see him in the week. Then we'd go racing at the weekend and, unless I won, as I said, he'd be angry at me. It was only when my journey to Formula One didn't appear clear cut, that it dawned on me that he was away working to give me this chance. He was angry with me when I didn't win because he was putting so much effort in. We all had this dream, and if I didn't perform well, or at least give it my best shot, I would feel that I'd not only let him down, but my entire family.'

Russell responded to the pressure under the guidance of Mercedes, and won both the GP3 title in 2017 and the Formula Two championship in 2018, in which he beat Lando Norris and Alex Albon comfortably. The following year, he was to get his chance. With two prestigious trophies on his mantelpiece, he was ready to enter the big time. With Mercedes an engine supplier for Williams, Wolff and Vowles were able to place Russell at their storied customer team.* His first race was to be the season opener in Melbourne.

'I remember taking a photograph with my whole family in front of the garage on that first race day and my father crying, which was quite strange because I grew up with this tough man of a dad, who was so hard on me for so long. When I signed for Mercedes, he sort of let me fly, like releasing a bird, and suddenly his outlook on life and to me changed quite a lot. It was like he was passing the baton on to Mercedes. He had taken me so far, and now it was their duty. It just showed how much it meant to all of us, with my siblings there too, who've been such a huge part of my journey. But I was quite surprised, because when my helmet and visor went down, it felt like any other race.'

The three years he had with Williams were challenging. They finished plumb last in 2019 and 2020, but in 2020 he substituted in for Lewis Hamilton in the Mercedes at the Sakhir Grand Prix after Hamilton contracted Covid, a huge opportunity that Russell grasped with both hands. He qualified on the first row of the grid, just a couple of hundredths off pole sitter Valtteri Bottas. On Sunday, Russell got off the line quicker than his team-mate, took the lead and led for most of the race. It looked like being a fairytale victory, but a botched pit stop meant that Russell re-joined the race illegally with Bottas's front tyres attached, forcing him to pit again to fit his own set, which ultimately meant finishing down in ninth after he sustained a puncture and had to pit again. Nevertheless he did pick up his first points in Formula One, and it gave him a taste of what it was like to run at the front.

'I had some tough conversations with Claire Williams about trying to exit the contract for the 2021 season, which was made more difficult because they were in the process of selling the business. I had

---

* A customer team purchase their engines and other specified parts from an engine manufacturer. In the past, Williams did this famously with Renault and Honda, but in this case it was with Mercedes.

a sponsor ready and waiting to back me to terminate the contract, and Toto said that if I could get out of it the 2021 seat would be mine, but Mercedes weren't going to put ten million in to break it, when I was going to be in the seat for 2022. Financially it didn't make any sense.'

This is an example of how the business of Formula One works in the driver market. Russell was obviously desperate to extricate himself from an underperforming team who, at that stage, were living hand to mouth and on the verge of going bankrupt.

'When Claire made it clear that I wasn't leaving, that was quite tough to swallow. The results continued to be poor, but I saw how much hard work everyone was putting in. By 2021, it was a third year of survival at Williams, and yet I felt ready to fight for a world championship, especially as Sakhir had shown that I was more than capable of competing at the front. We carried on and managed to scored points that year for the first time in Budapest and that was the achievement that means the most to me, even to this day, because I saw first hand the grit and the pain that everyone was enduring during that time at Williams. It took us from tenth to eighth in the championship, and in the end was worth an extra $16 million.'

It was the first year that Russell had ended up in the black at the end of a season. Poverty isn't something you usually associate with Formula One drivers.

'In my first two seasons of Formula One I actually lost money. I had to take a loan because of the salary that I was on, minus the costs of my trainer, my sister who was my assistant and a number of other factors. But at the end of 2021, it was the first time in my life that I knew I could actually make a living from the sport.'

The next year, Bottas's seat was his. He had had to wait a lot longer than he had hoped and in front of him was the next challenge, his new team-mate, the greatest of all time, Lewis Hamilton. He and Mercedes were still processing the aftermath of Abu Dhabi when Russell arrived, but Hamilton immediately showed his class.

'I was very surprised by how welcoming he was. Whenever we did a joint activity, in a fan zone or at a sponsor event, where naturally all the attention was on him, he always made a very conscious effort to lift me up and never tried to steal the spotlight. If anything, he wanted to share it. That was really nice, and he gave me a huge amount of respect early on. I don't think he believed that I was going to be able to compete with him in the beginning, but I think very quickly he acknowledged that it was fair game and, even though we weren't winning as a team, there was a good battle going on between the two of us that motivated us both.'

Russell was also able to tap into the deep well of knowledge that Hamilton had gained from, at that stage, his 15 years in the sport.

'I learnt from a leadership perspective the impact the drivers can have on the team's morale, depending on what they say in the debrief or to the media. Every word he said went so far, and I learnt that it was important not to react with emotion, but also to give people a kick up the arse when it is required. He and Toto were the two driving forces and leaders of the team. From a driving perspective, his race pace is just so exceptional that it probably took me my first two years to get to his level. On outright speed, I have never doubted myself, but when it came to race pace you need a lot more experience, to be able to nurse the tyres and understand the little techniques required to make them go further, and he was the king of that.'

All things considered, it was still a sensational first year for Russell in an incredibly difficult car. It was the start of a new set of ground-effect regulations and the Mercedes struggled with porpoising (bouncing) and general performance issues. Russell, though, leant on one of his strongest traits, consistency, and finished the season in fourth, 35 points ahead of the seven-time world champion. Of the 22 races that year, he finished in the top five in 19 of them. A full season alongside Hamilton had allowed Russell to pick up on some of his 'techniques'.

'I call it my toolbox! What we do changes so much week to week. You might be in Melbourne in the rain, then in a sprint race on brand new tarmac in the freezing cold in China the next, and then you go to Saudi and it is boiling hot. Take whatever lessons you learn in different conditions, add them to your toolbox and then when you find yourself in that moment again you can reach into it and apply them. That is what I am trying to do with all my experiences. So being team-mates with Lewis meant I added a lot more tools to make me a more complete driver.'

More so than some, Russell is clearly a student of the sport and a sponge but, like all elite athletes these days, as we saw in the chapter on the performance coach, everyone is looking for an advantage over their competitors. So where does Russell get his?

'On a human performance level, things are evolving so quickly. Physically we are all in shape. When you compare this to 30 years ago, all of the drivers are in a much better place than they were. In the last five years, we've been talking more about psychology and mental health, and I feel that there is a lot more potential to tap into on this front. I work with a psychologist more to help me from a performance perspective, and to help me be happier.'

Russell's performance coach is Aleix Casanovas. The pair have been working together since his junior racing days and are constantly looking to push the boundaries. Casanovas is in charge of Russell's day-to-day physical health, nutrition, sleep plans, recovery and liaising with his psychologist. He also works with Russell's small group of engineers to understand how they can get the best out of each other. The devil is in the detail.

'I am looking at other ways to minimise the degradation of my body over time. Your eyes and brain worsen as you get older and you start to lose feel. We are working on techniques and exercises to help my eyesight and make sure my nerves are sharp and firing as quickly as possible. Ultimately, as a driver you rely on feel and if you lose feeling in your body you are going to lose feeling in the race car. I still don't believe many people are doing this. Rewind to 20 years ago, and no one would have been talking about it.'

It shows how much Russell and his team think about racing, away from the track. Gone are the days of James Hunt, drinking champagne the night before and firing up a cigarette as he stepped out of his car. Nowadays performance is all-encompassing for a racing driver.

'We live in a world where we look at the computer screen a lot, and that has an impact on our eyes and our brain as well. At night, I always wear my BluBlocker sunglasses. So before I go to bed I've always got the lights turned down, my phone brightness as low as possible [so that my brain realises that] it is night-time and time to wind down. Every day, first thing in the morning, I jump in the ice bath, which has such a massive impact on the body. I even had to get a structural survey for my balcony in Monaco because they were worried about the weight of it!'

He is also a driver who has a thirst for data. When he first arrived at Mercedes, he would drive his race engineer and performance engineer mad by pressuring them to give him more numbers to analyse. He soon realised that he needed to give them time and space to think and convert his feedback into an engineering solution on the car set-up. More data doesn't necessarily mean that you go faster as a racing driver. Between the three of them, they have found a balance about when to dive into the data and when to leave and get a good night's sleep.

'These days I don't need anybody to show me the data. I have it myself from different sessions and different years. There is so much now, that you can really use it to your advantage. I work the laptop and the programmes and know what it all says. Now, in our presentations, there is not much text, because I know what I am seeing from the graphs. When I was less experienced, I needed someone to guide me through what I was seeing, with all these squiggly lines and how they could make me go faster. Now I know which are the tyre temperature channels, the brake pressures, the car speed. I know everything that is required from looking at the graphs, where I am missing out, where I can find lap time versus my team-mate and where I can find lap-time myself.'

It's that language that Jock Clear and Gianpiero Lambiase talked about in previous chapters, between a driver and his engineers, that

Russell feels he has greatly improved in, and that's also now helping him drive the team forward better than ever before.

'If we are feeling something, we also need the ability to hop out of the car and show the engineers on a data trace exactly where it is. We talk about correlation in this sport a lot, of wind tunnel and simulator and X,Y,Z, but you also need correlation between the driver's feedback and the data, and that is where I need to be key. This is what I'm feeling, and I will show them on the graph where we've got the problem, and let them go away and do their magic.'

As well as the marginal gains Russell has begun to flex his competitive muscles. In Qatar, at the end of the 2024 season, Russell and Max Verstappen came to metaphorical blows after an incident in qualifying. Verstappen was adjudged by the stewards to have been driving unnecessarily slowly on the racing line in the final part of qualifying, thereby impeding Russell. It led to a one-place grid penalty for the newly crowned quadruple world champion. After arguing the toss in the stewards' room, Verstappen accused him of trying to 'screw him over' during the hearing. In response Russell revealed that Verstappen had threatened him in a private exchange and said he would 'put me on my fucking head in the wall'. At time of writing the two had still not shaken hands and made up. Seeing Russell stand up to Verstappen showed a different side to him, which we had seen flashes of before, but not to this extent.

'We are professionals, but it has always been ingrained in me, since I was a kid, that if someone is going to push you around in the playground, you don't let them and you push back harder, and show them that they've got a fight on their hands. We fight hard and we are all warriors on track but making things personal is something else. There was no strategy behind it from my side. I was just stating my views and my opinion and I made it clear publicly and I made it clear to him that I'm not going to take this shit. You might be able to do that with other guys, but you are not going to do that with me.'

So was Russell marking a line in the sand?

'It doesn't change how I am going to race him or anybody or how I go about my business. The fact is that I want to be a world champion and, in 2025, he is not the favourite. This year it is about beating the guys at McLaren, and that is the nature of this sport. One minute you are the king of the world, the next you are not. I've got no doubt he probably wouldn't have made those comments if he wasn't dominating the sport in the way that he was. Of course, Max is still one of the greatest drivers of all time, but I'm not going to accept people who are the leaders in the sport just saying what they want and thinking that they can get away with it.'

When Hamilton moved to Ferrari at the start of 2025, Russell found himself in position as the lead driver at Mercedes. His new team-mate is Kimi Antonelli, a teenager who arrived with a huge reputation. Many have questioned whether he is the next Max Verstappen. It provides a very different challenge for the Brit.

'It feels like a natural progression. I just feel like I am getting stronger every year. These past couple of seasons, because we haven't been fighting for a championship, it has allowed me to have trial and error in my approach. I knew I was probably too conservative in the past, but I have turned up the dial. I might have turned it up too much in 2024. It contributed to some incredible results but also to some crashes and uncharacteristic mistakes. I've gone back the other way a bit, and I feel that I have hit my sweet spot. I know what I need from the car, my tyres and what to look for from session to session, and I feel in the best place I've ever been in that regard. I'm the older, more experienced driver but I'm not thinking about anything other than winning and getting better and better every year, and I feel that I have a lot more to give.'

Now with six full seasons under his belt, Russell is on top of extracting the most out of himself from week to week, but how does he deal with the demands of the race weekends themselves where on top of everything, if you have a bad day, you are obliged to come and talk to the world's media? There is no hiding place in modern sport and at the top table in Formula One every single thing is analysed and talked about ad nauseam.

'I definitely realise that it is part of the job, but being totally honest, it drains me. Over the course of a race weekend, if my body had a percentage like an iPhone and every activity knocked that percentage down, only 25 per cent of that drain would be from driving. The rest would be split between sponsorship activities and the media. It's a very easy part of the job but it is very consuming and so I'm very conscious of my energy management over the weekend, because you are so hyped going into it. You can sometimes totally drain yourself on a Thursday, so I always like to be active on a Thursday and a Friday, whether that's going for a run or whatever. But I will cycle or scoot the track every evening, just to clear my head and get away from the noise. Race-weekend mentality varies, but a lot of places it's about building up to Q3, because that is where it matters most. I've got this mentality at every race now, that where you finish in the practice sessions and Q1 and Q2 is meaningless, as long as you get through. It is the last lap of Q3 that is the most important of the weekend.'

Russell has always been known as 'Mr Saturday' and it has undoubtedly been his strength. In 2024, he smashed Hamilton 24–6 in qualifying, including the sprints, and he knows he can rely on his outright speed to give him a decent starting position every single weekend.

'I feel like qualifying is the only place at the moment where I have reached my potential, but I'm nowhere close in terms of my whole race performance. It's why I have so much confidence in myself. If you are really quick in the race because you know how to get the most out of your tyres but you are two tenths off in qualifying, you can't overcome those last two tenths in raw speed and ability, but you can learn how to get the last two tenths out of your car or your tyres or whatever, come race day.'

Russell is clearly at an important moment in his career. This season he needs to show his young team-mate a clean pair of heels and, at the time of writing, he is still looking for a contract beyond the end of 2025. There have been rumours that Verstappen's camp have been talking to Mercedes, and their resources perhaps make them the favoured team as we go into the start of a new set of regulations. He knows he has to keep impressing to keep his seat, but his relationship with Toto Wolff goes way back and there is a great respect between the pair.

'He is an incredible human being and leader. I remember when I'd just joined the junior programme, and getting time with Toto was hard. I had been trying to get a meeting for a long time and at last we went for lunch in Brackley. We grabbed our food and suddenly he spots something in the canteen and before you know it he is having a 15-minute conversation with the cleaning lady about her job, the products she used and what more he could be doing to make her job easier and have a better impact on the factory. I was just sat there with my food in front of me thinking, *This is my one chance to have a chat with the boss and he's talking to the cleaner about cleaning products!* But that taught me so much about the person he is.

'He is so knowledgeable about the technical side of the sport and he's also a very good driver. We've done track days together and I'm not going to name names but he's been faster than some Formula One drivers. People have this perception that he's this good-looking businessman, but he is a fighter. When you see the boss pushing to such a degree in every single element you recognise that you've got to do at least the same.'

Russell is pushing every day to do that but, in the dog-eat-dog world of Formula One, that doesn't necessarily equate to another contract. When you have no certainty for the following year it must put a strain on a driver.

'It's pretty easy. You perform and everything works out. From my side, I know where I want to be for the long term and what I want to achieve, so I'm not going to stress over a contract. That can never positively impact performance. I'm going nowhere. I am just focusing on racing and winning, and I will leave the bullshit for another time.'

So what about the ultimate prize?

'I believe that my time is going to come. Whether that's this year or next. I will not lose motivation, after these years of minimal success, because no one can pre-empt when it will come. All I know is that I back myself fully. I have been team-mates with the greatest driver of all time, and I've shown what I am capable of. I want to be team-mates with Max Verstappen one day, to show what I can do. When you have been team-mates with Lewis for three years, nothing scares you.'

Now that's a pairing we would all love to see.

CHAPTER 23

THE HEAD OF BROADCAST AND MEDIA

While media duties might drain the drivers, as Russell knows, they are imperative for the millions of viewers who hang on their every word, and the extensive coverage is undeniably central to the sport's global popularity. Sky's coverage alone is broadcast in over 80 countries including the USA, Australasia, Canada, the Middle East and most of Africa as well as the home territories of UK and Ireland.

Formula One is one of the most complex sports in the world to film. In 2007 a centralised world feed was created so that every country received the same core footage. It was done to ensure consistent quality and neutrality because, prior to that, it was usually the responsibility of the host broadcaster to produce the coverage.

The man who was responsible for helping build this system, and who is now in overall charge of all broadcast and media in Formula One, is Dean Locke. Locke started working in the sport straight after he left university in 1997. At that stage, under Bernie Ecclestone, Formula One would provide additional services for the host feed, whether that be RTL in Germany or ITV/BBC in the UK, for example. They were adding the graphics and onboard cameras, and in addition to that, they set up a pay-per-view digital feed with two track channels – one focusing on the battles at the front, one at the rear – an onboard channel and a pit-lane channel for those obsessives who wanted to top up what was being shown on their television screens. Locke started as a researcher for Formula One before moving into the graphics department, and then started directing the track channels for the pay-per-view service. In 2002 Bernie pulled the plug on this and there were mass redundancies.

'I think it was a bit ahead of its time. It was difficult then to sell someone a service that was already free. Not so now, but in its infancy, it was. Sky entered the market at a time when some of the big American networks were pushing to develop sports broadcasting, and, with host countries only doing one race a year, it wasn't very easy for us to develop the coverage. So Bernie was keen to build the world feed. Myself and a couple of others were tasked with how we would do that.'

At that early stage, Locke and the team designed a system that would take the host feed and bolt on some extra bits and pieces, but there was a hesitancy around whether this would work in the long term. Formula One were also starting to travel to destinations like Bahrain and China, where they weren't sure that the host broadcaster had the capacity to work with the bolt-ons. It was agreed with the media rights team, led by Ian Holmes, to start negotiations with some of these host nations to see if Formula One could take over their coverage entirely.

'We started with three in 2004, Bahrain, Australia and China, and then took over five more in 2007, including Spain, Britain, Hungary, Belgium and Italy. We kept adding more races, year on year, and the last one to be taken over by us was Monaco in 2023. There were some legends directing the early iterations of the world feed, but Bernie saw the wisdom in having a staff director and thankfully entrusted me with the role.'

Locke became the primary director for the world feed in 2012, the year that Sky entered the sport. Sky have three add-on cameras that we use to cover presentation and my good friend Ted Kravitz in the pit lane, but these are our add-ons to the main feed that Locke was responsible for directing and that are beamed around the world. Every year there's more for him to consider.

'There are just so many different sources that go into the world feed nowadays. The amount of graphics that we are putting to air is incredible. Whether that's telestration, augmented reality graphics or tagging graphics. With regards to the team radio, that was fairly rudimentary in the early days; now we hear everything. There are also more onboard cameras now. Back then we only had four onboard lines, but now every car has one. We were standard definition, and four by three, so not the wider screen format that you see today. And we probably had 20 track cameras but, as the circuits have got longer in places like Azerbaijan and Saudi, they have got more camera hungry so perhaps we may have 27 or 28 in places like that. We had only three or four hand-held cameras and now we are up to five or six. We have "Rome" (remote operated mobile camera) cameras around the tracks (these are the high-angle camera positions usually placed on a crane or scaffolding to give sweeping views of the circuit) plus the helicopter and the wire cam that runs the length of the pits.'

There is no doubt that the coverage that the world feed provides takes us closer to the sport than ever before and, with the onboard technology available, it literally puts the viewer in the cockpit.

The most commonly used onboard shot is the T-Cam, or primary camera, which is mounted on top of the air intake, above the driver's head. This is the camera that gives the audience a clear view of the front wheels, steering movements and the track ahead.

Then there is the nose camera, which is embedded in the car's nose cone, or just above the front wing. This is perhaps my favourite view from onboard, as it is so close to the ground and makes everything feel 'fast'. It is fabulous when you are watching kerb-riding and wheel-to-wheel racing.

There are rear-facing cameras, situated behind the driver's headrest and on the rear wing, which are often used to demonstrate overtaking, a halo camera in the Halo safety device gives you a driver's-eye view, as does a tiny helmet camera embedded in the driver's helmet at eye level. These work particularly well in the night races, with the lights flashing by.

'We have 90 onboard cameras across the 20 cars, and we can switch on about 22–24 at any one time, because of bandwidth. There is a lot of jumping around from a roll hoop to a low nose to a rear-facing camera, and we cut these into the feed with track cameras via sub-mixes. The old-school way of directing in the TV truck, where a director calls out cut to camera four, mix to camera seven, wouldn't be fast enough for our sport with all the sources now. We never used vision mixers back in the day, because it would've been too slow. We used to cut the buttons ourselves. But that would be impossible now, so we moved to sub-mixes.'

Without sub-mixes, the director would have to manage hundreds of feeds at once. Instead, sub-mixes filter and prioritise the most important content, allowing the director to make quick decisions. They allow for smooth and dynamic coverage. There are different types of sub-mix available to the director.

The track sub-mix is the mix of the trackside cameras that capture the race from different angles, from corner to corner, and there is a dedicated trackside producer/director who selects the best trackside camera angles before sending the mix to the world-feed director. The director can either select these, or decide to switch to the onboard camera sub-mix, controlled by the onboard producer, who monitors all of the onboard feeds and picks the most relevant. There is a replay sub-mix, which is a pre-edited selection of replays created by a dedicated replay team and specialised operators that ensure that key moments are covered with the best angles. Then there is a pit-lane and team-radio mix, with a separate producer that can give quick access to relevant team radio messages and the relevant pit-stop action, without missing key on-track battles. On top of that is the data and graphic sub-mix of all the telemetry, timing and graphic overlays that enhance the broadcast, which is run by the data and graphics team based back at Biggin Hill in the UK.

'We have a split broadcast, so roughly about 140 people at Biggin Hill and about 100 people in broadcast at the track. The core track sub-mix is done at the track and that is sent via our fibre connectivity to Biggin Hill, where we cut in our roaming cameras, onboard cameras, graphics, replays and team radio. So we call it acquisition at the track, getting the data – the pictures and the audio – and then curation of all the products at Biggin Hill. The reason that we split it that way is so that the track director is on site and more tangible to all the camera operators, and also for disaster recovery. So, if anything goes wrong with our fibre lines and interrupts that connectivity, we can cut the pictures and produce the feed on site. Within seconds we can switch to a satellite uplink.'

Locke directed the world feed until Liberty took over in 2018, and was then asked to step into his current role overseeing the whole operation. Nowadays, he looks at all the products that Formula One provide in the broadcast and media space, but during the race still adopts an executive producer role.

'We have an editorial director choosing what the stories are; the world-feed director choosing how to shoot, cut and story-tell; and we, as producers and executive producers, are really keeping an eye on the narrative and trying to get ahead of the world feed. So we are a bit more pro-active than reactionary. I liaise between the track team and Biggin Hill, and with the on-site broadcasters, and oversee the post-production content, all our extra content channels, direct-to-consumer web and Formula One TV. In the last few years, I've helped with *Drive to Survive* and the *F1* movie. We also have a very active CEO in Stefano Domenicali, and I will speak to him throughout the sessions. He knows what he likes to see and has an incredibly astute eye. He will spot a wrong graphic before anyone else most of the time! I also deal with on-site management, for example if schedules change; the FIA; and the race director.'

It is fair to say that Locke is busy.

Over the past couple of years, it has been incredible to watch how a Hollywood movie has been shot on Formula One weekends. The filmmakers have fitted seamlessly into the ecosystem of the sport, and a lot of that is thanks to Locke and his team. The sight of Brad Pitt and Jerry Bruckheimer at the front of the grid has become reasonably normal. So normal, in fact, that at the British Grand Prix in 2023, Jenson Button, Naomi Schiff and I, who were waiting to come back in vision during Martin Brundle's grid walk, plucked up the courage to go and have a chat with Mr Pitt, who was stood about ten yards from us. He couldn't have been friendlier, and engaged us in conversation for a good five minutes before we had to leave to keep talking on air. It was only after the race had finished that we received a polite message from the production team to perhaps not do that again as Brad had been moments away from shooting an important scene. Alas we didn't make the final cut of the movie, I should imagine that is why! Having seen it though, *F1* takes the audience right to the heart of the action.

'I think the film is incredibly authentic. To the point where we filmed their car with our operators doing the pit stops, because they just felt that our operators made it look more authentic when compared with their teams. They had no cameras around the track, so all the track action is ours, but we had to change things like shutter speeds for them so that it looks more cinematic, and we talked about how we filmed speed. We gave them space for some onboard cameras of their own, and looked at their camera technology, which we may be able to weave into our future plans. They loved our cable camera and that was whizzing about all the time. They would sit in on our production meetings, and it was enjoyable working with the director, Joseph Kosinski. Brad came into our gallery on site one day when he found out that all our camera operators had had to come in at five in the morning to help shoot a scene for the film.'

But how did they shoot the racing scenes?

'They were utilising our camera systems for their car runs, so that it looked identical. If they were doing some off-site scenes, they were using follow cars and Russian arms [remotely controlled camera crane systems]. They used our helicopter footage a lot. We actually partnered with them and used the pilot that filmed a lot of scenes in Kosinski's other recent film, *Top Gun: Maverick*. We used our pilot in Austin and Vegas. Our operators all of a sudden became movie camera operators and wanted higher rates! In the actual race footage, they used our footage and the same technology from *Maverick* to superimpose their car into the actual racing scenes. It was a great experience and we are going to miss them at the track.'

That is until *F1-2* comes out!

With the expansion and firm foothold that sport now has in the States, there has been a slight shift of direction in the themes that Formula One wants to cover, as they try to cut through to a younger audience and retain them going forward.

'We are certainly diving into personalities in the world feed more than we ever have. Sky and other broadcasters do a terrific job of getting to know the personalities in their pre- and post-race shows, so it's not enough for us just to show a bit of racing. We have to dial into the characterisation. It is entertainment, but we don't want to alienate the hard-core fans by just showing celebrities. We have 20 young and engaging drivers, who are good-looking and carry themselves incredibly well. And we've got six rookies in 2025, so we wanted to get to know them.'

That, it seems, will drive more of the editorial of the world feed going forward but it won't distract from the main purpose.

'The racing is the key editorial and we never favour any particular team, except when it comes to championship deciders. We always dial into on-track battles, but that characterisation has becoming increasingly important. You can get closer to our stars than in a lot of other sports, even though they are under a helmet and in a cockpit doing 200mph. F1 75 was another example of that.'

As I mentioned in a previous chapter, F1 75 was the event at the O2 in London in February 2025 to celebrate the 75th anniversary of the sport. It was the first time in its history where every team's livery was unveiled at the same time and in the same place. All 18,000 tickets were sold out in a matter of 20 minutes and it showed the insatiable appetite that there is at the moment from the paying public. It demonstrated exactly what Liberty Media has brought to the sport: a blend of sports and entertainment and massive brand exposure for the sponsors of the sport and every team.

'The biggest challenge was to convince the teams that it was a good idea, and to do it uniformly. Being a competitive sport, it is not that easy to get everybody to agree. And I didn't think it was going to happen. Credit to the teams for trusting us, but it wasn't until they all agreed that I actually thought, *Right, I've got to go and sort out a broadcast for this.*'

Planning started in summer 2024.

'Once they had agreed, it was blow after blow. You don't get the venue until 24 hours before, and it was the biggest build that they had ever done at the O2. It was incredibly time consuming, but the value of the content and the event itself was incredible. I think we will be looking to do it again, and we probably won't need an anniversary to do that.'

There were a few pantomime boos on the night for Christian Horner and Red Bull and it was noticeable that Max Verstappen was the only driver not to speak. It was clear that he felt uncomfortable in front of the partisan British crowd and, perhaps, they might need to move the event to different countries in the future.

'There are a huge number of teams based in the UK so, logistically, it works quite well but, as we know, we are pretty damn good at logistics. So doing it on the way to the first race, for example, or at another point in the season, hasn't been ruled out.'

Each race these days is incredibly different and they all have their own unique personality. In this truly global sport there is a chance for Formula One to lean into different cultures, and events such as these provide another opportunity for Locke and his broadcast team to reach out and cut through to the younger fans. That was obvious from the audience on site and from the record numbers the launch generated on YouTube and the other free streaming platforms.

With the technology ever improving, the challenge for the broadcast and media team is to constantly improve the coverage and allow the fans to engage in the content in the way that they want to.

'We tend to look three years hence and we have to be in line with our broadcast partners as well. There is no point in us providing a crazy, immersive experience if we have no way of getting it out there. Our pictures in UHD and HDR already look the business. The first part we can improve is to be able to pull more camera feeds off the car and perhaps use the 360 cameras more. Very occasionally, we don't have the right angle, because we were looking at the rear-facing rather than the forward-facing camera during an incident. So being able to get all the footage off the car for the big incidents will improve the coverage. That is part of our technological roadmap, to get more bandwidth off the car. Personalisation of the viewership might be interesting in the future, where you'd be able to choose a graphics package for a hard-core fan or a lighter one. Plus, you will be able to choose the commentary that you really like. Some people want the car audio loud and some want Crofty and Martin louder. And just getting as much access as possible.'

Artificial intelligence is also something that, although in its infancy, is being phased into television, and will have a huge impact on the broadcasts in the future. There may be a time in the not-too-distant future that we can all sit back on a sun lounger and let the machines do our jobs. In the meantime, though, it will absolutely add to the coverage of sport. We had a presentation at Sky recently where we saw the cricketer Stuart Broad explain how he bowled an over in his own voice, translated and mimicked by AI so that he spoke perfect Hindi to an Indian audience – and all generated in real time. And we haven't even scratched the surface.

'We are working with some partners already, mainly around problem-solving and the accuracy of graphics. If you are about to generate an incorrect graphic, could it warn you before it goes to air? We are also building some systems around storytelling. We have some AI graphics, like battle forecast, that predict cars coming together in the future, but we are looking at a system that tells the whole story. It is hard to find producers who know the sport inside out and have a whole handle on everything that is going on in the race.'

In fact, it is almost impossible. Our commentators rely on a spotter and a person in our race control position to monitor team radio and the tracking graphics in order to stay one step ahead. AI might be able to help them with that in the future.

'What we don't want to do is, after the race, go back and realise that we missed an amazing battle and an important storyline. We will also be able to get real-time accurate transcription on team radio and of course subtitling.'

Locke, like many within our industry, keeps a close eye on innovation across other sports. Formula One is like golf, skiing or the Tour de France in that it is not a stadium sport where all the action is self-contained and played out in front of a live audience on the pitch. The on-site fan cannot be everywhere at once and therefore, holistically, it is better viewed from an armchair on a screen.

'I've just come back from the TPC at Sawgrass and had a look at their new remote facility there. Golf might be slower than us, but it shares the same issue of multiple things happening simultaneously, and therefore we are constantly having open discussions about how to help each other. One of the things I get asked a lot is why we aren't using drones so much. It works extremely well in skiing but, obviously, in our sport at the moment, the drones aren't fast enough yet. We are experimenting with them, though.'

And that is the point. The evolution within broadcasting continues at the same pace as the development of the cars that they are covering. Live sport is one of the few products that continues to grow. As one of Sky's taglines ahead of a season said, '*It's only live once.*'

It is an incredibly exciting industry to be part of and certainly the most exciting sport that I have been involved in in my 28 years of broadcasting. Locke joined Formula One at the same time that I joined Sky.

'I only really intended to stay for a couple of years, to see the world. I wouldn't be here unless it kept challenging me, and every single week there is a new challenge. Sometimes, that's also the negative, but there is always something where we have to lift our game. There is a continual buzz. We set ourselves some incredible goals and meet any challenge thrown at us, whether that be moving our infrastructure into garages in Japan to avoid a typhoon or doing an opening show in Las Vegas that was as big as many concerts. It's just the fast pace of Formula One and it is very addictive.'

It really is. Every year it keeps you coming back for more. Even in the slower seasons, when the narrative isn't so juicy, it is about finding the stories to make it interesting for the viewer. It's one of the things that Locke and his team do so well and that we hope we also do at Sky.

CHAPTER 24

THE COMMENTATORS

t was always going to be awkward writing about your friends and colleagues. Before I begin, I would like to apologise to them both for anything they are about to read, any glaring inaccuracies and any other stuff that I forgot to check before publishing the secrets of their 'art'. So to David Croft and Martin Brundle, sorry.

Where on earth do you start with David Croft? Well, I'll try and start at the beginning. I first met Crofty after Sky had secured the rights to Formula One in the UK, alongside the BBC, from 2012. I'd been made aware that I had been given the opportunity to be the presenter of the new Sky Sports F1 channel in the summer of 2011 and, while there was speculation about who the rest of the team would be, we knew internally, but were sworn to secrecy. And so, under the shadow of this clandestine TV embargo, I first met Crofty at the Abu Dhabi Grand Prix in 2011, while he was still commentating for BBC Radio 5 Live. Over several overpriced imported lagers, we bonded over a shared love of all sport, despite the fact that he supports West Ham. Imagine my horror when broadcasting legend Martin Brundle announced he was also a West Ham fan (I had assumed he was a Norwich City fan, coming as he does from East Anglia), although this was much later, in Miami, live on air in 2024.

Anyway, back then Crofty was half the man he is today. Lithe and standing over six foot tall, he was living proof that life begins at 40. Instantly good company, you could tell he would never be short of a word or two. He was also pretty adept at left-armed pub sports, a rivalry with me that has endured, globally, for 14 years. He was loving working in radio but, when Sky got the contract, it was his first proper opportunity in television and, for both of us, the thought of being part of a new channel was fairly daunting. Crofty had dreamt about it since he was a young lad in shorts.

'I used to watch sports on the telly, or listen on the radio, and think, *Now that is the greatest job in the world.* When David Coleman would shout "one–nil", or Sid Waddell would come out with amazing prose and John Motson, Barry Davies, Harry Carpenter and of course Murray Walker were doing their thing. These people used to get to go round the world, watch sport and talk about it for a living.'

When he was in the fourth year at senior school, a teenage Crofty was asked by his teachers what he wanted to do for a career.

'I want to be a sports commentator, sir,' he replied, his voice barely broken.

'And they laughed at me. What a ridiculous notion that you could ever do that, because who tells their teachers that they want to be a sports commentator? When they asked me how I intended to achieve this, at that stage, obviously, I had no clue. I mean they don't advertise for these positions, do they?'

So Crofty went off to work in the theatre.

'I joined the Gordon Craig Theatre in Stevenage as a stage-hand, and put my dream on hold. I was 16, still at school, but not very often because I used to bunk off to go to work instead, which explains why I ended up with one A level when I finished college. I never went to university because I loved working in the theatre. I moved on from the stagehand job into publicity and marketing for them and, whilst there, I struck up a friendship with a guy called Darren Isted. Now, of all the millions of people who have helped me over the years, it was Darren who set my career in motion. He took a job as a sports editor for the local paper and gave me my chance, writing 300-word match reports for the local Stevenage Borough games. From there, I started doing the club-call line, the

0898 numbers where people would spend £1.50 per minute to listen to me tell them about the game. It's where I first learnt that as a commentator you can, literally, get paid by the word. It was great training for Formula One practice sessions!'

From there Crofty continued filing local match reports, before landing a job at BBC Three Counties Radio. While a lot of people in our industry these days go through the traditional route of media studies at university before applying for roles and internship programmes, Crofty learnt on the job. He spent time volunteering at the radio station, learning to edit, produce, script-write and put bulletins together. It's why he feels that the ecosystem that BBC local radio provides is so important, as it is a great training ground.

He was still working at the theatre when his first commentary opportunity came along for the world feed at the Toulon U20 international football tournament in summer 1995. It was in Provence, France. Crofty's fee was £100, plus expenses. Bargain!

'My first game was France against South Korea, and all I remember was that Robert Pires scored from a corner and I was awful, but I did one match a day for two weeks and it was like an intensive commentary course. I could make as many mistakes as I liked because it was all edited down into highlights.'

Off the back of this, the producer of the tournament put him forward for a job as the third commentator for West Country TV, which he did for a year. Crofty would fill in when teams like Plymouth played away at Darlington, too far for the other commentators to be bothered to travel. He was working all the hours God sent and still freelancing with Three Counties when he was awarded a full-time contract with the station. When I say full time, it was a month. But he risked it all and sacked off his job in the theatre and at West Country TV for his big break with the BBC and the promise of a longer contract if it worked out. It did. He spent three years there, before applying for a position as producer for BBC Radio 5 Live.

'I was the worst producer on the planet. I can barely organise myself, let alone someone else. But at the time, they were just launching their digital service and doing pilots for Radio 5 Live Sports Extra and were looking for commentators. Initially, I didn't apply, because I'd only just secured a full-time job as a producer, and knew I was onto a good thing, but someone convinced me to do so, and I then spent a year broadcasting to nobody apart from those listening in on the BBC's internal system. We'd go to Royal Ascot, the cricket and cup finals. Again, it was great training as virtually no one could hear your mistakes and it led to my opportunity as a full-time reporter, doing late nights with Fi Glover. She is such a naturally gifted broadcaster, and we covered more than just sport. I remember doing the Tory party conference from Blackpool and ended up doing a diet challenge with Ann Widdecombe! I beat her by about two pounds over the course of the conference and celebrated by eating a bucket of KFC live on air.'

Glamour!

After four years as a reporter on Radio 5 Live, he knew that he wanted to specialise. He was doing the odd football commentary and, from 2004, some darts commentary for TV for the BDO world championships at Lakeside, when another friend at the BBC, Jason Swales, who produced the Formula One coverage for Radio 5 Live, convinced Crofty to audition.

'As part of the pitch I made up a lap of Monza off the top of my head for USP, one of the production companies who were tendering for the rights, and it helped them win the Formula One contract for the BBC.'

So again, Crofty risked a steady job as a Radio 5 Live producer/reporter for a year's contract with the production company. It paid off, and he set about prepping for his first race as lead commentator for Radio 5 Live, in Bahrain in 2006. His summariser was Maurice Hamilton, a hugely respected Formula One journalist.

'For the first two or three years, Maurice was part of the team, until Anthony Davidson joined. To spend time in the company of people like Maurice is a great education into Formula One, the history and the right way to do your job in the sport. And just to have that person next to you who knows everything, when I felt I knew nothing, was invaluable. I was on my knees after about ten minutes, thinking, *How the hell am I going to keep this going for another hour and a half?* But somehow I did, and it got a bit easier with more time and more races, as anything does.'

There is nowhere to hide, though, as a broadcaster, when things go wrong and, invariably, they do. Everyone makes mistakes, and it was a steep learning curve for Crofty in the early days of his commentary career. To this day, his major regret was during the 2008 championship decider. It had come down to the last race in Brazil, with Lewis Hamilton leading the championship by seven points. If Ferrari's Felipe Massa won his home race, Hamilton needed to finish fifth, or better, to take the title. It is one of the most dramatic finishes to a season in the history of the sport. Massa was leading for the majority of the race, and Hamilton was running in fifth for most of it. With rain beginning to fall in the final few laps, most drivers switched to wet-weather tyres. On the penultimate lap, Sebastian Vettel passed Hamilton, dropping him to sixth and potentially costing him the championship.

'We were so focused on Lewis needing to get past Vettel that nobody in the commentary box, not Maurice, Jason or myself, spotted him getting past Timo Glock, who had stayed out on the slicks and gained track position. We only had one timing screen and a monitor and I just wasn't watching where Glock was. It was a salutary lesson in trying to understand every bit of the story when you are commentating, and not just the bit that you think is relevant. It also taught me to keep alive the possibility that anything can happen, right to the end. I was watching the Brazilian crowd, and the grandstands were going absolutely wild, because Massa had won the race and with it, they thought, the championship. But because it's radio, and you don't always have to talk to the pictures, I was reacting to the crowd and I just gave it, "Massa crosses the line, he's the world champion unless Lewis can do something in the next 30 seconds." I didn't realise that Lewis had already got past Glock until

Massa crossed the line and the FIA timing screens changed. I was late with it, and only then did I say, "And he's gone past Glock, that's amazing." I still kick myself for that moment, I really do. I should've known better.'

As a broadcaster, you can only learn from your mistakes, and Crofty is the first to acknowledge when he does. It's why he's so good at his job, because he strives to get better with every race.

As a youngster, I spent four years living in Perth, Australia, and was brought up on the peerless Channel 9 commentary team that covered the cricket. Led by Richie Benaud in his array of cream jackets, it featured Bill Lawry, Tony Greig, Ian Chappell, Mark Taylor, Ian Healy and Michael Slater. They were all such distinctive characters with incredible voices, and it was their cama-raderie and innate knowledge of the game that made me fall in love with cricket. It was a line-up so iconic that they were paro-died by the comedian Billy Birmingham, and I listened to his tapes constantly as a kid. Great commentators bring sport to life. Effortlessly describing what is in front of you and explaining what is happening to an audience of all ages is a rare skill. Before I moved into Formula One, I had the pleasure of working with Miles Harrison, who, as a lead commentator, was a genius. He was the voice of Sky rugby, remembered especially for the British and Irish Lions tours that he covered, starting in 1997 with the iconic win in South Africa. I played a few times for his village cricket team, which also featured the football commentators Peter Drury and Jon Champion. It was always amusing when the ball came to you and one of them would make a comment. You felt like you were playing in a live match on television. All three of them came through BBC local radio, as Crofty did, and I put them all in the same category. Crofty is simply the best at what he does. He also has the added complication of commentating on the fastest sport in the world so, when he got the opportunity to become part of the Sky team and move into television, he was aware it was a very different challenge.

'I'd done some TV but, in commentary terms, to go from radio to TV was a massive step up, into a job that not many people had done either. As leads only Ray Baxter, Murray Walker, Martin Brundle, James Allen and Jonathan Legard had come before me. I questioned myself when Sky offered me the gig, but I went back to my mantra, "Always find a reason to say yes". I thought long and hard about how I'd come an awful long way only to say no now, and I got over my mental hump that way. But I was still so nervous.'

As we all were. But Crofty received some sage advice and words of encouragement from the undisputed master.

'I have to confess, the night before the Sky Sports F1 team was announced, I phoned up Murray Walker to tell him that I had got the job. He was so enthusiastic for me and so positive about it. I thought, *Well if Murray believes in me then I shouldn't have any doubts either.* It meant so much.'

The man that Crofty has shared the commentary booth with ever since is Martin Brundle. Brundle retired from full-time racing at the end of the 1996 season. He started at Tyrrell in 1984 and drove for six other teams including Benetton, Brabham and McLaren. He achieved nine podiums in a 12-year career and won Le Mans with Jaguar in 1990. As soon as he finished racing, he moved straight into the box with Murray and their combination was to become legendary to motorsport fans the world over. He, too, received some wisdom from the great man before they started their time together for ITV.

'We had dinner in London on the eve of heading out for the first race in Melbourne. I was still quite grumpy, because I wanted to be on the grid in 1997. But I hadn't got a drive, and it had dawned on me that I was going to be a commentator, so I asked him what this broadcasting lark was all about. He said, "I will give you one piece of advice. We are here to inform and to entertain," and I live by that today. It's never about you. You leave your ego at the door. It's a highly complex, fast-moving sport and you have to explain it to people without talking down to the broad church that is the audience. Let people understand it, so that they can get more pleasure from it.'

Brundle and Walker worked together for five seasons at ITV between 1997 and 2001, and their dynamic was unique. Walker had boundless energy and was prone to the 'Murrayisms' that made him a national treasure. Brundle provided the knowledge and expertise straight from the cockpit and into your living rooms.

'Murray was just so passionate, understood broadcasting and what the audience wanted. Some of those early races in my commentary career were as boring as hell and they needed Murray's energy, especially when Michael was winning all the time with Ferrari. He was just a very easy man to like, whether you knew him or not. He became part of the fabric and people were comfortable with him, whether they were watching rallycross or touring cars or Formula One. His enthusiasm was contagious and he brilliantly traded off, and became loved for, making errors. Not many people can get away with that in their careers.'

In those days there were far fewer tools at the commentators' disposal, and the information available to them was much more limited. Nowadays, there are a bank of screens for Crofty and Brundle to refer to. In the box now, they have the main television screen that shows the world feed for them to commentate on. They have one simple timing screen, which shows the three sectors and the last lap time in race order, plus one screen that displays stewards' decisions and weather conditions in real time, which comes from race control. They have another TV that shows what is going to air on Sky Sports, two driver trackers, one on Crofty's side and one on Martin's. Crofty will commentate off these around the pit stops, if the main feed isn't showing them. There's another screen that conveys top speeds, one that has mini-sector times that is more detailed than the main timing screen, and a tyre screen that informs them which compound each driver is on and how old each particular set is.

'Technically,' says Croft, 'it's one of the hardest sports to commentate on, certainly that I've done, because most of what goes on, you can't see. The driver is encased in the cockpit, you can't see the engine and the gearbox, it's hugely strategic and the teams have to think one step ahead. Things don't happen straight away, they evolve. And as the narrator, you've got to be onto the story early, and go with the evolution and explain why things are happening the way that they are. But I think the most difficult part of Formula One commentary is [that], unlike any other sport, there are so many stories taking place at the same time. Linking those strands together, and keeping people as abreast of the complexities of the race as you can, is hard. It's not just about the front two. You may be seeing more of them on the screen, but I'm looking at pictures, timing screens and data and the action can change rapidly and without warning. So it's about being able to react to what is going on and make sense of it, so the viewer can understand.'

Crofty never scripts any of his words but prepares meticulously and produces an elaborate set of notes that he pins to the wall next to him in the commentary box for quick referral. He compiles these from the stat packs that we all receive on the Monday before each race. Knowing him as I do, he has an incredible capacity to retain this trivia and use a stat at the appropriate time over the weekend. Martin, on the other hand, has never taken a note into the commentary box in almost three decades apart from 2011, when he was lead commentator for the BBC alongside his good friend David Coulthard. Hence the difference between the lead and the colour commentator.

'My job is to put people on the pit wall, in the pit lane, on the grid or inside the cockpit. Usually, whatever happens, I've seen it before or it's happened to me, and I don't need notes for that. I have to call incidents there and then and, hopefully, we usually get it right. I read the sporting regulations three times a year, and I always have a copy close to hand on my phone or iPad, because they are so complex and hard to keep on top of as a commentator. You have to hold it in your memory, and these regulations are over 100 pages long. When you read something like that, essentially a legal document, every word matters and so you have to read them very carefully. Crofty has an overview of them, but it's not really his role. He is the continuity guy who calls the action. I am the one that has to give his opinion but I absolutely need to be on top of the rules.'

Between the pair they have commentated on some of the great races of the modern era but the one that everyone still talks to them about is Abu Dhabi in 2021. Was it the hardest call of their lives?

'Looking back on it, probably,' says Crofty. 'In the moment, it was unfolding like a commentary normally unfolds. The race was meandering towards a conclusion, and then changed dramatically. I'm happy that we got over that what was unfolding wasn't necessarily correct and within the regulations that were written down. It's not my job to complain at the time, or get outraged at what is going on, because we are broadcasting to the world. The referee made a mistake, Martin made mention of the procedures not being followed. My job is to say what is happening and what that meant. I was proud of what we did. I thought we summed up everything in the last lap, and that my words at the end were the correct words. I said, "Max Verstappen, champion of the world," but if I'd have said, "Max Verstappen, champion of the world but that's not right and that shouldn't have happened," then I would have been doing Max a disservice and probably Lewis as well, as I'm not sure he would've liked that description either.'

It is hard to describe the impact of Abu Dhabi 2021. Hamilton fans were, rightly, aggrieved at the decision and, subsequently, it has led to a polarisation of the fanbases of Red Bull and Mercedes that has endured and that I'd never witnessed in the sport before. A lot of vitriol was aimed at us but, as broadcasters, ultimately we describe what we see in front of us. Commentators have the hardest job of us all, in that they must call it as it happens.

As Jackie Stewart famously said, 'Motorsport is dangerous, it says so on the ticket,' and there have been moments when they have had to talk over horrific accidents such as Jules Bianchi's crash in

Suzuka in 2014, and Romain Grosjean's in Bahrain 2020. It's one of the trickiest parts of the job, as Martin explains.

'You don't want to be too funereal because you don't immediately know the circumstances. You need a certain gravity to it. We had that with the Grosjean situation, until we knew that somehow he had miraculously got out of that car that had pierced the barriers and caught fire. There is a balance to it. You can't be too positive or too negative. You just have to explain what is going on, what it all means, how it happened and what the challenges and ramifications are.'

The pair now have an innate understanding and a massive level of respect and trust that has built up over the many years that they have been working together.

'Crofty is so easy to work with because he always has a word and, having done lead for a year, I know how hard it is to have something pertinent on the tip of the tongue. He's great at segueing from one element to the other but, when they say cue and you've got to say relevant stuff and keep saying it, that's a huge skill in itself.'

'It's just so simple with Martin because he is a very generous broadcaster, both with his time and his knowledge. His contacts are second to none and you know that when Martin says something that he has researched it and knows it to be true. Really, it's like standing there and having a chat with your mate.'

Martin is kept busy on a Grand Prix weekend because, on top of his commentary, there is also his world-famous grid walk that takes place all the way up until the national anthem, about ten minutes before the start of the race. He barely has time to catch his breath before he is straight up to the commentary box. The first time he tried it was at the British Grand Prix in 1997 and it was instantly a hit. It is some of the best access in sports television as he can talk to the drivers just minutes before they get into their cars. It started when he was at ITV, and the bosses there told him to go onto the grid and say what he saw. Since then, it has grown into something that is synonymous with Formula One and there are many who have tried to imitate him.

'Back then, I had the place to myself and I remember the very first one. I sat on the track and got the cameraman to come up behind me to show what it was like from the driver's eye. Then I mooched around from week to week, and it grew from there. In those days, drivers were keen to talk to you, for example I had Michael Schumacher and Gerhard Berger at the same time once. I had raced against all these guys, and they would say to me, "You haven't been to see me recently, come and talk to me," and it used to be just a delight. There was no social media, you didn't have any *Drive to Survive*, the teams didn't have all their own media departments, no Formula One TV, so we were the kings of the castle. But now, the drivers get to the grid and they are fed up of seeing another microphone and camera, because they've been at it since Thursday.'

But how does he prepare for it?

'Again, no thought has ever been put into it or discussion and there is a car-crash nature to it. I don't know what is going to happen next, and I think the fans like that edginess. Some work, some don't and some feel awful to me. I've never, ever watched one back since 1997. I've seen some of the bits that go viral, but I've never sat down and watched one and I couldn't bear the thought of doing so! It's sort of taken on a life of its own, which kind of bothers me, because I'm not a stand-up comedian and I'm not a person who likes being cheeky and interrupting people. It's so not my personality. This alter ego of mine running around causing chaos is terrifying, to be honest with you. It's sometimes 15 minutes of unscripted television, which is hard to do.'

These days, a list of the talent attendees is provided in advance of a race weekend and updated each night. In the States, the list can run to 60 or 70 people, some of whom, certainly when it comes to the influencers, a few of us of a certain age can find difficult to recognise. The grids these days are absolutely packed, and it makes Martin's job even trickier.

'It's still fun, don't get me wrong, but it sort of annoys me, because it defines me and is my legacy, and I want to be defined as a decent quality sports commentator who won some fantastic races and somehow stayed in Formula One for ten years; not as the guy who got ignored on the grid or got knocked over by some bodyguard.

'On the other hand, though, I've met some wonderful people on the grid – what a privilege. Actors, musicians and athletes from every sport imaginable. Really, I always want to talk to the drivers, but now they just want to focus on what they are doing. There is no respite for them.

'There is so much pressure and so much expectation, and the grid walk gets no thought until Sunday morning. But on the flip side of the coin it gets me excited and the adrenaline going. It's the only thing that makes me about 30 per cent as nervous as I was when I was racing. As racing drivers, we are all adrenaline junkies and I still get a rush when I do the grid walk.'

It is clearly a part of the job that divides Brundle's opinion, but either way, he knows it is seminal sports television and nobody does it better. The musician Stormzy, himself a massive Formula One fan, even wrote a lyric about him in his song 'Angel in the Marble'.

You know you've made it your own when that happens.

Brundle has now been involved in the sport for 42 years as a driver and broadcaster. Since Liberty Media took over from Bernie Ecclestone, Formula One has changed beyond all recognition, and he has welcomed the evolution of the sport he is inextricably linked with.

'In all my time, it's in the best shape I've seen it. Everything about it is high quality and it attracts the best people, whether you are a truck driver or in catering, in media or a technician, because it's a very exciting business to be a part of. I think there's been over 150 teams that have gone out of business in the history of Formula One, which is why I run the Grand Prix trust. We've had such turbulent times, teams going broke, all sorts of dodgy people coming through. Right now, it is as sharp, focused and professional as I have seen it, and by some margin. Couple that with the fact that the teams are merging with their technology and aerodynamics, and it is closer than ever. I would say that this is a high point for Formula One.'

And, as Crofty says, when Martin says it, you believe him.

I have been lucky enough to travel the world with these two for the past 14 years. If it all ended tomorrow, I have more than enough great memories to last a lifetime. We are a tight team at Sky Sports F1 and, if you get too big for your boots, someone will shoot you down. I've always believed that if you are friends, the audience will pick up on that and, perhaps, that is one of the strengths of our group. As I said at the start of the book, we spend as much time with each other as we do our families and, although we may, at times, be a little bit dysfunctional, we have shared some wonderful moments together. We hope that comes across on screen.

CHAPTER 25

THE LEGACY ENGINEER

Petrosynthesis
noun

The artificial creation of organic compounds (synthetic petroleum/petrochemicals) and oxygen from inorganic precursors (principally water and carbon-dioxide) using non-biological energy (such as hydro, wind, solar, tidal, nuclear, geothermal); the industrial equivalent of photosynthesis, using neither energy nor material produced by either concurrent photosynthesis (plants) or legacy photosynthesis (fossil fuels).*

Petrosynthesis is not a word recognised by the *Oxford English Dictionary*.

Yet.

Of all the people that I've ever met in Formula One, Paddy Lowe is undoubtedly one of the smartest. An engineer, he studied at Cambridge and entered Formula One in 1987, working in the sport for four decades, during which time he was involved with cars that won 12 world championships (seven drivers' and five constructors'). He began with Williams and, alongside Adrian Newey and Patrick Head, oversaw the development of the active suspension

---

* Patrick Lowe, 'PETROSYNTHESIS: The Completion of the Industrial Revolution', white paper, 15 November 2021.

system that helped Nigel Mansell win the world championship in 1992. He moved to McLaren in 1993 where, when he was chief engineer, Mika Häkkinen won back-to-back championships and Lewis Hamilton won his first title in 2008. From 2013, he moved to Mercedes as technical director and was instrumental in the most dominant era of all time. He was to finish his Formula One life back at Williams, before leaving the sport in 2019.

And then it got *really* interesting.

In 2020 Lowe set up Zero Petroleum, the first British company to make synthetic fuel in a completely fossil-free process. The technology behind it is extremely exciting, and Lowe's belief that it's the future of the planet is unwavering. They have the buy-in of the Royal Air Force, who have been key in their early-stage funding, and have also received a grant from the Department of Transport, as the country tries to remain on course for becoming net carbon zero by 2050.

With Formula One moving to 100 per cent sustainable fuels in 2026, Zero are in position to be a supplier to many of the teams. They are already involved with Audi but how does Zero's technology differ from other sustainable fuels? Lowe has written a white paper on it and when you read it, it gives you hope that there are some very smart people working very hard and applying their huge intellect to one of the world's most imperative and immediate problems.

And just as a by-the-by, this is not an advert!

Currently, most of the world's energy is still derived from the burning of fossil fuels. The alternatives to generate power are:

1. RENEWABLES

Energy generation has been developed in the form of hydro, solar, wind, tidal, geothermal and nuclear power.

These renewables all generate electricity, either directly or indirectly, from heat and are typically unsuited to the generation of power directly at the point of use. Lowe rules out electrification for the future of mobility on the planet.

'This may be controversial, but it is just physics. You cannot electrify something like a Formula One car. The batteries are simply too heavy for the amount of performance you need and the amount of time you need it. People come to Formula One to watch energy at work. It's a big display of energy and it is what creates the drama, makes the cars go fast and hit the wall. With all due respect to Formula E, they do a good job, but it's in a very constrained context. That just wouldn't work at the scale of drama that you need to create for Formula One. If you did it with batteries, a Formula One car would weigh four tonnes. That's not a car, it's a truck.'

To store the same amount of energy as 1kg of gasoline, a lithium-ion battery would need to weigh about 50kg. It's clear then that if the world is to electrify, battery technology will have to get so much lighter and more efficient to provide any long-term answers.

2. HYDROGEN

Hydrogen fuel cell technology permits the reconversion of hydrogen's chemical energy back to electrical energy at the point of use. Synthesised hydrogen is produced by the electrolysis of water by renewable power and returns to water when combusted or reacted to release its energy.

'Hydrogen is not much better than batteries in the future of mobility. It's a very high-energy material, but it is a gas and, to constrain it in a reasonable volume, you need very heavy containers. You end up with roughly five times the weight of the equivalent in gasoline. These numbers still don't work for performance or for any commercial vehicle. I'm not exaggerating here, but if you had a hydrogen-powered 737 aeroplane, you'd go past row six or seven in business class, pull back the curtains and there'd be a hydrogen tank. There'd be no economy class!'

3. BIOFUELS

A huge range of biofuels have been developed over several decades including biodiesel and bioethanol. First-generation biofuels use sugarcane or maize and convert the sugar and starch to energy. Second-generation biofuels use agricultural waste as the feedstock by converting the cellulose to energy.

'There is simply not enough global land capacity for this to be a viable long-term option. There is also the threat, of course, to biodiversity. But as a good example of this in terms of the restrictions on scaling, if you wanted to fly the entire British Airways fleet for a year on biofuels, you would need all the agriculture of Ireland to do so. It doesn't work. It's the same with the fuels produced from waste cooking oils or municipal waste, there just isn't enough material.'

No one said trying to solve the world's energy crisis was going to be easy!

'I'm a systems guy. For me it's only worth working on something that's going to work for the whole thing, otherwise you are just wasting your time and it's a distraction. So you have to have something that will truly solve the problem in its entirety.'

For Lowe, none of the above are solutions.

'It's got to scale and it's got to be feasible and it's got to meet reasonable cost levels. So that's what Zero is all about. Synthetic fuel can be any hydrocarbon, anything that you can get from crude oil that you drill out of the ground. It can be diesel, jet fuel or gasoline. Or it could be gas, so propane or butane. It can even be chemicals like the ones used to make plastic. We can make these hydrocarbons from scratch. Hydrocarbons are just hydrogen and carbon. Another way of looking at it is what comes out the exhaust of your car. When you burn petrol (a hydrocarbon) what comes out of the tailpipe is carbon dioxide from burning the carbon, and water from burning the hydrogen. So all we are doing to make synthetic fuel at Zero is reversing that and reconstituting the fuel.'

This is what Lowe terms 'Petrosynthesis'. Simply, Zero are trying to recreate what a forest does in a factory.

In nature (and you might remember this from school) the basis of all life on earth employs carbon, oxygen and hydrogen as the primary chemical elements to capture, store and distribute energy and construction material for use by plants and animals. Plants capture solar energy by photosynthesis and convert atmospheric carbon dioxide and water into hydrocarbons such as sugar, oil, fat, starch, protein, wood and fibre. It's why your garden grows in the summer when there is enough solar energy for the plants to harness. Animals either eat these plants or they decompose and are returned to the earth. Deposits of the decomposed matter have been forced underground over millions of years and, since the industrial revolution, we have dug them up in the form of coal and then, more recently, drilled for them in the form of oil and gas.

Prior to the industrial revolution the planet was largely in balance when it came to this so-called carbon cycle, but since then, with the accelerated burning of the hydrocarbon deposits, that has changed and created an imbalance of the atmospheric carbon dioxide levels, causing global warming. In essence, everything that has been done so far to try to solve the world's energy crisis and reliance on fossil fuels has failed.

'An industrial carbon cycle works in the same way as a biological carbon cycle. The animals are the equivalent of a combustion engine, consuming hydrocarbons from either plants or other animals, and what we are doing is replicating what the plants are doing on an industrial scale. To reconstitute the fuel, you need to put in energy because you've received the energy when you've burned it. So that energy needs to be renewable, and I believe that the components that we need to do that are solar power at a vast scale.'

In simple terms, Lowe and his team have developed a process that was invented a century ago by two German scientists, Franz Fischer and Hans Tropsch. They used a series of chemical reactions to convert a mixture of carbon monoxide and hydrogen into liquid hydrocarbons. At this stage, Zero take the hydrogen from the electrolysis of water, and the carbon from the CO_2 by the fermentation of sugars. To scale, they will eventually need to use direct carbon capture.

'Our technology is a very specialised variant of the Fischer-Tropsch process, with a far superior performance to the original that has been extensively developed over the years. The unique thing it allows us to do is make refinery-grade fuels straight from our process. So out of our chemistry we are directly making a gasoline that can go into your car and in 2021 we flew the first aeroplane with the help of the RAF, on 100 per cent synthetic fuel, and got the Guinness world record. We can now also make a complete replica of standard jet fuel that goes into aircraft. Nobody else in the world can do that.'

Other synthetic fuel manufacturers are making hydrocarbon products that then need to be refined, more like a synthetic crude oil. Zero are effectively their own refinery, and can recreate the molecular compounds of any of the different fractions of oil. The chemistry is extremely advanced and the first five years of the business have been about proving the concept.

Based in Bicester, they are extremely close to motorsport valley and have direct access to Oxford University. Now at 60 employees, Lowe and his team are a mixture of academics, engineers and chemists from the petrochemical and automotive industries, a fair smattering of whom formerly worked in Formula One. Many Formula One teams have an applied sciences department, taking the technology of the sport and adapting it for use in other sectors. Zero is perhaps the ultimate extension of this. They are currently looking at a $90 million funding round for the next phase of development.

'The really big story is that we've explained and proved that we can make synthetic fuel from air and water and renewable energy. So then we have to talk about scale and cost, which is where I started. Does this work? And the answer is yes. Firstly scale. So if I made a huge solar farm that was 25 per cent of the land area of Saudi Arabia, mostly uninhabitable desert, that would make enough electricity to make the equivalent, via our process, of all the oil we use today on earth.'

Let that sink in for a bit.

The reason that Lowe believes that solar power is the answer is that solar panels have a long lifetime of between 50 and 100 years, have fewer working parts to go wrong, so require less maintenance than wind turbines, and the cost point is coming down rapidly. They are made largely from silicon, which is plentiful on earth and therefore relatively cheap.

'At the moment Zero's fuel is roughly four to five times the cost of fossil fuels. But we have modelled it and this may sound extreme to you, but we reckon that in as little as ten years we will be at cost parity. And I need to nuance that with the fact that we won't be able to compete with the extraction costs of oil in Saudi Arabia but in the UK, those costs are some of the highest in the world, so we could be competing with North Sea oil within a decade. The idea is that in 20 to 30 years the world has migrated completely away from drilling in very difficult places for fossil fuel. This is not imaginary, it is very real. In the past people moved from the horse to the car.'

Of course there will be naysayers and those, particularly in the oil and gas industries, who won't want this technology to prevail while there are still dollars in the ground. And this is why there are remarkably few companies in the world doing what Zero do, but the upside to society is surely going to be the driving factor in this sector.

'There are perhaps only ten companies in our sphere doing this. In 20 years' time, I think people will realise that there is no point trying to locate and drill for oil in a really difficult place out at sea, when you can build a synthetic fuel plant on land, in a stable place, own it for ever and have a limitless supply of oil, that is better and cheaper. For me it is inevitable because it is an entirely industrial process, this manufacture of oil. It's all machinery and it will keep getting better and cheaper, like all industrial products in history. It sounds extraordinary to say now but we will literally wean ourselves off the drilling and mining, and we will be making it.'

Right now Zero has their first plant, 0.1, which is in production at an engineering scale. Within 0.1 are plants that are producing different volumes of different hydrocarbons, while they still experiment and improve their processes. The small plant produces 100cc per day, the medium can produce three litres per day and the large, which is not yet conditioned, will make 30 or 40 litres per day. The sole focus of 0.1 is to improve the efficiency and try to create more fuel for less energy.

Plant 0.2 is the next step and will be capable of producing quantities suitable for market. As you can imagine, with no product to sell up until this point, the business has been extremely capital intensive and reliant on the support from the RAF, the government grant from the Advanced Fuels Fund and private investors. As they transition to their next phase, they are looking for institutional money.

'If I was to really summarise it: we need liquid fuels, there is simply no way we can electrify the planet, not by a country mile. And the only way that we can deliver liquid fuels at the scale of consumption that we have today from the fossil fuel industry, is by synthetics. There is enough land in the world to do it. The difficulty for us at the moment is evangelism. It frustrates me that most people don't even know about it. They have no idea that you can make oil. Even I didn't think you could make oil until six or seven years ago.'

That is not the only issue.

'The main headwind to the process is cost. We need to reconstruct the entire upstream section of the oil industry. If I had ten minutes at COP29, or whatever the next one is, I would say, "Look, everyone, talk around us all you like, but what we have to do is stop drilling oil out of the ground and the only way to do that is to replace oil with a synthetic version." And we've just got to get on with it. And that is the capital challenge.'

So how much would it cost?

'My range is quite wide and the costs will come down but it's something between $200–400 trillion.

'"Oh," I hear you say … "Shit!"'

'If you read the papers on it, this is the cost needed to de-fossilise the earth over the next 30 years. Currently the investment in the oil and gas industry runs at $1 trillion per year. But it requires a paradigm shift and I'm not even sure the governments have got their head round the fact that you can have your own asset that makes unlimited oil, rather than buying it off an oil company.'

Unlike Formula One, there is no rule book for what Lowe and his team are trying to achieve. it reminds him of the time when he first joined Formula One and innovation was at its most pronounced.

'In 1987, the rule book was very thin and the only limitation was capability. We'd only just come out of the "back of a shed" phase, as an industry. I arrived in the first wave of academically trained engineers. Nowadays, the top universities recognise Formula One as a fantastic career. That wasn't the case when I started. So now you have incredible intellect deployed, much larger budgets and extraordinary capability. In fact, Formula One has overtaken its peer sectors, like aviation and the rest of the automotive sector, in terms of the tools it works with, like CFD [computational fluid dynamics] and aerodynamics. It's far more advanced than most other industries. That has come through 30 or 40 years of continuous growth in the calibre of engineers and the amount of investment in technical capital.'

Lowe was ever present throughout that time. Four decades spent watching from the inside, as the pinnacle of the automotive engineering sector improved to the level it is at today. He watched and worked with many of the greats behind the wheel, as legends perished and champions were crowned. Lowe is now channelling all that energy and brain power into the biggest challenge mankind has ever faced. And while barriers such as industrial-scale carbon capture, renewable energy production, conversion inefficiencies and attitudinal shifts will take time and require money, they are not insurmountable. If the field of sustainable fuels can advance as Formula One did under Lowe's watch, then perhaps there is a chance that the planet won't suffocate. Surely it is time that we invest in making hydrocarbons rather than burning what already exist. And let's hope that sometime very soon everybody has heard of the word that Lowe invented. Remember it; it's pretty important.

Petrosynthesis.

CHAPTER 26

THE ENGINE GURU

At the start of 2026, Formula One will change its regulations again. It will be the start of a new cycle, a reset. Usually when this happens, we see one team exploit the regulations better than the others and surge ahead. It happened with Brawn and their double diffuser in 2009. It happened with Red Bull in 2022 with their solid grasp of ground effects, courtesy of Adrian Newey, who wrote a thesis on it at university, and it happened back in 2014 with Mercedes, who were top of the class in building the new turbo-hybrid engines.

The man who led the design and development of that power unit is the former managing director of Mercedes AMG High Performance Powertrains (HPP) and now CEO and team principal of the Aston Martin Formula One team, Andy Cowell.

'I've got my dad to blame for being who I am. He still races home-built sprint and hill-climb cars and, from an early age, I helped him build them and go racing. It was absolutely at the amateur level, no sponsors. Build your own car, build your own trailer and go racing.'

Cowell went to a state school in Blackpool and then to Lancaster University to study mechanical engineering. As he was graduating, his dad spotted an advert in the back of *Autosport* for Reynard racing cars, who were looking for graduates.

'I had never thought of having a career in motorsport. I thought I would follow the route of doing motorsport at the weekend as a hobby, and a normal professional engineering job during the week.

I went along to Reynard, and suddenly my eyes were opened to the fact that there was a semi-professional motorsport engineering industry. I finished my degree and applied for motorsport jobs as well as normal ones, like British Aerospace and so on. Adrian Reynard offered me a job paying £6k per year, and Cosworth [automotive engineering company] offered me a job paying £11k per year. So I took the money and that's what got me started in engine design!'

Cowell spent 12 years at Cosworth, joining on the graduate scheme and working his way through the assorted technical departments, before specialising in the design of Formula One engines. Ford bought Cosworth in 1998 to strengthen their involvement in the sport. They rebranded their engine division as Cosworth Racing and supplied engines for Stewart Grand Prix. It was Cowell who, that year, headed up the engineering group for the innovative CK engine, which powered the team to a win at the European Grand Prix in 1999 with my good friend and former colleague Johnny Herbert at the wheel.* It was to be their first and only victory before they rebranded as Jaguar Racing in 2000.

Cowell joined Mercedes in 2004 and worked on the Mercedes-Ilmor V10 engine project. In those days, Mercedes were an engine supplier in Formula One for the McLaren and Jordan teams. The following year Mercedes took 100 per cent ownership of Mercedes HPP.

'Ola Källenius joined at the end of 2004, and he was one of the best leaders that I have ever worked for. It was simply the best or nothing, for him. He set us up with the equipment and processes to give us the wherewithal and the approach to win.'

It's difficult to understate the importance of Ola Källenius to the success of the Mercedes Formula One team. He is now the chairman and CEO of the Mercedes Benz group, taking over from Dieter Zetsche in 2019. We will come back to him.

_____

* We once jumped out of a Hercules plane together strapped to a couple of sailors – it was exhilarating.

With the best equipment at his fingertips, Cowell and the team at HPP set about working on hybrid cars after the KERS regulations were first published at the end of 2006. They then had a two-year period of development before they went racing in 2009 as a supplier to Brawn GP, Force India and McLaren.

KERS means kinetic energy recovery system and its use was optional for the teams in 2009, and was a precursor to the ERS system adopted in 2014. The system allowed cars to recover energy during braking and store it for use as extra power during acceleration, giving them a temporary boost. However, not all the teams chose to use it in 2009 because of the complexity of the system, the added weight and the reliability factors. It was still very much an experimental phase for engine developers like Cowell.

'That was the period when we started developing high-powered batteries, electric motors and power electronics and so on, and it was fun seeing engineers adapt. There were lots of engineers that had previously worked in a purely mechanical environment that then had to transfer across and learn electrical engineering. At HPP, we were always determined to have all the systems created in the factory at Brixworth. You are integrating the heart of an electric motor into an internal combustion engine, and you want to marry them together as closely as possible. If you can look at where the first big-end bearing is on the crankshaft, and where the gear drive is, and where the electric motor is going to go in, you can merge it together and balance the requirements, because it is all yours, it's all Mercedes, the whole environment. You are not having to work with two separate companies.'

Brawn GP chose not to use KERS in 2009, but still won the championship with Jenson Button, thanks to their innovative double diffuser concept. But, at the end of the year, Mercedes took the huge decision to re-enter the sport as a works outfit, as their parent company, Daimler, wanted to enhance the Mercedes brand's visibility and image. It was then that the pressure on Cowell and his team began to ramp up. As the engineering director at HPP, he took the learnings from the KERS project and applied it to the next huge set of regulations that were to start in 2014, when the cars became 1.6 litre V6 turbos.

'Another system was added on with the turbo charger. This system uses a compressor to shove the air into the engine, and a turbine to extract energy from the exhaust stream and an electric machine called the MGU-H, which captures and utilises this energy. Again, it is about stripping it back to basics. What's the system diagram? What are the power and energy restrictions? What does that mean in terms of the size of the compressor, the turbine and the electric motor? And then you just play around with where you position the components. If you own all the real estate and you understand that every single race car designer doesn't want a great big barnacle on the side of the engine cover, or anything that pushes the gearbox cluster rearwards, then you are doing your job. The engine will always sit in the shadow cast by the driver's shoulders, and then taper in. So, with that in the back of your head, everything just gets laid out. If you can do that without losing thermal efficiency, then you will produce something that will be pretty impressive in the back of a race car.'

And it was. The power unit that Cowell and his team provided for the works team in 2014 was a work of art. It was the basis of the prolonged success that the Mercedes team enjoyed for eight straight constructors' championships and seven straight drivers' championships in the turbo-hybrid era.

'I think Mercedes had two major advantages over our competitors in that period. Firstly, as we have mentioned, having everything under one roof so that it limited outsourced parts, and secondly, that we got on with it as soon as possible. Time is your enemy, whenever you are developing something. The sooner you make an example and measure what it can do, the sooner you learn whether your calculations are real or not. Mercedes are big fans of going around a learning loop. So, you have a theory, you do some calculations and CAD drawings. You make it, you assemble it, you test it, you look at the results and you see if the results tie in with your original theory. The more you do that, the more you learn. As soon as the regulations were being talked about, we got on with it.'

It meant that when the new regulations came in, they were ready to hit the ground running. But when that happens it is a monumental task for every team just to get everything in place for the first race, let alone to continue developing to stay ahead of the rest. In 2014 there were 19 races on the calendar, and more have been added since. It takes its toll on the teams.

'One of the biggest challenges of that period, in spite of the fact that we were winning, was how to make success sustainable. You are racing all the time, whilst at the same time developing for the following year. So you need to set the organisation and the methods up so that you can develop and go racing, without relying on individuals. And that is what I mean by sustainability in an engineering sense. People aren't creative if they are tired and under pressure. You need to set up an environment of healthy pressure, so that the creativity thrives and an environment where everyone is self-critical, and therefore constantly thinking of what's next and how to improve. Celebrating was brief during that time!'

You can see why Aston Martin recruited Andy Cowell. He started as CEO in October 2024 and, at the start of 2025, also assumed the role of team principal, taking over from Mike Krack. Lawrence Stroll is extremely ambitious, and has poured money into the project since he bought the team, then Force India, out of administration in 2018. Stroll's expectations are high and he is not afraid to make changes to his organisation: Cowell is the third team principal since his takeover. But with the new set of regulations due, Cowell is being trusted as the man to pull it all together. What can he take across from his time at Mercedes, a team he left in 2020 after seven successive winning years?

'I guess I keep coming back to some of the things that Ola Källenius did at Brixworth. This way of running a business whilst staying focused on going racing. We are in a cost-cap era, so financial resources are limited, and it's the same for everybody. So the amount that you can deliver within that cost cap is the game that we are all in. Lessons I learnt from working on a small budget at Cosworth and the business approach that I learnt from Ola rattle around in my head. And Ola's absolute bravery with asking questions and learning new things. It's just listening and challenging and setting a vision of where we are trying to get to. Which Ola was brilliant at, at Mercedes.'

The difference for Cowell this time around is that he is overseeing a project that isn't all under one roof, like it was at Mercedes. In May 2023, Aston Martin announced that they would be partnering with Honda as their engine supplier from 2026. What's more, the two roofs couldn't be further apart, with Honda's Formula One engines manufactured in Sakura, Japan. Cowell will need to ensure the two companies are working in harmony.

'Honda have won several world championships in recent times, and are mighty competitors. Their capability to provide a championship-winning power unit is not questioned. I guess what I am trying to do is provide an understanding to people within Aston Martin of what the power-unit people are thinking, and also provide an understanding to Honda of what the race-car creators are thinking. I'm dancing either side of two engineering groups to try and get them to understand each other. It's different perspectives.'

On top of the language barrier, there are the time and cultural differences to overcome in making the partnership a success.

'Honda's engineers are super creative, motivated and technically highly capable. They have an incredible supply base as well. They've got reach to all the Japanese and European suppliers and they are in a unique position on that front. Its advantageous to us because they can access different companies and therefore opportunities. They can pick the best from the east or the west.'

Now, 99.9 per cent of Cowell's time is spent on helping to create a fast racing car, which sounds obvious but he is less hands-on now, in engineering terms, than he was in the early part of his Mercedes career.

'Probably for the last four or five years of my time at Mercedes I was the leader of the business, rather than the chief engineer of the power unit. There was Formula One, which was the largest aspect, but also Formula E and the Mercedes-AMG ONE. One of the things I personally learnt through 2014 was that, to make it sustainable, you need a breadth of people, a group of chief engineers to look after the current power unit and the following one. That transition to leading a business rather than engineering something was what I went through at Mercedes.'

Cowell aspires to keep everyone at Aston Martin across how they are performing as a business. He sees it as his role to make sure the whole team is aware of where they are at, what they are trying to achieve and that the work that is done is well balanced across the business. That is not just management speak. It feels like an experienced engineer applying his incredible logic to solving a business problem, rather than a technical one.

'You need every single department to be equally strong. You need HR to be strong so that we recruit and retain the best people. Operations needs to be strong so that we can make things quicker than we have ever made before, but with the quality still maintained. Every week you can leave the aerodynamicists in a wind tunnel is probably worth 50 milliseconds gained to a fixed race point. So what can operations do to condense their lead time? That's how they contribute to lap time. So how do you link the purpose of every single department to the performance of a product, whether that is a power unit or a whole race car?'

Cowell wants everyone to come to work thinking the same thing.

'I'm here in order for that race car to win. And everybody knows how far away from winning we are, what we are trying to do and the investment is balanced across every single department.'

But how do you operate better than others in a cost-cap era?

'As much as possible I've always tried to run a business where the financial side is looked after by a group of people and the creative engineering side is looked after by another group of people and you work hard so that you never have to say no to the creative group. They are the geese that you want to lay the golden eggs. You want them to just sit there laying egg after egg after egg. One thing that pisses off creative types is worrying them about money. So every time they think of a new toy, or say they want someone new to help them, just say "YES" and remain poker faced when you walk off thinking, *Shit, how are we going to pay for this?!'*

In the power-unit world, these geese are the combustion engineers.

'It is a group of people that chase combustion efficiency and the whole thermodynamics of the engine. They are the group of people that you show huge amounts of love to. You don't bother them with man–management challenges. You never say no to them financially because it is an area that brings lap time.'

On the race-car side, Cowell doesn't like saying no to the aero-dynamicists for the same reason. Much of Stroll's investment has gone into creating a state-of-the-art facility next to Silverstone with a wind tunnel that came on stream in early 2025. They hope it will be the final piece of the jigsaw to become consistent championship challengers. Only seven short years ago the team was bankrupt, and about to go out of business. Despite living hand to mouth, though, the team were still managing to go racing and be competitive.

'Half of the team come from that era, and half have come in from other teams and other industries. And my challenge is how you bring 900 people together so that we aren't thinking we are Force India or Mercedes or Dyson, or wherever everybody has come from. We are Aston Martin Formula One team and are entrusted with this amazing brand that is attracting strong sponsorship, and how do we carry that winged logo forward and write our own bit of history? And what would we class as great? It is winning races, winning a championship and then back-to-back world championships. With that as a vision, it is then a case of what do we need to realise this? What is the equipment, what are the methods? What are the ways of passing the baton from person to person in order to create better ideas than anybody else, and get them to a race track? Because until they are at a race track, and actually making a car go quicker, you are just in the investment phase, not in the benefiting phase.'

Cowell has that vision and knows what it looks like in reality because he achieved multiple titles with Mercedes. With money no object, Stroll has assembled a dream team. Alongside Mercedes's former engine guru, he has made perhaps the biggest designer coup in the history of the sport in luring the great Adrian Newey from Red Bull. Stroll has paid top dollar for them both, and it is not lost on Cowell that his boss expects to be at the sharp end in 2026.

'It's hard to describe what it is like working for Lawrence. It's probably going to be ten years before I can say it succinctly. He genuinely thinks about it 24/7 and is 100 per cent focused on winning and being the best. He's incredibly intelligent, passionate, totally determined and a friend. But the goal is that, in the short term, the time we put in on the factory campus delivers lap time on the track. This needs to happen regularly. In the medium term, how does the rate at which we do that become quicker than our opponents? Because then it's just a question of time before you overtake them and are at the front.'

Cowell has a way of simplifying everything. He can make the extremely complex seem glaringly obvious. Everything comes back to basics and making sure that all 900 people working for Aston Martin understand their roles and the direction in which the team is heading. Only time will tell whether his methods will bring championships, but with him and Newey at the helm, and 39 world titles between them, you'd be reluctant to bet against them.

Oh and, by the by, some of you might be wondering why there is not a chapter about a technical director. Adrian Newey wrote a book on it, called *How to Build a Car*, so I didn't think I'd bother, as I believe he had most things covered, so please refer to that!

CHAPTER 27

THE CEO

Someone who has recently understood how to take a team to the top is Zak Brown. He is, by his own admission, a workaholic. He is also one of the most approachable team bosses in the paddock. Boundlessly energetic, he has overseen a turnaround in McLaren's fortunes that has been several years, one boardroom coup and one pandemic in the making. In transforming the team from what it was to what it is now, he has cemented his place in the annals of racing history, something that has been an ambition of his since he was a boy. Because, first and foremost, Brown is a racer.

I had known of Brown before he took over as the top man at McLaren, through his role as CEO and founder of his sports marketing agency, JMI. Several friends from my university days have worked for him, and not one of them has a bad word to say. In fact, many of them owe their careers to Brown, and they will admit that. He is one of those leaders, as Nick Martin explained, that leads by example, works seven days a week and expects huge levels of commitment across the board. He is relentless in everything that he does, and that is one of the main reasons why he has turned around a floundering organisation. When he arrived in 2016, McLaren had Honda as an engine partner.

'I came in and everyone was telling me that it was a power unit problem. "It's all their fault." And I know that McLaren is almighty, so at first I believed them. No, it fucking wasn't. Yeah, the engine was a disaster as well, but the problems ran so much deeper than that. And it was overwhelming because of how pissed off everybody was. So the first thing I had to do was rally the troops. And that's not easy and it takes time.

'You've got three groups of people: those that like to follow your lead right away, those that are on the fence because this place had been a revolving door and then there's the people who aren't with the programme and you just need to throw them off the fucking bus. But it takes a while to get the big boat turned around, throw the excess water off and get out of the marina to be able to pull back the throttle.'

Brown's responsibility, when he initially joined, because of his background, was to get the commercial side of the organisation functioning again. As we've heard in previous chapters, McLaren was in a dark place, metaphorically and literally, with a struggling grey car and a dearth of sponsors.

'It was the easiest place for me to start because I had been doing that a long time. A lot of sponsors weren't just pissed off with the results but also by how they were being treated. There was an arrogance from some who thought, *We are McLaren, who cares that we're ninth, we're great,* and a lack of empathy with our commercial partners, even though we were not delivering. When I first stood up and did one of my town halls in front of a thousand people, most of them were looking at me and thinking, *How long is this fucking guy going to last?* There is nothing worse than talking to that many people and getting nothing back.'

So, as well as setting about the commercials of the business he set about changing the leadership team one by one.

'I didn't come in with that in mind. I didn't come in thinking I'm going to clean the house and do it my way. It was more, I'm coming in, let me see what's going on and then make some decisions. It wasn't long before I understood why that department sucked, or why that department was disgruntled. So I changed every single leadership member, one at a time, after I had given them all a chance. It started with a fight at the boardroom level. The troops want to follow the leader, but when the leaders are following, where do the troops go?'

When Brown came in, there was a transitional period, with long-term boss Ron Dennis eventually forced to sell the remainder of his shares in the company after this boardroom coup. Dennis had had a long-standing conflict with the majority shareholders, particularly Mumtalakat, Bahrain's sovereign wealth fund, and the TAG group, led by the late Mansour Ojjeh, who disagreed with his management style and the future direction of the company. In 2016 Dennis attempted to buy out the other shareholders with backing from a Chinese investment group, but the deal was rejected and the move worsened the relationship. The McLaren shareholders placed Dennis on gardening leave in November 2016, effectively forcing him out as CEO, before he stepped down in June 2017, ending his 37-year association with McLaren. Brown immediately got to work unravelling the mess that the company had got itself into.

'Back then I had seven people report into me and all seven leaders went. A couple of them left of their own accord, because they knew what was coming. I needed to get people around me that would challenge me. So you would think that my management team now hate each other half the time, but that's what I want. People are fully encouraged to give me their views and we'll debate it. Sometimes I put my foot down but other times I will come in, put a firm idea on the table and get everyone to start challenging it. I might walk out of that exchange having done a 180-degree turn. I have no problem doing that if they convince me that I'm wrong.'

That transparency and openness has been a feature of Brown's McLaren. He is the type of leader who inspires respect because he lays it all out as it is. But how would he describe himself as a leader?

'I'm a variety of things. I work hard. If you can't keep pace, it will be evident in two minutes. I'm brutally honest. And I like to have fun, because I think if you are working seven days a week, who wants to be around miserable people? Plus, I find that I can push people harder if we are having fun. I will berate my team, but the minute I'm not, that's when you've got to worry. I get the most out of people by beating the shit out of them – in a fun way, but so they also know I'm not joking. I try not to be an asshole, but if I am an asshole, I'm deliberately doing it with a smile on my face. But I will be getting my message across. So it's just a style!'

In a world that is increasingly petrified about behaviour in the workplace, I find Brown's honesty refreshing. It seems perfectly obvious that the best way to treat each other is with respect, and doing the right thing should be standard procedure. It appears that the culture in McLaren is based around this tough-but-fair ethos, which stems from Brown's childhood. Brown was born in Los Angeles in 1971 and attended several different high schools without ever graduating. By his own admission, he was a difficult student.

'Unless I wanted to do it, I wouldn't. I was a defiant kid. I ditched, I fought, I got thrown out of schools. I was less about making everyone follow me, and more about doing it my way. And if I wasn't interested in doing something, I wasn't quietly not interested. I was an in-your-face troublemaker, class clown, attention-seeking punk. I've matured a little bit since then!'

Brown has taken aspects of the disruptive side of his personality into business. He clearly had a head for money early on and even appeared on *Wheel of Fortune* as a child, winning a cash prize that he used to help fund his early racing career in competitive karting. He won 22 races between 1986 and 1990, and then moved to Europe to compete in Formula Ford 1600. Over the years, Brown has competed in more racing series than most people could ever dream of, and he's done it on both sides of the Atlantic. From the Formula Opel-Lotus Benelux series to British Formula Three, Indy Lights, German Formula Three, endurance racing at Daytona and Sebring, Ferrari Challenge and the British GT Championship to name but a few. The guy is totally obsessed. He loves racing anything, anywhere and he continues to do so to this day. He knew early on that he wasn't ever going to make it to the top level, so he made his hobby his work and grew his motorsport marketing agency, JMI (Just

Marketing International), to become the largest of its kind in the world. In 2013 he sold that business to CSM and by then had forged a reputation as one of the world's leading sports marketing executives. It was that nous and head for a deal that attracted the McLaren board and secured Brown his dream job.

Brands and sponsorship had been Brown's life, and when he arrived, he also knew that the McLaren brand was in urgent need of a refresh.

'The rebrand to papaya was huge. I remember when we did it, a couple of the old-school people within the organisation asked me if I was only changing it to get the fans back onside. Err, was that a fucking trick question? That's exactly why we're doing it. I felt like we didn't have a very warm identity.'

Brown is at pains to point out the *Star Wars* analogy. McLaren were Darth Vader and they wanted to be more Luke Skywalker.

'I'm not a big *Star Wars* person, but I think that analogy makes sense. We look at our building, the MTC, and the sport that we are in. Darth Vader is cool and domineering but that was cool 20 years ago. Now, cool is Lando and Oscar stopping for autographs and being fan friendly; the papaya played into a new era for us, and Lou was critical to that. She has done an incredible job bringing our brand to life in a modern, fun way. McLaren, as cool as it was, was cold, clinical and hard. That was awesome and one way to do it. It wasn't wrong but our new era is summed up by our young drivers, whose personalities fit our brand so well.'

The McLaren that we see these days and the mantra Brown has brought to the team is all about authenticity. His vision about being a successful brand is utterly rooted in that principle. To get the fans behind you, they have to believe in you and what you stand for. It's as true in business as it is in life.

'You can't go wrong if you are just constantly telling the truth. You don't have to remember what you've said, or spin it, if you just tell the truth. I've never been one to believe in trade secrets. I think that's all voodoo and nonsense. Just be transparent, open and honest, and if you do get it wrong just hold your hands up and go, "Guess what, we got it wrong!"'

But was there a specific moment when Brown realised McLaren were on track to where they are today, the 2024 constructors' champions?

'When I moved Andreas Seidl out and Andrea Stella in.'

Andreas Seidl was the team principal of McLaren between 2019 and 2022, and was Brown's appointment.

'When we won in 2021 and we had a pretty good year, people thought that was down to Andreas Seidl, Tony Salter [former head of aerodynamics] and James Key [former technical director]. It wasn't.'

In 2021 Daniel Ricciardo and Lando Norris finished first and second in Monza at the Italian Grand Prix. It was McLaren's first win since Jenson Button in Brazil, in the last race of 2012. It was seen by many as a turning point in their fortunes and, when they finished fourth in the championship, a sign that they were getting back to where a team of their stature belonged. With the benefit of hindsight, these green shoots of recovery were a false dawn.

'In 2019 we were developing the car for 2020. That was Pete Prodromou [head of aerodynamics], Andrea Stella [racing director] Gil de Ferran and Pat Fry. They built a good car in 2020, and all we did in 2021, because it was Covid, was change engine supplier from Renault to Mercedes. We got five podiums and won a race. That was my 2019 team. My 2021 team was Seidl, Salter and Key who, for the first time, built the 2022 car.'

The 2021 team, though, were responsible for the upgrade packages throughout that year. Despite the win in Monza, Brown had his Damascene moment earlier that year, after the French Grand Prix.

'We had a massive upgrade package at the French Grand Prix in late June of 2021, and it didn't work. And the response from my leadership team was not what you would expect from a leadership team. You don't have to act like it is a crisis but, as far as I was concerned, it was. So before the summer break, I gave them a scolding report card. Out of 13 categories, 12 were red and one was amber. I think that pissed them off. I then got the message from Seidl towards the end of the year that he was going to see his contract out until 2025, and then leave and go to Audi, and I just said, "You know what, go tomorrow." It was a blessing in disguise.'

Andreas Seidl left McLaren at the end of 2022. Andrea Stella immediately replaced him.

'The moment I put Andrea in, I had him assess what was going on. He came back to me with a detailed report two weeks later. Even though we hadn't touched the car yet, at that point we called out that our 2023 car was going to be bad. But I could tell by Andrea's actions, communications and the restructuring that he started to put into place, that this was a guy who gets it. As a CEO, you have kind of a gut instinct and, when you get a good gut feel, the results kind of follow but then my gut feel was that we were heading for a disaster, and that's what happened. But I knew Andrea was going to be able to turn it around and unlock the potential of the team. The interesting thing was that, out of the thousand people we have in the Formula One team, at that stage I only changed the three most senior leaders and so the same 997 people who gave us the car at the start of 2023 were the same 997 that we just won the world championship with, and that is the power of great leadership.'

Brown believes in Stella. He has total faith in his team principal these days, and so he should. That transformation from plumb last in the championship after the first couple of rounds in 2023 to constructors' champions in 2024 was one of the most remarkable turnarounds in the history of the sport.

'Andrea leads by example and is a fantastic communicator and listener. Hard as nails but in a polite way. Extremely articulate but he doesn't suffer fools, so you can't bullshit him. He's effectively a technical director with a team principal's roles and responsibilities. He restructured the technical department and brought back Pete Prodromou in charge of aero, brought Rob Marshall in, elevated

Neil Houldey, promoted Mark Temple. He took people that we weren't getting the most out of, gave them clear goals and authority. He's just a fucking awesome leader.'

Within that, it is important not to underestimate the recruitment of Rob Marshall from Red Bull. Now the chief designer, he joined McLaren at the beginning of 2024. Wherever Marshall has gone in Formula One, success has followed. He joined Benetton in 1994 as a race engineer for Giancarlo Fisichella and stayed with them as they transitioned to Renault in the early 2000s, helping steer the team, technically, towards Fernando Alonso's two world championships. In 2006, he joined Red Bull as chief designer, working with Adrian Newey and playing a key role in all of Sebastian Vettel's championship wins and the first three of Max Verstappen's.

'He never talks down to you. He breaks technical things down simply and is a creative genius. He's gotten the team comfortable with living life on the edge. So flexi-wings, brilliant, they were totally legal, they were visible to everyone, but he pushed it right to the edge. When I started here, we were of the mindset that we were trying to be as good as the "Big Three". We were defeated before we started. He was like, "Fuck that, we are the big four now." And he brought a confidence and an ingenuity and a belief that there is nothing that they are doing that we can't do better. His hands are dirty all the time. He's never in his office. Any time I see him, he's under the floor of the car. He looks like he works in a petrol station half the time! The team love him for it. He doesn't sit in his ivory tower, drawing.'

What McLaren achieved in 2024 was particularly remarkable, because they beat the Mercedes works team. More often than not, the works teams have prevailed in Formula One. Brown believes that the cost-cap era might spell an end to that.

'You have one big disadvantage as a customer team. The works team gets earlier visibility to what is going on so when they are designing and packaging, they have a head start. Now that you can't change the engine mapping, you can take our engine and swap it with theirs and there is no difference. The works teams have just happened to be the best teams.

'Over the past few years. Benetton won as a customer team and so did Williams, so I've always thought that you could win as a customer, and I've been proved right.'

Brown, like many who work in the sport, thinks that the cost cap is creating a more competitive field. All of the teams are now operating at the cap and have sufficient funds to spend the maximum that they are allowed. So does that mean that there is a future where there are six or seven teams fighting for the wins?

'Undoubtedly the level of competitiveness is going to grow, but I think that the one variable is that the best people are going to want to work for the best teams. Do I think that we will get to a stage where all ten teams are fighting for wins in the future? No, maybe five or six, because the drivers' salaries aren't included in the cost cap. So the likes of Mercedes, Red Bull, Ferrari and ourselves will always have an advantage as we can always pay more to have the best drivers. But I do think it is only going to get tighter.'

As the CEO, like in any organisation, Brown has the closest ties with the board and reports directly into them. In McLaren's case, the majority shareholders are the Bahraini sovereign wealth fund, Mumtalakat. Like Brown, the crown prince of Bahrain is a racer himself, and the Grand Prix that they put on over there is a massive passion project for the royal family. After McLaren won the championship, the crown prince was pictured in the centre of the team photo. It summed up how passionate he and his team are for McLaren, and it was the reward for their years of backing that hadn't borne fruit.

'You couldn't ask for a better board, because they are totally supportive. They let me get on with it and they are racers first. They want to win and they understand the brand. Formula One is not a normal business so you need someone who understands the sport.'

For Brown though, now that they have tasted success and lifted the constructors' championship, there is a thirst for more from all the stakeholders, especially the Bahrainis. So how will he do that?

'We've got to keep the politics out of the team, not only our team, but the politics and disruption people are trying to bring onto our team. If you look at Red Bull, they have a great driver, huge budget, great technology, why are they sliding backwards? Because they lost half the pit wall and because I think the boss there has lost the dressing room. Rob Marshall has gone, Adrian Newey has gone, Will Courtenay is leaving, Jonathan Wheatley has gone. You look at the dynasties, it's when the teams stay together. The Ross Brawn, Jean Todt, Michael Schumacher, Rory Byrne era at Ferrari. The Toto Wolff, James Allison, Aldo Costa, Lewis Hamilton era at Mercedes. It was the same at Red Bull. I need to keep what we've got intact, and not let anything disturb it for as long as possible. So just as I went shopping for Red Bull's top people, every team is going to come and try and poach mine. And whilst I can contractually protect myself, I've always believed you don't steal people, you lose people.'

That, in itself, is the skill of a good CEO especially in a sport where winning is everything and every single team up and down the paddock wants exactly the same things that you do.

'I need people to want to be here. So I've got to take care of them, I've got to treat them well, I've got to pay them well, I've got to give them opportunities and the right recognition. I can't be an egomaniac, where it is all about me. That's why you'll never hear me pretend I'm doing something on the pit wall that I'm not. My racing team know that the pit wall is not run by me, and I would never want to pretend that it was, in order to get all the glory, and then have my own team lose respect for me. One of the nicest things that Tom Stallard [Oscar Piastri's race engineer] said to me was, "Zak, you never say anything on the pit wall." I'm not the guy coming on the radio, and you know which ones that I'm talking about, that come over the top of the team, to get some airtime and make it look like they are in charge. I'm totally comfortable in my role and the people that I'm most concerned about are my own race team and what they think about me.'

Brown is always looking to the future. He has a rolling five-year plan and, within that, a yearly plan that he ensures everybody within McLaren is fully aware of, so that they know what needs to be done to feed into the longer-term strategy. Every year he refreshes the five-year plan in order to stay ahead.

'At the end of [each] year, I will look and see what we have achieved and where are we in every championship that we have entered. OK, here's what we are going to do in 2026. Andrea's job is to worry about today and tomorrow. My job is to worry about next week and next year.'

We saw Zak Brown the competitor in full flow for the first time in 2024. While he had gradually built McLaren back up into an organisation that could compete at the sharp end, by restructuring and getting the commercial flywheel to sync up with on-track development, he had kept his own counsel and didn't often go head-to-head with those that were clearly winning. But, as the team began to believe that they were in contention for a championship, he seemed to relish going toe-to-toe with Christian Horner and his competitors to try to derail their pursuit of glory. But that works both ways, they are all at it! He has become, once again, the disruptor that he was as a teenager, relishing the scraps that defined his youth. He believes that his team in 2024 had the most successful commercial season in the history of the sport. That has given him a strong financial bedrock to support his talented racing set-up. Now he faces his greatest challenge yet: keeping McLaren at the top.

'That's the hardest part. We need to be passionate but not emotional. Emotion is dangerous, it can make you erratic and [there] is a fine line between both. These are the best days of my life, right now, but I know how quickly it can change.'

One thing you do know is that whatever happens, Brown will be working incessantly to keep his team at the front. Formula One waits for no one, and Brown is not someone who is going to stand around wondering.

Formula One is a complex ecosystem in which the pursuit of speed is reliant on everybody operating as close to perfection as is humanly possible. But that is the point. We are all human, and therefore by nature imperfect, which is what creates the jeopardy and the minute differences between the competitors. As we've seen, it takes up to 1,500 people to produce the most technologically advanced cars on the planet. In this book, I hope I have given you an insight into how they perform at the highest level and under the most intense pressure. It is something that I am privileged to be a tiny part of; sport's finest continuous soap opera that keeps you wondering what is around each and every corner from race to race and season to season. That's what makes it so addictive. Here's to the next chapter, the many after that and to all those people who make it happen.

IMAGE CREDITS

SECTION 1

Andy Hone / Stringer / Getty Images (Image 1)

Peter Fox – Formula 1 / Contributor / Getty Images (Image 2)

Guenther Iby / Contributor / Getty Images (Image 3)

James Moy / Staff / Getty Images (Image 4)

Anadolu / Contributor / Getty Images (Image 5)

Aflo Co. Ltd. / Nippon News / Alamy Stock Photo (Image 6)

Sutton Images / Stringer / Getty Images (Image 7)

Mark Thompson / Staff / Getty Images (Images 8 and 9)

Giorgio Piola (Images 10, 11 and 12)

SECTION 2

Sutton Images / Stringer / Getty Images (Image 1)

Mark Thompson / Staff / Getty Images (Image 2)

XPB Images Ltd / Alamy Stock Photo (Image 3)

Independent Photo Agency / Alamy Stock Photo (Image 4)

Xinhua / Alamy Stock Photo (Image 5)

Sutton Images / Stringer / Getty Images (Image 6)

Qian Jun / MB Media / Contributor / Getty Images (Image 7)

James Moy / Alamy Stock Photo (Image 8)

Glenn Dunbar / Stringer / Getty Images (Image 9)

Myung J. Chun / Contributor / Getty Images (Image 10)

Mark Sutton / Staff / Getty Images (Image 11)

John Keeble / Contributor / Getty Images (Image 12)

Clive Mason – Formula 1 / Contributor / Getty Images (Image 13)

Jayce Illman / Contributor / Getty Images (Image 14)

ACKNOWLEDGEMENTS

I want to thank all of the kind people who spared the time out of their busy lives to talk to me for this book. Without them it simply wouldn't have been written. To the team at Ebury, Penguin Random House, especially Lorna Russell, thank you for your relentless positivity and guidance for a novice author.

To Anthony Davidson, who kindly fact-checked it for me to ensure that I wasn't talking utter nonsense. It says everything you need to know about 'Big Tone', who is one of the most generously spirited people I have ever met. Thanks, mate.

To my family and most especially to my wife Ronie, our two wonderful kids Harry and Rosie, and our dog, the one that looks like Donald Trump (Isla). Without their patience and understanding I wouldn't be able to have the privileged job that I do. I have missed so many important occasions and you have never once complained. To my mum and dad (Jane and Terry) for their love and support. To my sister Sarah and her family, Guy, Jess, Jack and Frank.

To Martin Turner, the godfather of Sky F1, the man who set the channel on its way, for giving me my chance in telly and being a great mentor to me and so many others. I am extremely grateful.

To my colleagues, I'm sorry that I could only include Crofty and Martin as you all do such incredible jobs. To Ted, Anthony, Karun, Natalie, Rachel, Naomi, Bernie, Jenson, Danica, Nico, PDR, Johnny and Damon. It has been a total blast and it's a pleasure to have shared these experiences together.

And the same to all the crew past and present. Thin Henry the eighth, FBS, T-Bass, The Marine, The Sad Crow, Wor Jackie Lad the disco egg, Georgia, Emma, Ferrans, Razor, Jim, Haguey, Tiger, Tim Davies, Clifto, Si Graham, Georgie, Woodo, Roddy Holder, Ben, Sandy, Georgie, Paddy, Phil, Helen, Sniff, Lisa, Colesy, Billy,

Jess, Moggsy, Tim, Seth, Potter, Sam, Nige, Jimmy G, Dammo, Tommo, Tim, Sean, Sam, Will S-C, Gabby, Holly, Heather, Adam, Harry, Don, Sexy Chris, Martin T and, of course, the Spaniel. To any of those that I've missed from 14 years on the road, apologies, you know who you are and you've all played your role in making this the finest crew in the world. A team is only as good as the sum of its parts and this is the best I've ever worked with.

And that is what it's all about.

Long may it continue.

Cheers,

Simon

X

INDEX